The Politics of Elite Transformation

The Consolidation of Greek Democracy in Theoretical Perspective

Neovi M. Karakatsanis

Westport, Connecticut
London

Library of Congress Cataloging-in-Publication Data

Karakatsanis, Neovi M., 1964–
    The politics of elite transformation : the consolidation of Greek democracy in
theoretical perspective / Neovi M. Karakatsanis.
        p.   cm.
    Includes bibliographical references and index.
    ISBN 0–275–97035–3 (alk. paper)
    1. Democratization—Greece.   2. Elite (Social sciences)—Greece.   3. Political
leadership—Greece.   4. Greece—Politics and government—20th century.   I. Title.
JN5147.K37   2001
949.507′6—dc21   00–061171

British Library Cataloguing in Publication Data is available.

Library of Congress Catalog Card Number: 00–061171
ISBN: 0–275–97035–3

First published in 2001

Praeger Publishers, 88 Post Road West, Westport, CT 06881
An imprint of Greenwood Publishing Group, Inc.
www.praeger.com

Printed in the United States of America

The paper used in this book complies with the
Permanent Paper Standard issued by the National
Information Standards Organization (Z39.48–1984).

10 9 8 7 6 5 4 3 2 1

Copyright Acknowledgment

Chapter 7 is based in large measure on an article published in *Armed Forces and Society* (24:2,
1997). The publishers of that journal, Transaction Periodicals Consortium, has kindly allowed the
article to be reprinted, in slightly altered form, here.

For Jonathan

Contents

Preface

This research would not have been possible without the contribution of many. First, I wish to thank Richard Gunther, Vassilios Lambropoulos, and Felipe Agüero. Their careful reading and many theoretical and substantive contributions to earlier drafts of this study improved it enormously and were truly invaluable. Additionally, Constantine P. Danopoulos and P. Nikiforos Diamandouros proved to be tremendous sources of knowledge and insight on Greek politics and civil-military relations, to say nothing of diligent, careful readers of several chapters of this study. I feel fortunate indeed to have enjoyed the support and guidance of such insightful, dedicated scholars as these.

Two individuals made an invaluable contribution to my understanding of the junta years in Greece by providing me access to archival materials at their disposal. Adamantia Pollis made available to me taped interviews—then held at New York University's Alexander S. Onassis Center for Hellenic Studies—with key Greek and international political elites of the period. Stephen W. Rousseas also allowed me to review usually closed archival materials at Columbia University's Butler Library. I sincerely wish to thank them for their generosity and the contributions they have made to my research.

This research was also made possible by the generous financial support of a number of organizations in both the United States and Greece. First, I wish to express my gratitude to the U.S. Educational Foundation in Greece and The United States Information Agency, which provided me with a Fulbright Grant, allowing me to conduct research for a year in Athens. Additional financial support was provided by The Ohio State University Graduate School (Graduate Student Alumni Research Award), the Ohio State Chapter of the Phi Kappa Phi Honor Society (Graduate Enrichment Award), the Hellenic University Club of New York, and The Democratization Program of the Mershon Center at The Ohio State University. An Ohio State University Graduate School Presidential Fellowship allowed me an entire academic year to complete the writing of this study. Finally, a post-doctoral fellowship at Princeton University's Program in Hellenic Studies/Foundation for Hellenic Studies provided me with several months of support as I undertook additional archival research at Firestone Library and began revising the manuscript.

The support and encouragement I have received from family and friends went a long way toward making this study possible. I thank the Priovolos family in Athens for their friendship and warm support, particularly in the early stages of this research. My deepest gratitude goes also to Artemis Leontis; my mother-in-law, Patricia Swarts; and my sisters, Ioanna and Areti Karakatsani, without whose moral support and encouragement this study might never have been completed. There are no words to express my gratitude to my parents, Michael and Ploumi Karakatsanis. Throughout my entire life they have made tremendous sacrifices for me, always supporting me in the pursuit of my goals and aspirations, and teaching me—through their own example and efforts—the importance of persistence and hard work. I thank you for teaching me the Greek language, taking me to Greece often, and always inspiring in me a deep interest for things Greek. My love and gratitude to you is written across every page of this study.

The contributions of so many Greek political and military leaders who offered me hundreds of hours of personal interviews will never be forgotten. I found these men and women to be generous with their time, candid with their responses, insightful, and courteous. To these interview respondents I wish to express my utmost gratitude and respect. Without your willingness to assist me in this effort, my research would never have been possible. To all of you I extend a heart-felt, "Σας Ευχαριστώ." Finally, I also wish to acknowledge the editorial assistance of Maureen Melino and Bobbie Goettler. Maureen offered her assistance in the early stages of production, while Bobbie, a careful reader of the manuscript, offered valuable editorial assistance in the final stages.

Above all, I wish to thank my husband, Jonathan Swarts, who was with me at every phase of this project, guiding and encouraging my every step and providing steadfast support during the entire period of my writing. Words cannot express the countless scholarly contributions he has made to this study. I am truly grateful for his excitement, constant devotion, encouragement, and the interest he has shown for my work. This book is as much his work as it is mine. It is to him that I dedicate this work.

From Transition to Democracy: Greece in Theoretical Perspective

A well-known Athenian intellectual, writing anonymously in the colonels' Greece, could not possibly have known in 1972 of the uncharacteristic atmosphere of self-restraint, patience, and responsibility that would characterize Greek politics after the demise of the military junta. Yet, as if he could foresee what was to transpire years later, he wrote[1]:

If we are willing to collaborate, if needs be, with the communists, who previously attacked democratic institutions with armed force, why should we refuse to collaborate with ... those who are simply suspected of having had antidemocratic designs in 1967? What counts is everyone's present inclination, not their former sins, real or imagined. There is reason to believe that the whole of the right, including the king, has learned a lesson from its terrible experiences under the present dictatorship, and that it will in future respect democratic processes. ... It is not likely, moreover, that the great majority of the left will demonstrate or make extreme demands to upset the right. Whatever its present leaders may say, the rank and the file will be far too happy to be freed from the present nightmare to think of provoking dangerous confrontations. For the left also have a lesson to learn on the virtues of moderation and patience, as well as the dangers of verbal braggadocio. All this demands, above all, the greatest possible unity ... among the different political groups. We will contribute to our liberation not by fighting against each other, even if only with words, but by agreeing on a co-ordinated action programme toward a minimum common goal: liberation pure and simple. ... Patience and systematic effort should replace amateurism and a taste for spectacular and immediate results.[2]

Certainly, this Athenian could not conceivably have known in 1972 that Constantine Karamanlis, once a symbol of the repressive post–civil war state and the first prime minister after the fall of the Greek junta, would address the nation with words of moderation and conciliation upon his return to Athens from self-imposed exile. Further, the Athenian could not have sensed that the words of the politician entrusted to lead Greece from seven years of oppressive dictatorship to the full restoration of democracy would echo his own; and yet, almost as if the Athenian *did* know, on 25 July 1974 Karamanlis announced to the nation:

I assume the responsibility of governing the country in critical circumstances for it and for all Hellenism. I am sustained by the deep conviction that even the greatest difficulties can be overcome by mobilizing all the forces and virtues of the nation. ... My government's ... task will be to outline rapidly the procedure that should lead to the creation of a genuine and progressive democracy in whose context there will be room for all Greeks. The transition from dictatorship to the full restoration of democracy is always crucial. Political maturity is needed if we are to benefit. My government has ... neither a partisan nor a political character; it is clearly a national Government.[3]

Moreover, Karamanlis was not the only Greek evincing self-restraint and patience in rhetoric and behavioral style in July of 1974. Years of postwar "guided democracy" and subsequent dictatorial rule appeared to have taught many Greek political elites that patience has its merits in politics, and that if one demands too much too quickly s/he may be endangering democratic stability and consolidation.[4] For example, Elias Iliou, a leader of the United Democratic Left, announced that his party would follow a "moderate line" to avoid "pushing people to extremes."[5] Similarly, the Communist Party of Greece-Interior adopted a conciliatory attitude toward the Karamanlis regime: "Where he [Karamanlis] takes positions opening up things we support him. ... On the political level, we are with him against the dictatorship." Even Charilaos Florakis, first secretary of the pro-Soviet orthodox branch of the Greek Communist Party, called for the formation of a broad front of democratic forces to "confront the dangers of a relapse."[6]

Unlike the Athenian, most other observers of twentieth-century Greek politics might not have expected these traditionally antagonistic and warring elite factions to evince such self-restraint and moderation at the time of the transition to democracy.[7] Based on their interpretation of the unpredictable nature of twentieth-century Greek politics, most observers expected a repeat of the serious conflicts between parties and the political crises that frequently challenged the legitimacy of the regime and allowed recurrent military involvement into politics throughout the twentieth century. And yet, not only did instability and crisis not take place in the post-1974 period, but a remarkably stable and consolidated democracy came into being,[8] thanks in large part to elite self-restraint and moderation.

The processes through which a stable, consolidated, and fully democratic regime came into being in Greece in the 1970s and early 1980s are examined in this study. The case of Greece provides a rich and challenging opportunity for the testing of theoretical propositions concerning consolidation processes. However, in contrast with the other Southern European transitions—Spain, Italy, and Portugal—there have been relatively few accounts of its transition and consolidation trajectories. From the standpoint of theory-building, this is most unfortunate, since the transition trajectory followed in Greece was rather distinct from other Southern European transitions. Considerable analytical leverage will be gained in this study by exploring the Greek case with the same level of theoretical rigor as the others.

THE CASE OF GREECE

As we will see, the Greek case challenges existing theoretical explanations. First, traditional democratization theories, which focus on socioeconomic,[9] cultural,[10] historical,[11] and other prerequisites of democracy, are not fully supported by the Greek case. Greece is one of several countries, along with Portugal and Spain, that experienced authoritarian rule despite significant ongoing socioeconomic modernization. Specifically, the country underwent phenomenal economic growth during the postwar period. Its economy, surpassing every EEC country, expanded at an annual average growth rate of over 6 percent from 1957–66. Driven by foreign investment, industrial production skyrocketed, increasing five-fold from 1950 to about 1965.[12] As classical modernization theories predict, this economic development and concomitant rapid industrialization had a tremendous social and demographic impact. Primary among these social changes was urbanization, as the percentage of the population residing in urban and semi-urban centers steadily rose.

Development, however, was uneven, leading to social dislocation and disintegration—phenomena directly related to the social unrest and political mobilization of the late sixties.[13] Specifically, increased geographical mobility weakened traditional loyalties and orientations, widened the social horizons of villagers, and made increasing social inequalities both more visible and less acceptable.[14] By the mid-1960s Greeks had matured politically, realizing the importance of both the vote and of direct personal involvement in politics. In fact, it was at this time that the liberal George Papandreou, promising not insignificant social, political, and educational reforms, was elected. However, the victory of his Center Union party over the conservative National Radical Union (ERE) was evidence that the politically exclusivist parliamentary system—Greece's "guided democracy"—could not survive without fundamental change.[15]

As some observers have argued,[16] the 1967 coup should thus be regarded as an attempt by extreme-right forces to safeguard their political supremacy by preventing the political participation of recently mobilized sectors of the population that were calling for liberalization and for the elimination of Greece's "guided democracy." Thus, despite tremendous economic development and concomitant social-structural change, a successful *coup d'état*—not increased democratization—took place in 1967. In short, Greek socioeconomic modernization was neither a necessary nor a sufficient explanation of democratization; socioeconomic factors were certainly not determinative in bringing about the 1974 transition to democracy.[17]

Moreover, as will be discussed in some detail in chapter 2 of this study, Greek political culture and history did not preordain democratic stability and consolidation either. In fact, deep political cleavages, partisan animosities, and political instability characterized the Greek polity throughout the twentieth century as Greece experienced a bloody and divisive civil war (1944–49), ten major military revolts, and three periods of military/authoritarian rule. One cleavage was the *Ethnikos Dikhasmos* (National Schism), which served to divide the middle class into polarized camps of royalists versus republicans—a division rooted in the conflict over Greece's participation in World War I.[18] Four of the seven *coups d'état* that took place during the interwar period arose directly from this conflict. The second source of regime instability had at its root the almost uninterrupted domination of politics by the right, which, with the exception of the 1950–52 period and the 1963–65 period, held power almost continuously from 1935 to 1967—often acquiescing in the use of manipulation of the electoral laws as well as fraud and political violence at the polls.[19] The most divisive schism, however, was the result of armed confrontation between nationalists and communists in a bloody civil war as the communists engaged in armed rebellion against the established order. Related to this was a deep division in the Greek polity associated with the right's deep hatred of communism and its incessant efforts to delegitimize the left. This division had a long-standing impact on Greek politics by leading to a protracted period in which illiberal civil war–era emergency measures were allowed to function alongside a liberal democratic constitution. The result was selective repression and discrimination against the war's vanquished by its victors. In fact, it has been argued that postwar Greece functioned according to a "paraconstitution" that divided Greeks into "nationally minded" and "suspect" citizens, the latter subject to various forms of repression and denials of civil and political liberties.[20] Thus, rather than putting an end to the hatreds and animosities that had been bred by that war, the post–civil war period prolonged and kept alive this schism.

A fragile party structure also contributed to democratic instability throughout this period as Greek political parties (except for the communists) consisted primarily of a small number of notables, party leaders, and local politicians. There were no grassroots organizations, no organized party members or militants, and no real party ideologies[21] to distinguish between the many political camps. Instead, both national and local leaders campaigned on a personal basis, holding mass rallies that relied more on charisma than on ideology. Voters, for their part, identified primarily with leaders rather than parties.[22] Thus, politicians with strong patron-client ties could afford to switch parties frequently without losing electoral support. Instability ensued as voters transferred their allegiances from party to party, following their patrons whenever they switched political camps. In nine postwar elections the average shift of the popular vote from one political camp to the other amounted to thirty percentage points.[23] Thus, despite a relatively long parliamentary tradition and contrary to structuralist theories, Greece in the 1960s and 1970s was lacking both a tradition of democratic stability as well as a homogenous and democratic political culture.

Apart from the hatreds, animosities, and illiberal measures that characterized postwar Greek politics, both structural-systemic problems of the exclusivist post–civil war period as well as the nature of politics at that time—where emotionalism, rancor, rhetorical exaggeration, and demagoguery prevailed—engendered a situation in which the legitimacy of the entire state apparatus—the monarchy, the army, the police, the gendarmerie, the Greek Central Intelligence Agency (KYP), the parliamentary right, as well as the entire left wing of the political spectrum—was repeatedly called into question. This contributed to a political climate in which society became polarized, politics became unstable, and a pretext was given to a small group of colonels to intervene.

Despite such divisive cleavages, a tradition of political instability, various aberrant characteristics of its transition, and problems with the quality of Greek democracy, however, Greece became a consolidated democracy in the early to mid-1980s.[24] There are multiple indicators of democratic consolidation in Greece that stand in sharp contrast with the past. The Communist Party of Greece is now a legal and loyal contender in the democratic game, signaling an end to the systematic delegitimation of the left and the closed nature of the Greek political system. The issue of monarchy versus republic has also been definitively laid to rest with the 1974 referendum (in which 69.2 percent of the electorate voted in favor of an "uncrowned democracy") and with the absence today of any significant groups that challenge the present republican form of government. More broadly, there are no antisystem parties with significant levels of electoral support, and the semiloyal stances originally adopted by the Panhellenic Socialist Movement (PASOK) have given way to ones of loyalty to the present regime, its rules of the game, its institutions, and its international commitments. Perhaps the most dramatic sign of democratic consolidation was the formation of the 1989 communist/conservative coalition government—a development (albeit temporary) that would have been absolutely inconceivable in earlier years.

At the mass level, extensive survey data also indicate that democratic consolidation has occurred and that the Greek masses have a great respect and admiration for the present democratic regime. In fact, a comparative study of Spain, Portugal, Italy, and Greece found that Greeks exhibited exceptionally positive attitudes toward democracy relative to other Southern Europeans.[25] As Table 1 indicates, diffuse support for democracy in 1985 was highest in Greece (where 87 percent of Greek respondents indicated that "democracy was always preferable") than in any of the other three countries. In addition, Greek respondents appear to be more consistently critical in their evaluations of the authoritarian past, and they perceive their current democratic regime to be more efficacious than do other Southern Europeans. Moreover, according to a 1992 Eurobarometer survey, Greeks even have a more positive attitude toward democracy than do most other Community members. Ninety percent of Greek respondents indicated in that survey that democracy was preferable to other forms of government, far exceeding the European Community average of 78 percent. (Only Denmark, with 92 percent, exceeded Greece on this item.)

An additional aspect of democratic consolidation considered here is the military's new attitude toward civilian supremacy. In contrast to the military's deep involvement in politics prior to 1974 as well as to several alleged coup attempts and conspiracies undertaken by officers between July 1974 and February 1975 (under the Karamanlis government) and two reported military disturbances under the Papandreou government (in 1982 and 1983),[26] by the early to mid-1980s the Greek military appeared to have learned that both its mission and corporate interests lie in the barracks and not in politics. Military officers have thus behaviorally and attitudinally submitted themselves to democratic government.

Table 1
Attitudes Toward Democracy in Southern Europe, 1985

	Portugal	Spain	Italy	Greece
DIFFUSE LEGITIMACY				
Democracy always preferable	61%	70%	70%	87%
Authoritarianism preferable				
in some cases	9	10	13	5
All the same	7	9	10	6
"Don't know" or no answer	23	11	7	2
OPINIONS ON THE PAST				
Bad	30%	28%	37%	59%
Part good, part bad	42	44	43	31
Good	13	17	6	6
"Don't know" or no answer	15	11	14	4
PERCEIVED EFFICACY				
Our democracy works well	5%	8%	4%	35%
Many defects, but it works	63	60	61	46
Getting worse and will not				
work at all	11	20	28	14
"Don't know" or no answer	21	11	6	4
NUMBER OF CASES	2000	2488	2074	1998

Source: Leonardo Morlino and José R. Montero, "Legitimacy and Democracy in Southern Europe," in Gunther, Richard, P. Nikiforos Diamandouros, Hans-Jürgen Puhle. *The Politics of Democratic Consolidation: Southern Europe in Comparative Perspective*, p. 236, © 1995. The Johns Hopkins University Press.

The remainder of this study will analyze the processes by which elite consensual unity was achieved and democracy consolidated in Greece. It will analyze the transformations in rhetoric and behavioral style of the left, the right, and the military[27] that forged the consensual unity required to establish a stable and consolidated regime. Understanding that elites do not act within a political vacuum, however, elite actions and interactions will be analyzed in the light of contextual and environmental influences as well as elite-mass linkages, which, it is posited, influenced elite decisions and behavior. First, however, we turn to a review of dominant theoretical models of democratic consolidation and assess their relevance in the Greek context.

MODELS OF DEMOCRATIC CONSOLIDATION PROCESSES

Elite Settlements

For a democracy to become stable and consolidated, previously warring elites must come to respect a common set of procedural rules, norms, and institutions and to no longer challenge the legitimacy of democracy. This usually involves an acceptance of basic social, economic, and political institutions, a commitment to elections and parliamentary procedures as the means to power and the attainment of one's goals, and an abandonment of violence and revolutionary methods. When a critical mass of disunified and conflicting elites reach such agreement, consensual unity is said to have been achieved and democratic consolidation is likely to occur. The achievement of such unity is thus a hallmark event in the life of a new democracy.

This study explores two models of democratic consolidation processes. The first model is that of an elite settlement[28] or elite pact.[29] Scholars contend that settlements between powerful elites in political parties, trade unions, military units, and mass movements can play a decisive role in the consolidation of new democracies. Private, face-to-face negotiations between powerful elites can lead to collaboration and compromise on fundamental disagreements, thereby resolving traditionally divisive issues that have been major sources of democratic instability and forging elite structural integration and the mutual civility required to establish a stable and consolidated democracy. Put simply, a transition characterized by a progressive and gradual process of elite bargaining should be more successful than one characterized by the lack of such a process.

As theory has it, abrupt transitions should hinder a country's prospects for successful consolidation insofar as they tend to be polarizing and potentially destabilizing.[30] Second, the presence of a single, partisan individual playing a dominant role in the transition can drastically bias the outcome in favor of one political or social group or coalition of forces, and encourage majoritarian, winner-take-all behavior that often leads to the rejection of the regime by the losers in a partisan struggle. Unlike transitions through progressive but gradual processes of interelite discussions (as was the case with the Spanish transition), abrupt transitions that take place in the absence of elite negotiations (as in the early stages of the Portuguese transition) are potentially unstable and polarized.

At first glance, it would appear that, in Greece, warring elite factions did not enter into an elite settlement or pact during the transition to democracy. In fact, the Greek democratic transition was extremely abrupt, was dominated by a single partisan individual—Constantine Karamanlis—and did not evince any formal negotiations between elites. As will be illustrated in chapter 3, and as scholars who have studied the Greek transition to democracy argue, Constantine Karamanlis possessed virtual *carte blanche* powers[31] or "a disproportionately dominant role"[32] in determining Greece's transition trajectory. Karamanlis single-handedly chose the members of his 1974 national unity government, personally decided the timing of the first post-junta elections and the referendum on the monarchy, legalized the Communist Party of Greece, lifted all of the restrictive post–civil war measures, and commuted the junta leaders' death sentences to life imprisonment. In light of this evidence, scholars have concluded that interelite negotiations were absent in the Greek transition to democracy.

Despite the absence of formal negotiations, however, scattered evidence seems to indicate that the Greek transition process was more complex and nuanced than the literature would have it. Informal interelite negotiations did in fact take place during the dictatorship as various factions opposing the colonels' regime engaged in private talks about ways to rid Greece of the colonels. A formal compromise or agreement was never reached, however. Rather, these negotiations appear to have been stifled by partisan rivalries, mistrust of one's opponents, and a general unwillingness to compromise.

The failure of these talks to reach a formal elite settlement notwithstanding, it is important to note that they nonetheless positively influenced the prospects for democratic consolidation and stability in a different way. These face-to-face contacts between previously warring elites served to forge a diffuse sense of unity and mutual civility between them—a requirement for democratic consolidation and stability. Thus, talks during the seven years of military rule, while not providing an explicit outline for Karamanlis' actions in 1974, probably facilitated greatly the building of mutual respect between members of the post-junta right and all politically significant opposition forces, thereby contributing to consensual unity over the long term. Even though these informal negotiations had a significant positive impact on democratic consolidation, they remain totally unexplored in published studies of the Greek transition. This study is the first of its kind to examine the contents of a number of such negotiations to determine the extent to which they facilitated democratic consolidation in Greece.

Elite Convergence

A second theoretical perspective posited to lead to democratic consolidation is the two-step process of elite convergence.[33] In step one of this process, one segment of the political spectrum enters into sustained, peaceful collaboration in electoral politics in order to win elections and enter government. In step two the opposition realizes that the only way it can emerge from opposition status is by beating the dominant coalition at its own game—by acknowledging the legitimacy of existing democratic institutions and by pledging adherence to democratic rules of the game. In sum, agreement among political elites concerning the rules, procedures, and institutions of the new democratic regime is driven by the desire to win parliamentary elections.

Elite convergence appears to fit the Greek left's moderation quite well. The factual case for this moderation is clear. After the fall of the colonels' dictatorship, Karamanlis' conservative *Nea Demokratia* emerged victorious from the 1974 and 1977 elections. Initially, Andreas Papandreou, leader of the Panhellenic Resistance Organization (PAK), criticized the accession of Karamanlis and argued "that the new government represented no real change in Greece." Upon founding his Panhellenic Socialist Movement (PASOK), Papandreou's stance had the appearance of threatening democratic consolidation: he questioned the status and the prerogatives of the President of the Republic, he vigorously opposed the "reinforced" proportional representation electoral law, and he refused to support the new constitution, denouncing it as authoritarian.

Over time, however, a significant transformation occurred as PASOK's radical rhetoric was replaced by manifestations of loyalty to the regime. Distancing himself from some of the more extreme and polemical factions of his party and allying himself with the more pragmatic parliamentary wing, Papandreou repeatedly asserted that PASOK would remain democratically accountable to the electorate and to Parliament and that it would act as a responsible democratic party, rather than a revolutionary movement.[34] Given this dramatic turnabout, the analysis of PASOK's moderation in chapter 6 will raise several theoretically important issues. First, it will raise the issue of potential obstacles to consolidation: There is no reason to believe that democratic consolidation is a unilinear process that guarantees perpetual democratic persistence. In fact, the emergence of semiloyal parties, as PASOK appeared to be upon its founding in 1974, can pose serious obstacles for a fledgling democratic regime. In this respect PASOK's radical positions provide us with an opportunity to study the potential effects of antisystem or semiloyal parties on democratic consolidation and stability. Had PASOK carried out many of its radical electoral pledges when it came to power in 1981—that is, had it refused to respect the constitution ratified in 1975 and had it withdrawn Greece from NATO and the European Community as it pledged to do—Greece's democratic regime might not have become fully consolidated. An analysis of PASOK's radical stances will provide us the opportunity to study some of the potential obstacles that could have ultimately prevented consolidation from occurring.[35]

The second important point to arise from this analysis of PASOK is that a rhetorically antisystem stance does not always translate into explicit antisystem action and democratic deconsolidation. In fact, contrary to earlier formulations of the elite convergence argument that moderation of programmatic and ideological stances is necessary for democratic consolidation and stability,[36] the analysis of PASOK indicates that the party's radical position in the early years of Greece's transition to democracy actually *facilitated* democratic consolidation. It did so by attracting the support of dissatisfied and disaffected antiestablishment voters who might otherwise have withheld their support from the newly established democratic regime had PASOK not initially served as a channel for their disenchantment. Later, as PASOK moderated all of its antiestablishment positions, its supporters followed suit, thereby being coopted into support for the established democracy. The analysis of PASOK will also point up a critically important point: the moderation of antisystem positions must be seen as distinct from the moderation of public policy positions. Programmatic and rhetorical radicalism—so long as it does not call into question the very institutions and rules of the new regime but remains confined to issues of government policy—can continue long after democracy has become consolidated and stable.

Like PASOK, the communists also opposed the reinforced proportional representation electoral law, the timing of the first post-junta elections, and many aspects of the new constitution. Nevertheless, even the Marxist-Leninist

Communist Party of Greece (KKE) behaved in a restrained and constructive manner during and after the transition as, for example, when in 1974 it pledged adherence to democratic, parliamentary government.

Since the *motives* for moderation are central to the logic of the elite convergence model, I carefully examine the motives and perceptions of the communist leadership. To put it succinctly, why did these parties moderate from their original antisystem stance? Was it simply the result of electoral tactics, international influences, or a nonpartisan concern for democratic stability and consolidation that would, in turn, ensure conditions of legality and development for the party?

In chapter 5 I contend that in light of the communist split in 1968 (into a dogmatic Marxist-Leninist party and a revisionist Eurocommunist party), moderation on the part of some leftists appears to have begun even before the transition to democracy occurred in 1974. In fact, interviews indicate that, with regard to certain communists, moderation began almost immediately after the civil war as recriminations between "old" and "new" communists broke out following the left's defeat. With regard to other communists, however—most notably the leadership of the dogmatic Marxist-Leninist left—a tactical decision was made during the dictatorship that as long as a common enemy existed, the KKE would be willing to temporarily accept bourgeois democracy and to cooperate with all antidictatorial parties committed to an overthrow of the dictatorship, the establishment of political rights and freedoms for all Greeks, and the convening of a constitutional assembly.[37]

While moderation on the left of the political spectrum appears, *prima facie*, to be consistent with the elite convergence model, moderation on the right of the political spectrum does not. As important as the moderation of PASOK and the communists was the appearance in 1974 of a democratic party of the right, in contrast to the antidemocratic or pseudo-democratic orientation of the right in past decades. In many respects, Karamanlis' decisions and actions in 1974 to legalize the Communist Party, to hold a referendum on the future of the monarchy, and to limit the prerogatives of the military were catalysts for the appearance of a democratic right-of-center party.

The right's moderation was fundamental to the achievement of democratic consolidation and stability in Greece. Had *Nea Demokratia* maintained the right's traditional commitment to zealous anticommunism and its attachment to the monarchy, Greece's new democracy may have been stillborn from the start. Significant political groups and their supporters would have effectively been denied personal liberties, and ideological cleavages based on the politics of the pre-junta years would have fostered feelings of regime illegitimacy among large sectors of the population. The post-1974 attempt at democratization would thus have been seriously threatened.

The right did modernize, however. But the right's moderation does not fit neatly into the elite convergence model and leaves a fundamental question unanswered: Why did *Nea Demokratia* adopt a fully democratic stance? It was certainly not the product of the kinds of calculations of opposition parties hypothesized by the Higley/Gunther model, which argues that such "convergences" are mainly reactive responses of opposition parties against their failure at the polls.[38] This model fails to apply in the Greek case because Karamanlis and *Nea Demokratia* were not opposition forces that had suffered defeats at the hands of voters.   The reality was quite to the contrary. Karamanlis played a disproportionately dominant role in directing the transition, and his party proceeded to win both the 1974 and 1977 elections. *Nea Demokratia*, unlike PASOK, was not an opposition party needing to change its electoral tactics in order to win parliamentary elections and enter government. Thus, although the moderation of *Nea Demokratia* appears to mirror the moderation of the left, the fact is that the motives underpinning increased moderation must necessarily be different from those of PASOK and the communists. By focusing on this theoretically important challenge to the model, this study will offer a fresh and valuable insight to theories of democratic consolidation.

As with the left, specific attention is paid to the *motives* of prominent members of the right, particularly Constantine Karamanlis. A number of such motives are explored. Moderation due to national or regime interests, partisan politics, and the need to build a modern, well-organized, and democratic political party are among the factors that are considered in this study. Specifically, did the colonels' regime, which repressed all political parties in Greece (including the right), teach Karamanlis and other prominent members of the right that a common interest (opposition to the junta) was shared by *all* civilian elites? Was Karamanlis' "awareness of the fragility"[39] of the regime or his "historical memory"[40] of instability and polarization the motive behind his moderation? Furthermore, did Karamanlis' long years of self-imposed exile in France, his view of Greek politics from afar, as well as his many visits from political elites (both Greek as well as foreign), contribute to his own personal "modernization?" These and other themes are explored by this study.

Finally, the literature on democratic consolidation also pays attention to the ability of militaries to impose limits upon democratic transition and consolidation processes. Efforts have been made to incorporate the military dimension, both theoretically and substantively, into these studies and the military's role has been included as an integral part of definitions of democratic consolidation. Specifically, in order for a democratic regime to be regarded as consolidated, all significant political groups (including the military) must regard the key political institutions of the regime as the only legitimate framework for political contestation, and they must adhere to democratic rules of the game.[41] As long as the armed forces challenge democratization and remain politicized, democracy cannot be considered consolidated. Thus, militaries must not only be effectively removed from power positions outside the defense area but must also acknowledge and respect civilian political superiors even in areas of defense for democratic consolidation to occur.[42] As Kohn puts it, one "cannot have democracy without civilian control."[43]

This definition of democratic consolidation contains both an attitudinal and a behavioral component. That is, the institutions, norms, and rules of the game of the established democratic regime must not only be *adhered to* by all significant political groups in order for the regime to be regarded as consolidated, but they must also be *regarded* as acceptable and legitimate by these groups. Insofar as a significant elite group (such as the military) withholds its behavioral and/or attitudinal support from the regime, the potential for regime overthrow remains real and tangible; in such a case, the regime cannot be regarded as consolidated.

Several explanations have been offered concerning the varying capabilities of militaries to place limits on democratization. These explanations have centered on (a) the nature of the outgoing authoritarian regime,[44] (b) the nature of the elite leading the transition to democracy,[45] (c) the particular characteristics of the transition path followed,[46] and (d) the cautious handling of military matters by civilian elites during the transition to democracy.[47] In sum, the achievement of democratic consolidation is inextricably linked to the nature of the transition trajectory.[48]

Little has been written about the Greek military's role in the transition and consolidation process, and much of the literature is highly descriptive and atheoretical. This is despite the fact that the Greek case is unique in that it is an example of a militarized authoritarian regime in which a traditionally politicized military comes to the eventual recognition that its proper role does not include intervention into the civil and political life of the nation. Despite a long tradition of parliamentary rule in Greece, numerous examples of military intervention into politics exist. As early as 1843, the army staged its first of many coups forcing the first king of Greece, Otto, to grant a constitution. Nearly twenty years later, in 1862, King Otto was ousted by another military-led insurrection. The military also took a politicized stand on the National Schism that culminated in several military interventions in politics. Then, after the communist defeat in the Greek Civil War, the military was active in playing the role of guarantor of internal order by helping to establish the repressive post–civil war anticommunist state. Therefore, according to theory, the fact that the colonels' regime represented a militarized authoritarian regime and that the Greek military was traditionally politicized ought to have precluded democratic consolidation in Greece.

Democratic consolidation did occur, however. The collapse of the colonels' regime in 1974 signaled the beginning of a continuous and cumulative transformation in military behavior and attitudes that would continue well into the 1980s. While several attempted coups and conspiracies reportedly took place between 1974 and 1983,[49] each successive conspiracy had diminishing levels of support from within the officer corps. The military was gradually, yet increasingly, becoming depoliticized. Had this depoliticization not occurred, the threat of continuous interventions into politics and even seizure of power by the military would have remained real.

In examining the depoliticization of the Greek military, the following question is addressed by this study: Why did the Greek military retreat to the barracks? Several explanations are offered: The first has to do with the fact that the Greek junta was a nonhierarchical regime—something Linz, Stepan, and Gunther contend ought to facilitate democratic consolidation.[50] A second factor is the humiliation of the Cyprus fiasco and its effects on the military. As chapter 7 argues, the debacle taught the Greek military an important lesson about the dangers associated with its interventions into politics. Moreover, the military was so engrossed in the national security issues confronting Greece at this time, as the possibility of war with Turkey loomed large, that initially it had little time for political meddling. The depoliticization of the military was also made possible by the cautious handling of military issues by civilian elites. In this scenario the military felt sufficiently secure in allowing its interests to be represented among the high counsels of state because it perceived that civilian elites—especially Karamanlis and Evangelos Averoff (viewed by the military as fellow conservatives, anticommunist, and "nationally minded")—were treating military concerns fairly and conscientiously. In assessing the depoliticization of the military, these and other themes are explored by this study.[51]

More importantly, however, by distinguishing two distinct elements of military withdrawal—the *initial extrication* of the military from politics and the *permanence* of that withdrawal—chapter 7 argues that factors conducive to the military's initial withdrawal from power, while facilitating democratic transition, are not sufficient to keep traditionally politicized militaries out of politics. Specifically, the Greek case illustrates that the proximate reasons behind the military hierarchy's decision to remove the military regime from power in July 1974 had to do with the specific interests of the armed forces (personal as well as corporate) and the military's perception of Greece's national interests. Extrication had little, if anything, to do with an intrinsic interest or a respect for democracy, democratic institutions, or democratic pluralism, *per se*. Withdrawal did not signal that officers no longer regarded themselves as legitimate contenders in civilian politics or that they wholly accepted the chain of command and their full submission to civilian rule. Consequently, long after the military had been confined to the barracks and had behaviorally submitted to civilians, military officers indicated in interviews that they reserved the prerogative to intervene in politics again "if necessary." Thus, I argue that while behavioral support for democracy is adequate in the short term, the attitudinal moderation that eventually occurred in Greece, signaling an acceptance of civilian supremacy and an acknowledgment of the official chain of command, is a necessary precondition for democratic consolidation in the long run. In sum, the Greek military's extrication from power highlights the importance of achieving both behavioral and attitudinal support for a regime before it can be considered consolidated.

SOURCES OF DATA AND PLAN OF STUDY

The research for this study consisted of a multimethod analysis of a variety of data and information sources: in-depth interview transcripts, party documents and publications, journalistic accounts, and the personal archives of some well-placed participants. The explanation of the moderation of the military's and the parties' programmatic demands, ideological precepts, rhetoric, and behavioral style required an extensive series of interviews with deputies, military officers, and party officials. The interview portion of this research sought to have as broad a representative sample of the political spectrum as possible for the purpose of collecting information as well as for scholarly objectivity. Thus, the respondents for this research were a cross section of opinion of people close to the top principals of each party (e.g., Karamanlis, Papandreou, Florakis, Kyrkos). Approximately ninety interviews were conducted with former and current deputies of the right, principally *Nea Demokratia* and its predecessor the National Radical Union (ERE), the former Center Union–New Forces party and its predecessor the Center Union, the Panhellenic Socialist Movement (PASOK), the traditional left (EDA, KKE-Interior, and KKE), and *Synaspismos* (the Coalition of the Left and Progress), as well as with retired officers of the Greek armed forces. The party interviews were conducted with both low-ranking deputies as well as high-ranking ministers and party leaders. Indeed, in the case of all significant political parties (with the exception of PASOK, which was in government at the time of research and whose only party leader was Greece's prime minister at that time), in-depth elite interviews were conducted with at least one or more party leaders. In the course of those interviews, I sought to determine the calculations and strategies that underpinned the political parties' and the military's moderation.

In addition to the analysis of these in-depth elite interview transcripts, the conclusions I draw in this study concerning elite negotiations are based on the analysis of approximately twenty interviews of key participants in those negotiations that were given publicly by the participants themselves prior to and immediately following the transition to democracy in 1974. The personal archives of some well-placed participants in that process were also made available to me and have served to illumine some of the behind-the-scenes activities of that process.

The remainder of this study will rigorously and systematically examine the processes that led to the establishment of a stable and consolidated democracy in Greece. To this end, four distinct transformations that forged the consensual unity required to establish a stable and consolidated democratic regime will be examined: (1) the modernization of the right from a questionable commitment to democracy before the 1967 dictatorship to a fully democratic stance in the post-1974 period; (2) the moderation of the communist left, which went from engaging in antidemocratic oppositional tactics for much of its history to loyalty toward the new democratic regime; (3) the moderation of the Panhellenic Socialist Movement (PASOK), which went from a seemingly semiloyaloyal stance in the formative years of the transition to one of full loyalty once in government; and (4) the transformation of the military's attitudes and behavior that led it to retreat from political involvement and to submit itself to civilian control.[52]

The next chapter will put the Greek case in historical perspective by focusing on those aspects of twentieth-century Greek politics—deep political cleavages, partisan animosities, and political instability—that theoretically should have been obstacles to the establishment of a stable and consolidated regime in Greece. Chapter 3 concentrates on the transition trajectory itself, placing Greece's transition in comparative perspective with those of Italy, Spain, Portugal, and France. It will highlight several aberrant characteristics of the Greek transition process—the rapidity with which the transition to democracy occurred in Greece, the virtual monopolization of the process by Constantine Karamanlis, a partisan member of the right, and the lack of any elite settlements or pacts.

Chapters 4, 5, 6, and 7 will discuss the modernization of the right, the moderation of the communists, the moderation of PASOK, and the depoliticization of the military, respectively. These chapters will examine the moderation in behavior and rhetoric of these political and military entities that, it is posited, contributed to democratic consolidation in Greece. An assessment of the motives behind these transformations that facilitated democratic consolidation will be offered in each of the chapters.

The concluding chapter of this study will evaluate current models of democratic consolidation in the light of the findings of this study. Since, as I will argue in the next two chapters, the Greek transition trajectory is not only unique, but aberrant, the final chapter of this study contends that the Greek case challenges some of the assumptions on which the theories of consolidation are based and forces a reassessment of these hypotheses. To this end substantial modifications and revisions to existing models will be offered in the concluding chapter.

As I will illustrate, the case of Greece defies easy theoretical explanation. It is not adequately explained by traditional theories emphasizing economic, structural, political-cultural, and historical "prerequisites" of democracy. While tremendous socioeconomic modernization took place in the 1950s and 1960s, these changes alone were insufficient to bring about the emergence of a stable and consolidated regime since the colonels' coup was in many ways an attempt to halt popular demands awakened by unprecedented socioeconomic modernization.[53] Rather, the weight of evidence in the Greek case indicates that *elite calculations and behavior* were central to the process of democratic consolidation.

And, yet, even current elite-centered theories—dealing explicitly with elite calculations and behavior—fail to adequately account for the consolidation of Greek democracy. First, the Greek transition was not characterized by the successful interelite negotiations and bargaining that scholars argue lead to elite moderation and the compromise necessary for successful consolidation. No formal interelite negotiations were ever held, and the informal, piecemeal negotiations that did occur ended in failure. Even though these early attempts at elite compromise broke down in the face of partisan and personal animosities, however, face-to-face contact between elites engaged in a common struggle against the colonels' dictatorship served to forge some degree of respect and civility among them. Therefore, even though formal agreement on the nature of the new regime was never reached, the experience of elite interaction laid the groundwork for the elite structural unity necessary for democratic consolidation. This study thus systematically analyzes the contents of these negotiations and the effect they had on the course of Greek democratization and on the gradual process of elite convergence there.

Two important points about convergence in the Greek case, however, distinguish it from the more "puristic" elite convergence model found in the theoretical literature. First, elite convergence as it occurred in Greece does not fully fit the logic of that model, which argues that such "convergences" are mainly reactive responses of opposition parties against their failure at the polls. In Greece, the primary motivation was not electoral. As will be shown in chapters 4, 5, and 6, in addition to electoral motivations for moderation, Greek elites were influenced most by a genuine desire to consolidate democracy. The repressive post–civil war years and the dictatorship to which those years led taught civilian elites that liberal democracy should be "the only game in town."[54] Most elites were therefore motivated by a desire to make democracy work. The second reason why convergence in Greece does not, at first glance, fit the model is that the origins of elite consensual unity in Greece clearly *preceded* the actual transition to democracy—indeed, the dictatorship itself. While the emerging literature on democratic consolidation treats transition and consolidation processes as distinct aspects of democratization, and while scholars recognize that in practice the two processes may temporarily overlap or sometimes even coincide,[55] by and large the implication of these studies is that elite consensual unity is the *result* of democratization. This implication is understandable: How can there be attitudinal support for a regime, its institutions, and rules of the game when the regime itself has not yet been established? The case of Greece appears to offer an answer to this question. First, it reveals that transitions to democracy are long-term phenomena, often requiring years, perhaps decades, before they become consolidated. Such was the case in Greece, whose transition to democracy should not be seen as a relatively rapid and simple transition from seven years of authoritarian rule but rather as a gradual, more long-term departure from the schisms, conflicts, and undemocratic practices of the entire postwar period. In such a long-term view of democratization, subsequent chapters will show how different elite groups moderated their behavior and attitudes at different times—some before,[56] some during, and others after the transition to democratic rule. They did so in response to different environmental stimuli, experiences, and lessons. As I will argue, a diffuse support—indeed, a demand—for democracy was so widespread among civilian political elites during and even before the dictatorship that the colonels faced nearly unanimous disdain for their seven-year experiment. In fact, by 1974 the desire for democracy was so great that political elites were willing to accept *any* new regime under *any* effective leadership so long as it would guarantee full civil and political rights of all Greek citizens (and thus be fully democratic) and preclude the reintroduction of another authoritarian regime. As in Spain under the last few years of the Franquist regime,[57] attitudes favorable to democracy and a general desire to fully democratize the restrictive, semi-democratic system were actually emerging in Greece before the 1967 military coup. This "diffuse support" for democracy—both at the elite and mass level—helped propel civilian elites toward a willingness to support democratization. As subsequent chapters will illustrate, some of the lessons for this and some of the steps toward the moderation preceded the dictatorship.

However, while contacts at the elite level during the the dictatorship appear to have established the roots of structural integration and mutual civility between previously antagonistic and warring factions—thereby contributing to elite convergence—these contacts were not successful in ironing out a concrete agreement on the specific nature of the new democratic regime—its specific rules, procedures, and institutions. As this study will illustrate, a number of opportunities arose for the newly established regime to collapse out of disputes and challenges from civilian and military elites alike over how the new system should be institutionalized and configured. In sum, democratic stability and success did not follow automatically from the general will to democratize. Thus, it is important that we understand the process by which the significant parties in Greece came into line, accepting the *specific* institutions and rules they originally found objectionable. To this end, the concluding chapter of this study will argue that a somewhat modified process of elite convergence appears to have forged interelite consensus on the specific procedures, rules, and institutions of the new democratic regime.

NOTES

1. The anonymous intellectual writing at the time of the colonels' coup was later identified as Rodis Roufos.

2. Athenian (Rodis Roufos), *Inside the Colonels' Greece* (New York: Chatto & Windus Ltd., 1972), pp. 179, 182–83, 191.

3. *Keesing's Contemporary Archives*, v. 20 (1974), p. 26668.

4. As subsequent chapters will illustrate, a process of political learning contributed to this end. See, for example, Nancy Bermeo, "Democracy and the Lessons of Dictatorship," *Comparative Politics*, 24: 3 (April 1992), pp. 273–91; and Arend Lijphart, "Consociational Democracy," *World Politics*, 21:2 (1969), pp. 207–25. Although from a different perspective, Víctor M. Pérez-Díaz, *The Return of Civil Society: The Emergence of Democratic Spain* (Cambridge, MA: Harvard University Press, 1993), points up the importance of long-term processes of societal change that shape the attitudes of elites. Discussions of these perspectives and their relevance to the Greek case appear in chapters 4 and 5 of this study.

5. *Facts on File*, v. 34 (1974), p. 735.

6. *Facts on File*, v. 34 (1974), p. 735.

7. On democratic transitions, see John Herz, ed., *From Dictatorship to Democracy: Coping with the Legacies of Authoritarianism and Totalitarianism* (Westport: Greenwood Press, 1982); Geoffrey Pridham, ed., *The New Mediterranean Democracies: Regime Transition in Spain, Greece, and Portugal* (London: Frank Cass, 1984); Guillermo O'Donnell, Philippe C. Schmitter, and Laurence Whitehead, eds., *Transitions from Authoritarian Rule*, vols. 1–4 (Baltimore: Johns Hopkins University Press, 1986); Larry Diamond, Juan J. Linz, and Seymour Martin Lipset, eds., *Democracy in Developing Countries* (Boulder: Lynne Rienner, 1989).

8. On democratic consolidation, see, for example, Scott Mainwaring, Guillermo O'Donnell, and J. Samuel Valenzuela, eds., *Issues in Democratic Consolidation: The New South American Democracies in Comparative Perspective* (Notre Dame: University of Notre Dame Press, 1992); Richard Gunther, P. Nikiforos Diamandouros, and Hans-Jürgen Puhle, eds., *The Politics of Democratic Consolidation: Southern Europe in Comparative Perspective* (Baltimore: The Johns Hopkins University Press, 1995); John Higley and Richard Gunther, eds., *Elites and Democratic Consolidation in Latin America and Southern Europe* (Cambridge: Cambridge University Press, 1992); Geoffrey Pridham, ed., *Securing Democracy: Political Parties and Democratic Consolidation in Southern Europe* (London: Routledge, 1990); Terry Karl and Philippe C. Schmitter, "Modes of Transition and Types of Democracy in Latin America, Southern and Eastern Europe" (unpublished manuscript); Philippe C. Schmitter, "The Consolidation of Political Democracy in Southern Europe" (unpublished manuscript); Leonardo Morlino, *Costruire la Democrazia: Gruppi e partiti in Italia* (Bologna: Società editrice il Mulino, 1991); Juan J. Linz and Alfred Stepan, *Democratic Transitions and Consolidation: Eastern Europe, Southern Europe and Latin America* (Baltimore: The Johns Hopkins University Press, 1996); Juan J. Linz and Alfred Stepan, "Toward Consolidated Democracies," *Journal of Democracy*, 7:2 (April 1996), pp.

14–33; Mattei Dogan and John Higley, eds., *Elites, Crises, and the Origins of Regimes* (Lanham, MD: Rowman and Littlefield, 1998); John Higley and Michael Burton, "Elite Settlements and the Taming of Politics," *Government and Opposition*, 33:1 (Winter 1998), pp. 98–115; Andreas Schedler, "What is Democratic Consolidation?" *Journal of Democracy*, 9:2 (April 1998), pp. 91–107. For a somewhat more demanding definition of democratic consolidation—one that encompasses such factors as democratic deepening, political institutionalization, and regime performance as well as a commitment to the norms, rules, and institutions of the democratic regime—see Larry Diamond, *Developing Democracy: Toward Consolidation* (Balimore: The Johns Hopkins University Press, 1999). Guillermo O'Donnell has also been a persistent critic of definitions of democratic consolidation that are "electoral" in nature. See his "Illusions About Consolidation," *Journal of Democracy*, 7:2 (April 1996), pp. 34–51.

9. Seymour Martin Lipset, "Some Social Requisites of Democracy: Economic Development and Political Legitimacy," *American Political Science Review*, 53:1 (March 1959), pp. 69–105; Daniel Lerner, *The Passing of Traditional Society* (New York: Free Press, 1958); Walt W. Rostow, *The Stages of Economic Growth* (New York: Cambridge University Press, 1960); and Karl W. Deutsch, "Social Mobilization and Political Development," *The American Political Science Review*, 55:3 (September, 1961). Despite the many criticisms launched against this classical modernization theory, empirical evidence has supported this hypothesis, showing high positive correlations between socioeconomic modernization and democracy: See, for example, Larry Diamond, "Economic Development and Democracy Reconsidered," in Gary Marks and Larry Diamond, eds., *Reexamining Democracy: Essays in Honor of Seymour Martin Lipset* (Newbury Park, CA: Sage Publications, 1992), pp. 93–139.

10. It was argued that political cultures that valued highly hierarchical relationships and an extreme deference to authority were a less fertile ground for democracy. See Gabriel Almond and Sidney Verba, *The Civic Culture* (Princeton: Princeton University Press, 1963); Samuel P. Huntington, "Will More Countries Become Democratic?" *Political Science Quarterly*, 99:2 (Summer 1984), pp. 193–218; Seymour Martin Lipset and Aldo Solari, *Elites in Latin America* (New York: Oxford University Press, 1967); John J. Johnson, *Political Change in Latin America* (Stanford: Stanford University Press, 1958); and David McClelland, *The Achieving Society* (Princeton: Von Nostrand, 1962).

11. Leonard Binder, James S. Coleman, Joseph LaPalombara, Lucian W. Pye, Sidney Verba and Myron Weiner, *Crises and Sequences in Political Development* (Princeton: Princeton University Press, 1971); Eric Nordlinger, "Political Development, Time Sequences and Rates of Change," in Jason L. Finkle and Robert W. Gable, eds., *Political Development, Time Sequences and Rates of Change* (New York: John Wiley, 1971); and Samuel P. Huntington, *Political Order in Changing Societies* (New Haven: Yale University Press, 1968).

12. See, *Ta Prota Penenta Chronia tes Trapezas tes Ellados: 1928–1978* (The First Fifty Years of the Bank of Greece: 1928–1978) (Athens: Bank of Greece, 1978), p. 495.

13. Diamandouros, "Regime Change and the Prospects for Democracy in Greece: 1974–1983," in O'Donnell et al., eds., *Transitions from Authoritarian Rule: Southern Europe*; and Nicos Mouzelis, *Modern Greece: Facets of Underdevelopment* (New York: Holmes and Meier, 1978).

14. For this argument, see Mouzelis, *Modern Greece*, p. 125.

15. Diamandouros, "Regime Change and the Prospects for Democracy," p. 144.

16. Diamandouros, "Regime Change and the Prospects for Democracy;" and Mouzelis, *Modern Greece*.

17. Despite this, it has often been argued that one of the reasons the military regime failed to take root was socioeconomic change and modernization. Nonetheless, it is also important to note that during the years of military rule, the Greek economy experienced a slowdown in industrial production as well as in agriculture, aggravating the country's chronic balance of payments deficit. Moreover, both the transition and consolidation of Greek democracy occurred during a period of economic stagnation as the country fell further and further behind the West European average.

18. As will be discussed later in this chapter, republicans wanted Greece to fight in World War I on the side of the Entente while the royalists preferred Greece to remain neutral.

19. Zafiris Tzannatos, "Socialism in Greece: Past and Present," in Tzannatos, ed., *Socialism in Greece: The First Four Years* (Aldershot: Gower Publishing Company Limited, 1986), pp. 4, 5.

20. Diamandouros, "Regime Change and the Prospects for Democracy."

21. I use the term "party ideologies" in the strict sense here. It is to be distinguished from the communist versus anticommunist political debate of the post–civil war period.

22. J. C. Loulis, "New Democracy: The New Face of Conservatism," in Howard R. Penniman, ed., *Greece at the Polls: The National Elections of 1974 and 1977* (Washington: American Enterprise Institute for Public Policy Research, 1981), pp. 50–51.

23. Roy C. Macridis, "Elections and Political Modernization in Greece," in Penniman, ed., *Greece at the Polls*.

24. In this study I treat democratic consolidation as distinct from issues regarding the quality of democracy. For a similar treatment of these concepts, see Linz and Stepan, *Problems of Democratic Transition*, pp. 5–6; and "Toward Consolidated Democracies," p. 16. For a somewhat more inclusive definition of democratic consolidation—one that incorporates variables related to the quality of democracy—see Diamond, *Developing Democracy*, chap. 3.

25. See Leonardo Morlino and José R. Montero, "Legitimacy and Democracy in Southern Europe," in Gunther et al., eds., *The Politics of Democratic Consolidation*. It is important to note, however, that the Greek survey was conducted close to the time of the 1985 national elections and the responses were therefore probably affected by the upcoming event.

26. See Constantine Danopoulos, "From Military to Civilian Rule in Contemporary Greece," *Armed Forces and Society*, 10:2 (Winter 1984), pp. 229–50; *Warriors and Politicians in Modern Greece* (Chapel Hill: Documentary Publications, 1985), pp. 147–48; *Daily Reports: Western Europe*, 7 (1 March 1983–22 March 1983) (Washington: Foreign Broadcast Information Service); *Keesing's*, 29 (1983), p. 32587; and Nikolai Todorov, *The Ambassador as Historian: An Eyewitness Account of Bulgarian-Greek Relations in the 1980s* (New Rochelle, NY: Aristide D. Caratzas, 1999). The veracity of the later coups has not been fully documented. Following the alleged 1983 disturbance, however, the government retired fifteen generals (stating, however, that the timing of the retirements was coincidental while denying all rumors of the coup attempt).

27. Although many studies dealing with Greece during the 1950–74 period include the military as part of the right, this study attempts to disaggregate civilians from military elites and treats them as separate actors.

28. Higley and Gunther, eds., *Elites and Democratic Consolidation*; and Higley and Burton, "Elite Settlement and the Taming of Politics."

29. O'Donnell et al., eds, *Transitions from Authoritarian Rule*, vols. 1–4; Karl and Schmitter, "Modes of Transition;" and Schmitter, "The Consolidation of Political Democracy." Although I am not distinguishing between pacts and settlements, Michael Burton, Richard Gunther, and John Higley, "Introduction: Elite Transformations and

Democratic Regimes," in Higley and Gunther, eds., *Elites and Democratic Consolidation* and Higley and Burton, "Elite Settlements and the Taming of Politics," argue that elite settlements differ from pacts in several important ways.

30. See, for example, Donald Share, "Transitions to Democracy and Transition through Transaction," *Comparative Political Studies*, 19:4 (January 1987), pp. 525–48; Donald Share and Scott Mainwaring, "Transitions from Above: Democratization in Brazil and Spain," in Wayne Selcher, ed., *Political Liberalization in Brazil* (Notre Dame: Notre Dame University, Office of Advanced Studies, 1985); O'Donnell et al., eds., *Transitions From Authoritarian Rule*, vols. 1–4; and Higley and Gunther, *Elites and Democratic Consolidation*.

31. See, for example, Richard Clogg, "Karamanlis's Cautious Success: the Background," *Government and Opposition*, 10:3 (Summer 1975), pp. 332–53; P. Nikiforos Diamandouros, "Transition to, and Consolidation of, Democratic Politics in Greece, 1974–1983: A Tentative Assessment," in Pridham, ed., *The New Mediterranean Democracies*; Diamandouros, "Regime Change and the Prospects for Democracy;" and Harry J. Psomiades, "Greece: From the Colonels' Rule to Democracy," in Herz, ed., *From Dictatorship to Democracy*.

32. Diamandouros, "Transition to, and Consolidation of, Democratic Politics."

33. Higley and Gunther, eds., *Elites and Democratic Consolidation*.

34. Constantine P. Danopoulos, "From Military to Civilian Rule in Contemporary Greece," *Armed Forces and Society*, 10:2 (Winter 1984), pp. 229–50.

35. It is worth noting that movement in the opposite direction—the deconsolidation of a previously stable regime—is also possible and that no democracy is immune from deconsolidation and possible breakdown over the long term. See Gunther et al., eds., *The Politics of Democratic Consolidation*; Juan J. Linz and Alfred Stepan, eds., *The Breakdown of Democratic Regimes* (Baltimore: Johns Hopkins University Press, 1978); and Linz and Stepan, "Toward Consolidated Democracies."

36. In a slightly revised version of this theory, John Higley, Michael Burton, and others argue that after consensual unity over government institutions, codes, and rules is achieved, elites may continue to be "affiliated with conflicting parties, movements, and beliefs." See Higley and Burton, "Elite Settlements and the Taming of Politics," p. 98; Burton and Higley, "Political Crises and Elite Settlements," p. 47, and Mattei Dogan and John Higley, "Elites, Crises, and Regimes in Comparative Analysis," in Dogan and Higely, eds., *Elites, Crises*, p. 18.

37. KKE, "Apofase tou 9ou Synedriou tou Kommounistikou Kommatos tes Elladas pano sten Ekthese Drases tes Kentrikes Epitropes" (Decision of the 9th Congress of the Communist Party of Greece on the Report of the Central Committee on its Activities), *Neos Kosmos* (New World), 3:4, p. 30.

38. See Higley and Gunther, *Elites and Democratic Consolidation*.

39. See Arend Lijphart, *The Politics of Accommodation: Pluralism and Democracy in the Netherlands* (Berkeley: University of California Press, 1968); "Consociational Democracy;" and *Democracy in Plural Societies: A Comparative Exploration* (New Haven: Yale University Press, 1977).

40. Richard Gunther, Giacomo Sani, and Goldie Shabad, *Spain After Franco: The Making of a Competitive Party System* (Berkeley: University of California Press, 1986).

41. Gunther et al., eds., *The Politics of Democratic Consolidation*; Diamond, *Developing Democracy*, p. 113; Linz and Stepan, *Problems of Democratic Transition and Consolidation*; and Higley and Gunther, eds., *Elites and Democratic Consolidation*. Also, on the need to eliminate veto groups for democratic consolidation to occur, see J. Samuel Valenzuela, "Democratic Consolidation in Post-Transitional Settings: Notion, Process, and Facilitating Conditions," in Mainwaring et al., *Issues in Democratic Consolidation*.

42. For an account of the limits imposed by the military on democratization see Felipe Agüero, "The Military and the Limits to Democratization in South America," in Mainwaring et al., eds., *Issues in Democratic Consolidation*, and "Democratic Consolidation and the Military in Southern Europe and South America," in Gunther et al., eds., *The Politics of Democratic Consolidation*; and Juan J. Linz, Alfred Stepan, and Richard Gunther, "Democratic Transition and Consolidation in Southern Europe, with Reflections on Latin America and Eastern Europe," in Gunther et al., eds, *The Politics of Democratic Consolidation*. On civilian control see Samuel E. Finer, *The Man on Horseback: The Role of the Military in Politics* (New York: Praeger, 1962); Claude E. Welch, "Civilian Control of the Military: Myth and Reality," in Claude E. Welch, ed., *Civilian Control of the Military* (Albany: State University of New York Press, 1976), and *No Farewell to Arms?* (Boulder: Westview Press, 1987); J. Samuel Fitch, "Toward a Democratic Model of Civil-Military Relations for Latin America," paper presented to the International Political Science Association, Washington, D.C., August 1988; Alfred Stepan, *Rethinking Military Politics* (Princeton: Princeton University Press, 1988); Samuel P. Huntington, "Armed Forces and Democracy: Reforming Civil-Military Relations," *Journal of Democracy* 6:4 (October 1995), pp. 9–17; and Richard H. Kohn, "How Democracies Control the Military," *Journal of Democracy*, 8:4 (October 1997), pp. 140–53.

43. "How Democracies Control the Military," p. 142.

44. Felipe Agüero, "Democratic Consolidation and the Military," 124–25, 140. See also Agüero, "The Assertion of Civilian Supremacy in Post-Authoritarian Contexts: Spain in Comparative Perspective," Ph.D. Dissertation, Duke University, 1991; and *Soldiers, Civilians, and Democracy: Post-Franco Spain in Comparative Perspective* (Baltimore: Johns Hopkins University Press, 1995).

45. Linz, Stepan, and Gunther, "Democratic Transition and Consolidation." See also Linz and Stepan, *Problems of Democratic Transition and Consolidation*.

46. For types of transition paths, see Donald Share, "Transitions to Democracy and Transition Through Transaction," *Comparative Political Studies*, 19:4 (January 1987), pp. 525–48; Alfred Stepan, "Paths Toward Redemocratization: Theoretical and Comparative Considerations," in O'Donnell et al., eds., *Transitions From Authoritarian Rule: Comparative Perspectives*; O'Donnell and Schmitter, *Transitions From Authoritarian Rule: Tentative Conclusions*; Guillermo O'Donnell, "Introduction to the Latin American Cases," in O'Donnell et al., eds., *Transition From Authoritarian Rule: Latin America*; Scott Mainwaring and Donald Share, "Transitions Through Transaction: Democratization in Brazil and Spain," in Selcher, ed., *Political Liberalization in Brazil*; Scott Mainwaring and Eduardo Viola, "Transitions to Democracy: Brazil and Argentina in the 1980s," *Journal of International Affairs*, 38:2 (Winter 1985), 193–219; Samuel P. Huntington, *The Third Wave: Democratization in the Late Twentieth Century* (Norman, OK: University of Oklahoma Press, 1991); and Josep M. Colomer, "Transitions by Agreement: Modeling the Spanish Way," *American Political Science Review*, 85:4 (December 1991), pp. 1283–1302.

47. See, for example, O'Donnell and Schmitter, *Transitions from Authoritarian Rule: Tentative Conclusions*; and Huntington, *The Third Wave*. For a detailed study of Argentina where civilian elites acted hastily to punish those involved in the harsh dictatorial regime, pushing military officers to intervene in the transition process, see David Pion-Berlin, "Between Confrontation and Accommodation: Military and Government Policy in Democratic Argentina," *Journal of Latin American Studies*, 23:3 (October 1991), 543–71.

48. Linz and Stepan, *Problems of Democratic Transition and Consolidation*, also emphasize prior regime type as having a great implication for the transition path followed and the tasks pursued as democratizing countries begin to consolidate their democracies.

49. See Danopoulos, "From Military to Civilian Rule."

50. "Democratic Transitions and Consolidation," in Gunther et al., eds., *The Politics of Democratic Consolidation.*

51. Averoff was the Minister of Defense during Greece's transition to democracy.

52. This study will not analyze the political center for two reasons: (1) change and moderation were most necessary for the left and right in Greece for democratic consolidation to occur, and (2) the center's electorate was largely absorbed by *Nea Demokratia* and especially by PASOK in the post-1974 period.

53. Diamandouros, "Regime Change and the Prospects for Democracy;" and Mouzelis, *Modern Greece.*

54. Juan J. Linz, "Transitions to Democracy," *Washington Quarterly* 13:3 (Summer 1990), p. 156; and Linz and Stepan, "Toward Consolidated Democracies," p. 15.

55. Richard Gunther, Hans-Jürgen Puhle, and P. Nikiforos Diamandouros, "Introduction," in Gunther et al., *The Politics of Democratic Consolidation.*

56. A similar argument can be made for elites of some postcommunist regimes who began to evolve their orientation even before the collapse of communism. See John Higley, Judith Kullberg, and Jan Pakulski, "The Persistence of Postcommunist Elites," *Journal of Democracy*, 7:2 (April 1996), pp. 133–47.

57. In 1975 a survey conducted in Spain indicated that of those respondents desiring a regime other than *Franquismo*, 43 percent indicated a preference for liberal democracy, 17 percent favored other kinds of regime, and 40 percent answered that they did not know or refused to state a preference. See Salustiano Del Campo, Manuel Navarro, and J. Félix Tezanos, *La Cuestión Regional Española* (Madrid: Editorial Cuadernos para el Diálogo, 1977), p. 95. For a discussion of these and other changes in Spain at this time, see Gunther, Sani, and Shabad, *Spain After Franco*, pp. 24–34.

CHAPTER 2

Political Instability and Breakdown, 1909–1967

The breakdown of Greek democracy in 1967 cannot be understood apart from certain fundamental historical and political-cultural features of twentieth-century Greece. Throughout the century and despite more than 120 years of parliamentary government, Greece has seen serious, recurring parliamentary crises, been rent by deep partisan cleavages, has suffered political instability, and has experienced military interventions into politics. As a result, the eventual consolidation of democracy was by no means predetermined by some propitious constellation of political, cultural, and historical factors. On the contrary, it was the historical legacy of endemic political instability that was in many respects responsible for the colonels' intervention and the demise of democracy in 1967. This chapter explores the nature of the deep partisan cleavages and political instability characteristic of twentieth-century Greece. It culminates in a brief analysis of those events leading up to and resulting in the colonels' seizure of power in 1967.

The single most important—and, for democratic stability, most problematic—characteristic of twentieth-century Greek politics has been a tradition of deep political division at both the mass and the elite levels. The origins of partisan division can be traced to the first major cleavage to split Greek political life—the *Ethnikos Dikhasmos*, or National Schism, which resulted from a deep partisan division over whether Greece should have fought in World War I or remained neutral. The Prime Minister, Eleftherios Venizelos, favored participation on the side of the Entente while King Constantine advocated neutrality. Increasingly, and especially after 1920, this cleavage divided the nation into two violently opposed camps of royalists versus republicans, led to political instability during the interwar years and ultimately contributed to repeated military intervention into politics. The nation remained divided by the National Schism until World War II, when this cleavage was largely subsumed by a second, more bitter and divisive political schism—that of communists versus anticommunists.

During the Greek Civil War, this second cleavage violently split the nation into two warring factions of "nationally minded" versus "suspect" citizens and led to a protracted period in which illiberal civil war–era emergency measures were allowed to function alongside a liberal democratic constitution. The result was an effective prolongation of the Greek Civil War as partisan animosities, hatreds, and fears led the war's victors to take discriminatory and repressive action against the defeated. Thus, rather than putting an end to the hatreds that had been bred by the war, the post–civil war period prolonged the schism. Ultimately, anticommunism provided the colonels an "excuse" for their 1967 *coup d'état* as they proclaimed their intention to save Greece from communist subversion. In many respects, then, the breakdown of democracy in 1967 can be attributed to the legacy of division and hatred so characteristic of the Greek Civil War and the succeeding period.

A second fundamental characteristic of twentieth-century Greek politics has been a tradition of military politicization and intervention. As this chapter will show, in the early 1900s the military intervened frequently in politics, deposing one civilian government and replacing it with another. After 1935, however, it also became virulently anticommunist. Liberal officers were purged from the armed forces and recruitment was restricted to those with *bona fide* anticommunist credentials. After World War II and the Greek Civil War, a largely homogeneous, stridently anticommunist officer corps increasingly adopted the mission of ultimate guarantor of Greece's external and internal security against the communist threat. This self-defined mission was only reinforced by Greece's membership in the NATO alliance and its client position *vis-à-vis* the United States, to say nothing of the prevailing anticommunist psychological climate of the Cold War.[1] In this light the 1967 military intervention into politics should also be viewed as the culmination of a protracted period of military politicization.

A third overarching characteristic of Greek political culture was endemic volatility and divisiveness at both the mass and elite levels. Political discourse and behavior eschewed consensus and compromise as a means of solving problems.[2] Rather, the rancorous and demagogic nature of Greek politics reinforced a situation in which the legitimacy of the entire state apparatus was repeatedly called into question by the opposition. This contributed to unrest and gave the colonels a pretext for intervention. To fully understand the origins and nature of the 1967–74 military regime, an appreciation of the deeply divisive and unstable nature of Greek political life is necessary. The task of this chapter is to analyze the roots of that divisiveness and instability.

SEEDS OF INSTABILITY

In 1909 a group of young liberal officers launched the first in the series of coups that would come to characterize twentieth-century civil-military relations in Greece. The officers replaced the "old political oligarchy" and invited the liberal Eleftherios Venizelos to be the new Prime Minister. Under the leadership of Venizelos, the military expanded in size, shed its aristocratic orientation, and became a modernizing force in Greek society.[3]

In 1915, however, the eruption of *Ethnikos Dikhasmos*, or the National Schism, served to divide the entire nation (including the military) into two camps over the issue of whether Greece should fight in World War I or remain neutral. Supporters of Premier Venizelos, a passionate anglophile with irredentist aspirations, favored participation in World War I on the side of the Entente. Supporters of King Constantine, however, advocated neutrality. As a result of this conflict, the king forced Venizelos' resignation twice in 1915. However, in August 1916, a pro-Venizelos coup was staged and a Venizelist provisional government was established in Thessaloniki, forcing the king's resignation in June of the following year.[4]

The ensuing royalist versus republican cleavage was at the root of much instability and conflict in the interwar years. In November 1920 Venizelos suffered a psychologically crushing defeat at the hands of a war-weary electorate, and a plebiscite held on 5 December returned King Constantine to Greece.[5] Once in power, however, the royalists, who had managed to receive popular support for the return of the monarchy by exploiting opposition to the war, continued Venizelos' irredentist campaign in Asia Minor. Their catastrophic defeat in 1922, known as the *Megale Katastrophe* (Great Catastrophe),[6] prompted a group of officers under Colonel Nikolaos Plastiras to launch yet another military coup, calling for the abdication of the king and the resignation of his government. Plastiras' coup was the first but not the last to occur in interwar Greece; from that point on, the military demonstrated an increasing willingness to intervene in politics.[7]

In 1924 the republicans, supported by the military (and by Asia Minor refugees), were returned to power and the monarchy was abolished.[8] Venizelos, who had been in self-imposed exile, responded to his supporters' pleas, returning to Greece in January 1925 to serve as Prime Minister. His Premiership lasted barely a month, however, and was followed by a number of ineffective and short-lived republican governments. This instability culminated in the military dictatorship of General Pangalos. Pangalos, however, was overthrown by yet another putsch in August 1926, only to have Venizelos return to power from 1928 to 1932. The period from 1933 to 1935 climaxed in an abortive *coup d'état* that attempted to return Venizelos to power.[9] In 1935 a rigged plebiscite, probably influenced by the military's support for the king, marked the formal end of the Greek republic and restored the monarchy.[10]

The deep division between monarchists and republicans persisted, however. In the elections of 1936, the royalists and their supporters won 143 seats to the republicans' 142, with the communists holding the balance of power. Much to the dismay of the king and the military, the major parties began negotiating secretly with the communists. Ioannis Metaxas, the general-turned-politician appointed Prime Minister by King George II, alleged that the state was in danger of a communist conspiracy. The king took action, deciding to suspend parliament, dissolve all political parties, and grant extraordinary powers to the police. Eventually, the king signed a decree suspending a number of constitutional provisions and making Metaxas a virtual dictator from 1936 until his death in 1941.[11]

The experiences of the 1930s and 1940s—the Metaxas dictatorship, the Axis occupation, the Greek resistance, and eventual civil war—transformed Greek politics. The National Schism was almost completely eclipsed, as these events overshadowed the old animosities and differences between republican and royalist officers. Many republican officers who had been purged from the military in 1935 were readmitted to active service when Greece fell to the Germans in 1941. Later, the more pressing problem of fighting communist attempts to overthrow bourgeois democracy during the civil war united many republicans and royalists against the threat of communism. The fight against communists also transformed the role of the Greek armed forces. The military, which prior to 1935 played a liberal interventionist role in politics, became an even more conservative and reactionary guardian of the anticommunist status quo.

OCCUPATION, RESISTANCE, AND CIVIL WAR

The legacy of a bitter and divisive civil war[12]—a war that lasted longer and was the cause of more deaths and destruction in Greece than World War II—so deeply divided the nation that the quest for national reconciliation appears to have been foremost on the agenda of democratizers during the transition to democracy.[13] Thus, it is important to understand both the origins of that war as well as its psychological consequences. Its origins can be traced to the emergence of a number of resistance groups that formed during the German occupation of Greece. The first, formed in December 1941, was the communist-dominated National Liberation Front (EAM) and its military wing, the National Popular Liberation Army (ELAS). While a number of other noncommunist organizations were also formed—the most important of which were the National Republican Greek League (EDES) under General Napoleon Zervas and the National and Social Liberation organization (EKKA) of Colonel Dimitrios Psarros[14]—EAM was the largest and most important resistance group to fight in occupied Greece.[15]

The Greek resistance movement was characterized by the inability and/or unwillingness of the various resistance groups to cooperate and form a common front against the Axis. So divided were they that on three different occasions conflict erupted between ELAS and the other groups. In December 1942 fighting broke out between EDES and ELAS. Eventually, the fighting spread to encompass all other resistance groups and, by February 1944, only EDES and ELAS remained. This was the first round of struggle between communist and nationalist forces. The second struggle broke out after liberation, in December 1944, when a communist-led demonstration turned violent and fighting broke out between police and demonstrators in Athens.[16] The internecine fighting that followed lasted for nearly six weeks and ended with ELAS's capitulation only after British reinforcements arrived from Italy. The ceasefire was followed by the signing, in mid-February, of the Varkiza agreement, which, in return for the disarmament of the communists, promised an amnesty for "political crimes" and agreed that elections would be preceded by a plebiscite on the monarchy. However, the extreme right—unwilling to forgive the left for the terror it had created during the occupation and infuriated by the fact that some of ELAS's hostages had been murdered—refused to honor the terms of the Varkiza agreement and began to take revenge against the left. Soon thereafter, when the liberal Sophoulis government announced that elections, the first since 1936, would be held, the left and much of the center protested the unfairness of holding elections in the prevailing climate of disorder and rightist intimidation. Then, in March 1946 the final struggle between ELAS and the nationalist forces began as the left, supported by progressive republicans who opposed the return of the monarchy, announced that they would abstain from the elections scheduled for that month. The left's decision to abstain and take to the mountains in August 1946 led to the third and longest struggle between the two groups—the Greek Civil War.

Lasting until 1949, the civil war was extraordinarily destructive and costly, both in material and human terms. What made the conflict so brutal was the fact that each side did not contain its fighting to clashes with opposing armed units but rather terrorized and executed civilians, sparking local acts of revenge and feeding deeply bitter personal animosities. By the end of the civil war, some 50,000 people were dead, with as many as 6,500 communists under sentences of death.[17] An even greater loss of population occurred, however, by emigration and imprisonment. From early 1948 the communists deported some 25,000 to 28,000[18] children from Greece into the Soviet-bloc—according to communists, for "protection against 'monarcho-fascist' reprisals;"[19] according to the Greek government, the evacuations represented "a new janissary levy."[20] Moreover, some 40,000 communists were sent to prisons and concentration camps within Greece for crimes committed during the civil war, and another 60,000 communists fled Greece for Eastern European countries.[21]

In order to fully comprehend the war's psychological consequences—indeed the deep national schism it created—one must understand the extent to which both sides' perceptions of how the war began were diametrically opposed. It is not too much to say that the fundamental communist/anticommunist division in postwar Greek politics turned on the basis of two completely opposed interpretations of the civil war. According to Greek leftists, the most powerful and genuinely national resistance force to emerge in occupied Greece, EAM,[22] and its military wing, ELAS, were pushed aside after liberation in favor of Greeks who had collaborated with the Nazi occupiers. Furthermore, the left became the target of a systematic, government-led military campaign to eliminate any and all progressive forces in Greece. Thus, in the view of the left, EAM/ELAS, in taking to the mountains, was engaged in self-defense against terrorist acts by extreme rightists and other dictatorial forces (such as the anticommunist Security Battalions[23]). As one report noted in 1948, "whatever the contributing factors—including deep poverty—Rightist terror [has] been the primary recruiting agent for the bands of the left."[24] Leftists argued that as the true democratic citizens of Greece, they had a constitutional right to kill rightist "terrorists" in order to defend their lives when assailed, and that people who took to the mountains did so to escape "terrorist" attack.[25]

Concerning the communist-led demonstration that took place in Athens on 3 December 1944, the left contended that police, completely unprovoked, fired on the demonstrators, thereby *pushing* communists into combat with government forces. Furthermore, when a truce was negotiated and a political settlement was finally reached in February 1945 between the Greek government and ELAS (the Varkiza agreement), it was the government and not ELAS that failed to keep its pledge: leftist guerrillas did not receive the amnesty promised them, even though they surrendered their arms to the government as agreed. The extreme right—unwilling to forgive the left's mistakes—refused to honor the terms of the agreement and continued to attack the left. And when the Sophoulis government called for new elections, it announced that they would precede—rather than follow—the plebiscite on the monarchy. This was a clear violation of Varkiza. Thus, it was the right, not the left, that failed to honor the peace treaty. While the left, the "true" resistor of fascism, was being persecuted, little was being done to bring suspected Nazi collaborators to justice. Moreover, the March 1946 parliamentary elections, from which the left abstained, as well as the referendum on the monarchy[26] held later that year, were shams according to the left, as ballot rigging and a climate of terror and violence pervaded the entire political process.

In sum, this interpretation of the civil war presents the left as the true democratic force in Greece, engaged in self-defense against extreme right-wing terrorist bands and fighting an oppressive, foreign-dominated, and antidemocratic state controlled by former Nazi "quislings." As a result of this intolerable situation, the communist leadership was *pushed* on to the offensive.

The right's interpretation of the causes of the civil war was strikingly different. According to nationalists EAM originated as a national resistance force in which Greeks of various political persuasions participated. However, EAM quickly became dominated by the Greek Communist Party's (KKE) leadership. When other resistance groups formed outside of EAM, they were either infiltrated, taken over, or attacked and destroyed by ELAS. According to nationalist interpretation, it soon became clear that ELAS's aim was not simply resistance to the Nazis but "the total transformation of Greek society on Soviet lines. ... [T]he Communists would only support the allied strategy so far as it suited their primary objective, which was to take control of Greece after the war."[27]

From this perspective the communists made, in fact, several overt bids for power. In October 1943, believing that Greece was about to be liberated and that the monarchy would return to Greece, ELAS launched an all-out attack on all other resistance forces. Later, in early 1944 an antimonarchist mutiny among Greek forces in Egypt[28] was fomented by leftist officers who wished to force the Greek exile government to create a government of national unity based on the communist-dominated Political Committee of National Liberation.[29] At the end of 1944, when guerrilla forces were ordered to disband, the leaders of EAM—which had been granted five out of fifteen seats in the postliberation government of George Papandreou—refused to disband ELAS and its ancillary organizations. Thus, when fighting broke out on 3 December 1944, after a communist-organized demonstration turned violent, the best units of ELAS, "conveniently" concentrated around the capital, attempted to seize Athens by force. Still later, even after the Sophoulis government declared a political amnesty, suspended some 60,000 prosecutions, and announced that elections would be held in March 1946, the KKE—still legal at that time—refused to participate in the elections and, in the summer of 1946, attacked the village of Litokhoro in Central Greece. This, argued the nationalists, set the stage for the KKE's third bid for power, the 1946–49 civil war.

To put it simply, the anticommunists, pointing to the communist regimes on Greece's northern frontier, the willingness of the KKE to collaborate with the communist parties of Albania, Yugoslavia, and Bulgaria and even to cede Greek territory to an independent Slav Macedonia, and to the ruthlessness of the Greek communists at home, claimed that in fighting EAM they were saving Greece from communism. A former deputy of *Nea Demokratia* argues:

Let's not forget that the [Greek] Communist Party had signed [an agreement] relinquishing Macedonia to the Bulgarians ... and then to Tito[30]. ... [B]asically, the goal of EAM and ELAS back then was to seize Athens. ... And that is why they launched the movement in the Middle East.[31] That is why they turned and carried out the *Dekemvriana*.[32]

And,

Greeks who believed in communism ... did so many horrible things to Greece. During the occupation—having committed crimes against the people, having butchered thousands of Greeks—they attempted [to seize power]. ... Then, in December, after having destroyed all other national resistance groups they tried [to seize power again]. ... The communists also went into the mountains with a so-called aim—the so-called pretext of fighting the occupiers—but essentially they went into the mountains with the aim of seizing Greece ... and putting into place a dictatorship of the proletariat.[33]

In sum, according to conservative opinion, "between 1943 and 1949 *parliamentary institutions were threatened from the extreme left, rather than the extreme right.*"[34] This communist/anticommunist division of Greek political life—this new National Schism—would have a deeply profound effect on the nature of postwar Greek politics.

A COUP IN THE MAKING, 1949–67

Emerging from the civil war as the victor over communist forces and homogenized from repeated purges of its liberal officers,[35] the Greek military became an extremely powerful and largely autonomous actor in post–civil war Greek politics. An institutional arrangement during the last year of the civil war, authorizing Field Marshal Papagos to pursue any military operation without the approval of the government or any other civilian body, formally institutionalized the military's autonomy. Thus, by the time the armed forces were placed under the authority of the Ministry of Defense in 1953, they had already become accustomed to their autonomous and highly politicized position. Moreover, approximately one year after the Middle East mutiny, a group of right-wing officers merged two officers' resistance groups and formed a secret organization known as IDEA (The Sacred Union of Greek Officers), a group with the avowed purpose to prevent a communist takeover.[36] Appointing themselves the guardians of the nation from external and internal communist threats, officers of IDEA soon came to control key positions within the army and played a decisive role in establishing a repressive, anticommunist post–civil war state. Frightened by the threat of communism, neither the political parties nor the king challenged the military's authority in the early post–civil war period—indeed they often actively supported it.

Although the civil war ended in 1949, it was legally prolonged until 1962 through the "theory of permanent civil war,"[37] in which parliament, shortly after enacting the 1952 Constitution, passed a resolution making it legally possible to enforce civil war emergency anticommunist measures, even if they contravened that new Constitution. This made it possible for courts to consider the "rebellion" (or the "bandit war" [*symmoritopolemos*] as it was legally referred to) as ongoing despite the fact that the communists had been defeated and the actual fighting had stopped. As a result, repressive legislation enacted during the civil war—legislation that would later be in contravention of the democratic Constitution of 1952—limited the exercise of civil liberties to the *ethnicofrones* ("nationally minded" citizens).

According to Public Law 509 (1947), for example, all communist and related activities were forbidden. Emergency Law 516 (1948) established "loyalty boards" with the authority to judge the loyalty of all present and prospective government employees based on any oral or written information received from any "pertinent available information source."[38] Testimony from the accused could not be heard and appeals of the boards' decisions to the courts were not permitted. Law 1612 (1950) reactivated the Metaxas Espionage Law 375 (1936), a provision that martial law courts could prosecute communists and other leftists as spies for the Soviet Union and could sentence them to death. Furthermore, the formal exclusion of the left from public life was enforced by a large police bureaucracy that engaged in systematic surveillance of hundreds of thousands of citizens and kept dossiers (*fakeloi*) on them. Until their abolition in 1974, these dossiers placed suspected leftists into various categories of threat to the state—categorizing them as *ethnicofrones* of the first grade (Epsilon one), the second grade (Epsilon two), "Alpha" leftists, "Beta" cryptocommunists, "Gamma" dangerous communists, and "Chi" unknown[39]—all in an attempt to eradicate leftist influences and to secure the loyalty of the masses to the established regime.

Thus, while the regime was formally democratic (i.e., elections were held regularly, parliamentary institutions functioned, and a democratic constitution was in force), it continued to display a number of illiberal—indeed, antidemocratic—features. In addition to those mentioned above, Greek citizens were also required to obtain certificates of "national-mindedness" for professional licensing, employment in the civil service, a driver's license, a passport, and (for a time) university entrance and scholarships.[40] Such certificates were granted by the police only to "nationally minded" citizens. All other Greeks, stigmatized as communists, or fellow-travelers, were denied these certificates. In a country where, according to one estimate,[41] approximately one-third of all urban employees and one-half of all nonmanual employees were on the state payroll, the ability to withhold such certificates gave the police great leverage over the citizenry. As a former centrist officer argued in an interview with the author:

Back then, we persecuted ideas. ... The Communist Party was ... illegal. And we did not persecute only the act; we also persecuted the convictions. The cleaning lady of the municipality could not be appointed [to this civil service position] if her brother had gone to the mountains and fought the Germans. If he had gone with ELAS, which subsequently was dominated by the communists, he was considered a communist when in actuality he had gone to fight the enemy.[42] And his sister couldn't be appointed cleaning lady to the municipality. Thus, from this point of view, [the post–civil war period] was antidemocratic. It was antidemocratic because it was totally controlled by the state apparatus and the military. No one could enlist in the armed forces if the gendarme of his neighborhood did not approve. An officer could not marry the girl he loved if the gendarme of his neighborhood did not say she was nationally minded.[43]

A former "suspect" centrist deputy added, "[U]ntil 1961 I was not given a passport. That is, my dream to go abroad to study was restricted. ... I did not have a driver's license either; I was not able to get a driver's license until 1961. They gave it to me ... as a favor—because some [nationally minded] acquaintances went and put in a few good words for [me]."[44]

All aspects of an individual's life had to be investigated both for documented wrongdoing as well as for potential "wrong-thinking." In order to acquire such information, "the petitions one signed, the groups one joined, the books one read, the friendships one had, and the statements one made" were all subject to surveillance.[45] Evidence of surveillance was given by the following officer who argued that "[o]fficers were watched to see what newspapers they were reading."[46] When probed as to how they were watched, he responds:

An [off-duty] officer would bring his newspaper with him [to the base]. Or they would go to the police and the police would ask the kiosk in Larrissa, Volos—in the small towns where people are known—[what newspaper the officer was buying]. When they saw that you purchased a newspaper that was [even] thought to be centrist, "Ah! He's a communist!", [they would exclaim.] If the newspaper was not a rightist paper, it was a communist paper. ... I took three exams to go abroad and all three times they rejected me because I read *Ta Nea*.[47]

A former PASOK deputy agrees: "I ... was a centrist and they would call us to the police station—me too. They called me to the police station as a teenager. My accusation was that I read a leftist paper. I didn't read a leftist paper! I read *Ta Nea!*"[48]

Repressive measures not only targeted habitual "wrong-thinkers" but also their acquaintances, friends, mothers, fathers, wives, husbands, brothers, sisters, and children. "Guilt by association" was often used to judge whether a person was nationally minded. As one respondent expressed, "The bourgeois class threw into the bag of the defeated all the moderate centrists which they pursued as leftists. They even said my father was a leftist and they took his passport from him. I, [too,] at the age of sixteen had a thick dossier."[49] Another parliamentarian adds, "If [one's] grandfather was in EAM or ELAS then [she] was suspect even if [she] had different political convictions. And this resulted in the inability to enter school [and] find a job."[50]

According to such respondents, then, the civil war was followed by a long period in which repressive legislation enacted at the time of the civil war continued to function to the advantage of some members of Greek society (the victors of the war) over others (the vanquished). They maintained that the entire post–civil war period was antidemocratic and repressive.

Interviews with others, however, revealed a very different picture of the post–civil war period. Unlike the first group, which viewed this period as repressive and antidemocratic, the second group believed that the legislation enacted at the time of the civil war was the means by which the Greek state was able to protect itself from communist subversion—thereby safeguarding liberal democracy. Even though many acknowledged that illiberal methods were used, they maintained that repressive legislation—the system of dossiers, the certificates of national-mindedness, and the outlawing of the communist party—was necessary to protect the Greek democratic regime—circumscribed and limited though it was. A Greek officer whose father was killed in the civil war argued:

Certainly they were persecuted since they were fellow-travelers opposed to the regime. What should the governments have done? ... The penal code ... enumerates certain wrongful acts—treason, disturbing the peace, mutiny, persecutions. ... Were they not antiregime when they tried to overthrow the regime? Does democracy entail regime overthrow? And does democracy entail bringing Tito's or Stalin's regime to Greece? Some injustices were committed. But no one was wronged for the sake of being wronged. He was wronged because he was believed to be of those persuasions—those persuasions that were illegal.[51]

Likewise, a parliamentary deputy argued that the outlawing of the Communist Party must be seen in this light:

We cannot call [the outlawing of the Communist Party] antidemocratic because a party which sits in parliament[52] while also having an army with which it attempts to seize government and to impose its own dictatorship ... would be outlawed in any country of the world. And, in my opinion, the action taken to ban the [Communist Party] was not antidemocratic at that time. It was a necessary measure of self-defense.[53]

Another deputy claimed that the system of dossiers used to classify all Greek citizens served the useful purpose of protecting the democratic regime: "For those who lived during 1940–46 or 1944–49, the imperative situation was one of self-defense—that is, to save the Greek and national idea [from] communism. ... Thus, the dossiers [were] an indispensable defense-shield of the nation."[54] According to a fourth respondent, even "the certificates of national-mindedness were an attempt of the bourgeois regime—of the free regime—to secure itself from overthrow. Thus, they were measures of protection."[55]

This group of respondents also claimed that the reason the emergency legislation was maintained long after the civil war had ended was that the communist threat did not disappear immediately after the defeat of the communists in 1949. In fact, many Greeks believed that a communist threat existed throughout much of the 1950s and 1960s. One respondent exclaimed:

What definitely did take place here was anticommunist propaganda. That is a fact; the war had just ended; the blood was still steaming ... and Zachariades[56] was threatening from abroad that he was [waiting for the opportunity] ... to invade Greece again. What was Greek democracy to do? Was it not supposed to defend itself? ... [Military officers] were taught about the dangers facing the fatherland—both internal and external. The internal danger was known—it was the KKE, which continuously aspired to seize government [by force]. And, besides, after their defeat when they had departed to the communist countries, [their leaders] ... continued to threaten that they [still] had weapons. ... Weren't the officers supposed to ... prepare themselves against an enemy which continued to declare that it was still present? ... [Thus,] despite the fact that they were defeated, they continued to plot, to threaten, and to prepare themselves for another round. And proof of this were the wirelesses they sent to Greece, various small bands which returned to Greece, the growth of clandestine organizations ... composed of individuals they were sending from behind the iron curtain, etc.[57]

In actuality, the benefit of hindsight has since revealed that manipulation of intelligence reports in the mid-1960s by the army and police led to an overestimation of the communist threat. Nevertheless, the *perception* of a threat was real for many people. Take, for example, Panayiotes Kanellopoulos, the moderate and well-respected leader of the conservative ERE from 1963 to 1974, who later wrote: "[I]n February 1965, because of some false information that was carried to me by some KYP[58] officials and others in the General Staff that the communists had brought weapons into Greece, I became alarmed and called the people of Athens to a rally."[59] As a prominent centrist argued in an interview with the author: "I was deceived. They would bring me reports, and I would believe them."[60] Constantine Karamanlis also indicated that he perceived a communist threat:

It is across our territory, *on* our national territory that the road from Eastern Europe to the Mediterranean passes. And that is why, since the time of Peter the Great, Greece has scarcely ever ceased to be subjected to pressure from the Slav-Communist mass. There is Russia but there are also the neighbors. Their covetousness moreover has scarcely ever ceased to cast an eye towards Greek Macedonia and Thrace. It grieves me to say that this threat is all the more formidable because there exists among us a Communist Party that is powerful, organized and entirely subject to Moscow. The Soviets have always pressed it to support from within Greece designs of Slav Communism, to create a Macedonian state, which naturally and from the beginning would be a satellite at the expense of Greece.[61]

In short, available evidence clearly indicates that a mixture of genuine fear of communist subversion—real or imagined—and a calculated exploitation of that fear by others for political and ideological purposes motivated many of the illiberal, repressive measures of the post–civil war period and provided a pretext for the colonels' coup in 1967.

Finally, an adequate understanding of this period cannot be had without also mentioning British and, especially, American foreign policy in the early years of the Cold War. Since Greece had experienced a civil war between communists and nationalists and given its strategic location in the Eastern Mediterranean, foreign intervention—first by Britain and later by the United States—was inevitable. In particular, U.S. policy was consistently aimed at containing and limiting the Greek left since it was assumed that should the Greek government fall to communism, this would lead to the fall, not only of the Middle East, but of parts of Western Europe itself—especially Italy and France—that had strong communist parties. Given this prevailing anticommunist Cold War mentality, American political, economic, and military aid was unhesitatingly granted to Greece and, in return, American policy-makers were given a direct role in Greece's internal affairs. As A. A. Fatouros writes, "No decision on any important matters ... [was] taken by Greek officials without consultation with, and normally the agreement of, the U.S. representatives at the American mission."[62] As Lawrence S. Wittner puts it: The United States "bolstered the power of the king, cooperated with British military intervention, excluded the left from the cabinet and even parliamentary representation, placed U.S. economic and military resources at the disposal of the right, flirted with military dictatorship, and narrowly limited political and individual freedoms."[63] Thus, it comes of no surprise that in the minds of many Greeks, the United States was culpable both for the repressive climate of the postwar period and of the colonels' dictatorship that followed.

BULLIES AND DEMAGOGUES

The style and tone of Greek postwar politics—characterized by rancor, emotionalism, irresponsibility, hyperbole, and demagoguery—also proved inimical to democratic stability and consolidation. It suffices to say that between 1946 and the victory of Papagos' Greek Rally in 1952, no less than twenty-five different governments came and went from power. The 1961 elections are but one example of the rancor and demagoguery that eventually contributed to democratic collapse in 1967. In those elections Karamanlis' conservative National Radical Union (ERE) won 50.1 percent of the vote to the Center Union/Progressive alliance's 34 percent. No sooner were the election results announced than Karamanlis came under fire from the opposition parties, which claimed they had been the victims of an "electoral coup d'état." The opposition, and especially the fiery and charismatic leader of the Center Union (EK), George Papandreou, accused the right of electoral malfeasance, intimidation, and violence and launched a "relentless struggle" against both Karamanlis and the monarchy.

While there is no doubt that electoral manipulation and intimidation did in fact take place in 1961[64]—albeit not on a scale extensive enough to affect the overall results of the election[65]—the important point about these elections is that the emotional and demagogic debate that developed around them set the stage for the political instability that immediately preceded the 1967 coup. The opposition's criticisms were fierce: Papandreou launched his "relentless struggle" against the "violence and fraud" of the right, as well as "the General Staff of the Army, the [Greek] Central Intelligence Agency, the gendarmerie, the National Security Battalions and other dark forces."[66] Both Papandreou's Center Union and the United Democratic Left (EDA—largely the legal cover of the outlawed KKE) contended that the army, with the acquiescence of the king and the right, had plotted and engaged in intimidation and electoral fraud in order to prevent a Center Union victory and to preclude an EDA resurgence reminiscent of the 1958 national elections when it had become the formal opposition. They alleged large-scale voting by "phantom" voters and maintained that in Athens alone more than 100,000 illegal votes had been cast. In 1963 the murder of left-wing parliamentary deputy Gregorios Lambrakis by right-wing fanatics in Thessaloniki lent credence to the opposition's claim that an unofficial "parastate" functioned alongside the official state: "A monstrous picture was assembled and presented to the public of a fascist monarchy, a police state, a corrupt and incompetent government, and a systematic oppression of national heroes in concentration-camps."[67]

The atmosphere created by these events reinforced popular perceptions of a right known for such "dynamic methods … as electoral manipulation, repressive techniques, royal and military intervention in politics, and monopoly control over the army and security methods."[68] Some claimed that Karamanlis and his party had tyrannically oppressed the left.[69] Still others argued that Karamanlis' "collaborators included a number of intolerant bullies who delighted in harassing communists. These men indulged in witch hunts, and kept in being emergency measures … long after their initial justification had disappeared."[70] A centrist deputy, George Mylonas, expressed this point of view:

He (Karamanlis) and his party should be blamed, and blamed very severely, for carrying on the civil-war, anti-Communist, and anti-progressive witch-hunting atmosphere in order to remain in power. They felt that if the country really reached a purely peaceful period and persecution of progressives dubbed "Communists" stopped, they would very likely lose the majority. That in my view is the great wrong committed by the Right in postwar Greek developments: wanting to keep the civil war atmosphere hot for as long as they could, so that they could exploit it from an electoral point of view.[71]

It was in this charged political climate that the old regime question of whether Greece should remain a monarchy or become a republic gradually reemerged. The monarchy's popularity suffered from the perception that it had participated in the electoral manipulation of 1961, in particular, as well as in the parastate, more generally. Further exacerbating this problem was the refusal of King Paul and Queen Frederika to take the advice of Premier Karamanlis in 1963 when he asked them to postpone a state visit to Britain, thereby embarrassing the government.[72] Eventually, this and other disagreements between the monarchy and Karamanlis culminated in the latter's resignation from government. Republicans stepped up their attacks on the royal family, accusing them of being, at best, an expensive and unnecessary luxury for Greece, and, at worst, a corrupt and repressive institution.

Capitalizing on the controversy over the monarchy, Papandreou's "relentless struggle" paid off in the elections of 16 February 1964 in which 53 percent of the vote and 171 of 300 seats went to the Center Union. Papandreou's term in office, however, was brief. In May 1965 his efforts to exert prime ministerial authority over the leadership of the army and of KYP (both under the leadership of IDEA members) by replacing senior officers with his own nominees brought him into conflict with his own Minister of Defense, Petros Garoufalias, who refused to carry out the sacking. At the same time Papandreou sought evidence of a right-wing army conspiracy that had allegedly plotted the electoral manipulation of the 1961 elections. Much to Papandreou's surprise, a left-wing conspiracy, known as *Aspida*, was instead uncovered in which the Prime Minister's own son, Andreas Papandreou, was implicated and accused of being the leader. Unwilling to carry out a purge in the army as the Prime Minister wished, Garoufalias was dismissed by Papandreou but refused to go, accusing Papandreou of using KYP to shelter the activities of *Aspida*.

A two-week dispute ensued between Papandreou and King Constantine. The king agreed to dismiss Garoufalias but refused to allow Papandreou to take the Defense portfolio himself, arguing this would be improper while his son was under investigation. A protracted parliamentary crisis followed: "[King] Constantine believed that he was protecting the armed forces from a demoralizing political purge. Papandreou considered that the young king was meddling in affairs which were not his business."[73] Papandreou thus left the premiership on 15 July 1965. According to some he resigned in protest at the king's political interference. According to others, he had been wrongfully dismissed by the king.[74]

In any event, King Constantine refused to call for new elections but instead attempted to induce other Center Union deputies to form a new government. While acting within his constitutional rights as Head of State, some argue that, in reality, the king "set about implementing a strategy of trying to split the Centre Union"[75] by giving mandates to three different Center Union deputies to form a government. A long period of rancorous politics and governmental instability followed. The first deputy, George Athanasiades-Novas, said on 15 July that the king had given him a mandate to form a new Center Union cabinet and declared that this verified the "King's firm resolve to cooperate with parliament's majority to respect the letter and spirit of the constitution."[76] Hearing this, George Papandreou denounced the new government and the young monarch: the "constitution has been violated. The peoples' government was forced to resign." In turn, he called upon Greek citizens to stage protests against "the government of traitors."[77] While some observers believed his call to be for peaceful protest, others concluded that Papandreou was virtually threatening revolution and the overthrow of the monarchy as he angrily shouted[78]: "A new struggle begins." On 19 July 1965, addressing a crowd of some 200,000 supporters in Athens, he declared: "The question now is who rules the country—the King or the people. ... I have ... explained to the King and I repeat it now. In the regime of a crowned democracy (i.e., constitutional monarchy) ... the King reigns but the people rule."[79] Throughout his speech shouts of "Plebiscite! Plebiscite!" were heard.[80]

A long period of unrest followed. On 16 July 1965, fifty-seven demonstrators and fifty-one policemen were injured in Athens when demonstrators protested the swearing-in of the new cabinet, shouting "Down with Novas' puppet government!" and "Fascism will not pass!"[81] The following day the General Confederation of Labor staged a mass rally of 25,000 Papandreou supporters, demanding the new cabinet's resignation. The day after that 20,000 demonstrated in Iraklion, Crete, chanting, "Plebiscite!"[82] On 21 July, one student was killed and 130 persons were injured when 10,000 demonstrators battled police during a protest demanding Papandreou's return to power.[83] Then on 20 August, severe rioting by Papandreou supporters broke out in the streets of Athens as 15,000 youths marched through the city chanting, lighting bonfires, smashing windows, and setting up barricades. Kanellopoulos, the leader of ERE who had warned parliament on 28 August of "large scale intimidations of the Greek people ... by Center Union bullies,"[84] was surrounded in a cafe by a hostile group of Papandreou supporters and had to be rescued by police.

Debate within parliament was no less rancorous and violent. During the entire summer of 1965, bitter debates and even fistfights periodically broke out on the floor of parliament as neither of the king's first two choices was able to receive a vote of confidence. Finally, Stephanos Stephanopoulos[85] won a vote of confidence and formed a government supported by the ERE, some Progressives, and forty-five breakaway Center Union deputies. No sooner was that government formed than rumors began that the forty-five "apostates"—as the Center Union defectors came to be called—had been bribed with money and cabinet posts by the Palace and the American Embassy. By this point charges of coups and countercoups were making front-page headlines and being openly discussed in public. To the supporters of the EK, the "apostate" government was wholly undemocratic in that Papandreou, who led the EK to victory, was no longer Prime Minister and ERE, which had lost the election, had helped to form the new government. Thus, while the new government was legitimate—in the sense of controlling a majority of seats in parliament—the perception that the government was a perversion of a democratic election result was common among the center and left.

Meanwhile, the investigation of the *Aspida* conspiracy was drawing to a close. In October 1965 an Athens court martial reached "the conclusion that there is sufficient evidence that the leader of the unlawful organization [*Aspida*] was Andreas Papandreou" and that his organization was plotting to seize political power.[86] In a series of follow-up articles and speeches, Andreas Papandreou countered that the United States, NATO, and the Greek monarchy were engaged in plots of their own, asserting that forces within Greece were either plotting to rig or prevent the elections scheduled for May 1967. He asserted that a dictatorship was being prepared by a "junta whose tentacles spread from the palace to foreign intelligence services, the extreme right and the economic oligarchy." This dictatorship was allegedly being secretly arranged by a group of senior generals in alliance with the king who were contemplating the use of emergency measures of relatively short duration to avert a "communist takeover."[87]

Seeing that the country had reached a fever pitch, George Papandreou, Panayiotes Kanellopoulos, and King Constantine reached a secret agreement in December 1966 to hold elections on 28 May 1967. As the time for elections neared, however, Andreas Papandreou and his supporters became more and more volatile, claiming that "the Prime Minister would be sworn in on election night in Constitution Square by a triumphant multitude, with or without the sanction of the King."[88] In addition, the tenor of George Papandreou's electoral campaign in April 1967 suggests that had the Center Union party been elected to power, Papandreou would have attempted another military purge. Moreover, to many who believed that Papandreou's "relentless struggle" had found "warm support" from the Greek communists (who quickly organized demonstrations and strikes on his behalf[89]), it now appeared that Andreas Papandreou—the more radical of the two Papandreous—had even formed an electoral coalition with EDA.

As it happened, the elections of May 1967 were never held. A small group of colonels, using a NATO contingency plan devised to counteract serious internal disorder, launched a *coup d'état* on 21 April 1967, catching the king, politicians, and senior military officers off-guard. An official publication of the dictatorial regime indicated that officers had become increasingly alarmed by the mass demonstrations and fights breaking out between deputies in parliament. Entitled *Why the Revolution of 21 April Occurred*, it reported that from April 1965 to April 1967, 80 percent of Greek trade unions went on strike and estimated that a total of 950 strikes took place. It argued that an estimated 60 percent of those strikes were organized or inspired by communists, and that 1,200 individuals (of which 300 were gendarmes) were injured and fifteen people killed during this unrest.[90] The publication further justified the coup on the grounds of preventing a total collapse of Greek politics and government, pointing out that governments had come and gone every five months on average during the previous few years.[91]

In reality, the origins of the coup of 21 April 1967 can be traced to the Greek Civil War and the secret anticommunist organization, IDEA. Most of the officers participating in the coup of 21 April were members of that organization and had fought against the communists at the time of the civil war. Thus, it is not surprising that an official explanation for the coup stressed that "the real danger was that Greece was again turning toward Communism."[92] In the words of several officers interviewed during the dictatorship:

We fought the Communists in Korea; we defeated them three times in Greece. Yet I was stunned to see them again on the sidewalks of Athens. (The national danger from Communist subversion was seen) when Athens was transformed into an arena of mobocracy. ... Demonstrations [took place] which had as their objective chaos and the destruction of Greece. ... The same events repeated themselves ... as they had in the period of 1944 to 1949. We had no other choice but to intervene.[93]

The first formal statement of the colonels gives a similar justification for the army's overthrow of democracy:

We have long been witnessing a crime committed against our people and our nation. Unscrupulous and base party compromises, shameful recklessness of a great part of the press, ... complete debasement of Parliament, all-around slander, paralysis of the state machinery, ... moral decline, secret and open collaboration with subversion, and finally, constant inflammatory slogans of unscrupulous demagogues have destroyed the nation's peace, created an atmosphere of anarchy, chaos, hatred, and discord, and led us to the brink of national catastrophe.[94]

In sum, according to the coup-makers, intervention was necessary to save Greece from communism.

CONCLUSION

To summarize, this chapter has argued that the 1967 military intervention was rooted in twentieth-century parliamentary crises, deep partisan cleavages, chronic political instability and a tradition of military interventionism. More specifically, the intervention was principally brought about by the divisive legacy of the Greek Civil War, which had devastating consequences on the Greek psyche for decades, ultimately contributing to a deep national schism between those Greeks considered to be "nationally minded" and those believed to be "suspect." The ascendence of the anticommunist ideology during the post–civil war period, the widespread fear of communist subversion (real or imagined), and the calculated exploitation of that fear by some nationalists provided justification for the colonels' coup. As the rest of the study will illustrate, the success of Greece's transition and consolidation trajectories thus depended in large part on the successful resolution of these divisions that ultimately had their roots in the civil war and post–civil war period. Resolution, however, was slow, taking place at differing speeds for different political actors and rarely having the support of all significant elites until the 1980s.

Specifically, the colonels' authoritarian regime remained in power from 1967 to 1974, and although unpopular both in Greece and abroad, it faced relatively little open resistance. In the first several years of authoritarianism, many Greeks appeared unwilling to admit a serious abnormality, optimistic perhaps that the regime would fall of its own accord, while others had little difficulty coming to terms with the dictatorship, preferring it over the chaos that had preceded its onset.[95] Even Greeks who were ideologically opposed to the regime remained relatively passive in their resistance. As the following chapter will illustrate, resistance organizations were formed, but little coherence, unity, or direction existed among them, and they remained largely factionalized and uninfluential. Writing during the dictatorship, an opponent of the junta explained these divisions: "The unification of resistance groups ... is prevented by the ideological differences and the mutual distrust that still exists between, for example, royalist and left-wing resisters; by the excessive individualism of the Greeks, and the petty jealousies and vanities which prevents one from taking orders from another, and vice-versa."[96]

Even Greek political parties that were unanimously united in their opposition to the junta never really managed to consolidate their efforts and present a united front against the regime. As will be illustrated in more detail in the following chapter, ideological, personal, and partisan differences proved to be formidable obstacles to the achievement of a united antidictatorial front.

NOTES

1. See, for example, Theodore A. Couloumbis, *Greek Political Reaction to American and NATO Influences* (New Haven: Yale University Press, 1966); Couloumbis and John O. Iatrides, eds., *Greek-American Relations: A Critical Review* (New York: Pella Pub. Co., 1980); Couloumbis, John A. Petropoulos, and Harry J. Psomiades, *Foreign Interference in Greek Politics: An Historical Perspective* (New York: Pella Pub. Co., 1976); Iatrides, "Britain, the United States, and Greece, 1945-9," in David H. Close, ed., *The Greek Civil War, 1943–1950* (New York: Routledge, 1993); Iatrides, ed., *Greece in the 1940s: A Nation in Crisis* (Hanover, NH: University Press of New England, 1981); Iatrides, *Revolt in Athens: The Greek Communist "Second Round," 1944–1945* (Princeton: Princeton University Press, 1972).

2. S. Victor Papacosma, *Politics and Culture in Greece* (Ann Arbor: Center for Political Studies, Institute for Social Research, University of Michigan, 1988), p. 1. On Greek political culture, see also Keith R. Legg and John M. Roberts, *Modern Greece: A Civilization on the Periphery* (Boulder: Westview Press, 1997); George A. Kourvetaris, *Studies on Modern Greek Society and Politics* (Boulder: East European Monographs, 1999); and Adamantia Pollis, "The Political Implications of the Modern Greek Concept of Self," *British Journal of Sociology* 16 (March 1985), pp. 29–47.

3. Many scholars have characterized the 1909 coup as a bourgeois revolution. See Tasos Vournas, *Goudi—To Kinima tou 1909* (Goudi—The 1909 Coup) (Athens: Tolides, 1957); Spyros Markezinis, *Politike Historia tes Neoteras Ellados* (Political History of Modern Greece) (Athens: Papyros, 1968); and Giannis Kordatos, *Historia tes Neoteres Elladas: 20os Aionas* (History of Modern Greece: 20th Century) (Athens: n.p., 1957). For a different point of view, see Nicos Mouzelis, *Modern Greece: Facets of Underdevelopment* (New York: Holmes & Meier, 1978); George Dertilis, *Koinonikos Metaschimatismos kai Stratiotike Epemvase: 1880–1909* (Social Transformation and Military Intervention: 1880–1909) (Athens: Exantas, 1985); and Thanos Veremis, *The Military in Greek Politics: From Independence to Democracy* (Montreal: Black Rose Books, 1997).

4. See George Th. Mavrogordatos, *Stillborn Republic: Social Coalitions and Party Strategies in Greece, 1922–1936* (Berkeley: University of California Press, 1983); George Ventires, *He Hellas tou 1910–1920* (The Greece of 1910–1920) (Athens: Ikaros, 1970); Keith R. Legg, *Politics in Modern Greece* (Stanford: Stanford University Press, 1969), pp. 188–89; Constantine Tsoukalas, *The Greek Tragedy* (Baltimore: Penguin, 1969); Thanos Veremis, *Hoi Epemvaseis tou Stratou sten Hellenike Politike, 1916–1936* (The Military's Intervention into Greek Politics, 1916–1936) (Athens: Odysseas, 1983); *The Military in Greek Politics*; and Richard Clogg, *A Short History of Modern Greece* (Cambridge: Cambridge University Press, 1986), pp. 105–32.

5. Richard Clogg, *Parties and Elections in Greece: The Search for Legitimacy* (Durham, NC: Duke University Press, 1987), p. 8.

6. On the Asia Minor defeat, see Thomas Doulis, *Disaster and Fiction: Modern Greek Fiction and the Impact of the Asia Minor Disaster of 1922* (Berkeley: University of California Press, 1977).

7. On the role of the armed forces in interwar Greece, see Thanos Veremis, "The Greek Army in Politics, 1922–1935," Ph.D Dissertation, Oxford University, 1974; in Greek see Veremis' *Hoi Epemvaseis tou Stratou sten Hellenike Politike*; and Mouzelis, *Modern Greece*, pp. 104–14.

8. Kourvetaris, "The Greek Army Officer Corps," p. 163; and Legg, *Politics in Modern Greece*, p. 189.

9. Yorgos A. Kourvetaris and Betty A. Dobratz, *A Profile of Modern Greece: In Search of Identity* (Oxford: Clarendon, 1987), p. 45.

10. Clogg, *Parties and Elections in Greece*, p. 11.

11. Clogg, *A Short History of Modern Greece*, pp. 130–32.

12. On the civil war, see Iatrides, ed., *Greece in the 1940s*; *Ambassador MacVeagh Reports: Greece, 1933–1947* (Princeton: Princeton University Press, 1980); C. M. Woodhouse, *Apple of Discord: A Survey of Recent Greek Politics in Their International Setting* (London: Hutchinson, 1948); *The Struggle for Greece, 1941–1949* (London: Hart-Davis MacGibbon, 1976); and William Hardy McNeill, *The Greek Dilemma: War and Aftermath* (Philadelphia: Lippincott, 1947).

13. Constantine Tsoucalas argues that "in terms of its ideological and cultural repercussions the Greek Civil War did not end until 1974." In "Ideological Impact of the Civil War," in Iatrides, ed., *Greece in the 1940s*, p. 319.

14. Both organizations were republican but ultimately anticommunist.

15. While noncommunist, both EDES and EKKA shared ELAS' determination to resist the Axis occupation as well as its aversion toward the exiled Monarchy.

16. On the fighting that broke out in December, see Iatrides, *Revolt in Athens*; and John L. Hondros, "The Greek Resistance, 1941–1944: A Reevaluation," in Iatrides, ed., *Revolt in Athens*; George D. Kousoulas, *Revolution and Defeat: The Story of the Greek Communist Party* (London: Oxford University Press, 1965); and Clogg, *A Short History of Modern Greece*, pp. 153–56.

17. Michalis Papayannakis, "The Crisis in the Greek Left," in Howard R. Penniman, ed., *Greece at the Polls: The National Elections of 1974 and 1977* (Washington, DC: American Enterprise Institute, 1981), p. 140.

18. Close, "Introduction," in Close, ed., *The Greek Civil War*, p. 9.

19. Clogg, *A Short History of Modern Greece*, p. 164.

20. By using "janissary levy" to describe this phenomenon, the government was alluding to the Ottoman practice in which Greek boys would be snatched from their parents and raised in Turkey as an elite military corps.

21. Papayannakis, "The Crisis in the Greek Left," p. 140.

22. On how EAM penetrated society during the resistance, see Angelos Elephantis, *He Epaggelia tes Adunates Epanastases* (The Promise of an Impossible Revolution) (Athens: Olkos, 1976); and Thanasis Hatzis, *He Nikefora Epanastase pou Chatheke* (The Victorious Revolution that Lost the Way), vols. 1–3 (Athens: Papazeses, 1977–79).

23. The "security battalions" were creations of the Axis occupiers staffed by collaborators and other individuals who regarded communists as posing a greater threat to Greece than did the occupiers themselves.

24. Frank Smothers, William Hardy McNeill, and Elizabeth Darbishire NcNeill, *Report on the Greeks: Findings of a Twentieth Century Fund Team which Surveyed Conditions in Greece in 1947* (New York: Twentieth Century Fund, 1948), p. 153.

25. For this view see, Ole L. Smith, "The Greek Communist Party, 1945–9," in Close, ed., *The Greek Civil War*, p. 134–35.

26. On the referendum see Ilias Nicolacopoulos, *Kommata kai Vouleutikes Ekloges sten Ellada, 1946–1964* (Parties and Parliamentary Elections in Greece, 1946–1964) (Athens: Ethniko Kentro Koinonikon Ereunon, 1985), pp. 147–55.

27. C. M. Woodhouse, *Modern Greece: A Short History* (London: Faber and Faber Limited, 1991), pp. 247–48.

28. For developments within the army during the resistance, see Panayiotes Kanellopoulos, *Ta Chronia tou Megalou Polemou, 1939–1944* (The Years of the Great War, 1939–1944) (Athens: n.p., 1964); Vassiles A. Nefeloudis, *He Ethnike Antistase ste Mese Anatole* (The National Resistance in the Middle East), vols. 1–2 (Athens: Themelio, 1981); and Veremis, *The Military in Greek Politics*. On the mutiny, see especially Hagen Fleischer, "The 'Anomalies' in the Greek Middle East Forces, 1941–1944," *Journal of the Hellenic Diaspora* 5:3 (Fall 1978), pp. 5–36.

29. The Political Committee of National Liberation (PEEA) was created in the Spring of 1944 to oversee the administration of the large rural areas of Greece under EAM control and established antibourgeois institutions in those areas. Its creation constituted a challenge to the exile government in the Middle East.

30. While there were many oscillations and policy reversals, many communists in the twenties, thirties, and forties followed the Cominform line and advocated an autonomous Macedonia within a Balkan federation.

31. The speaker is referring to March 1944, when EAM supporters had incited mutinies within the Greek armed forces stationed in the Middle East, demanding the formation of a government of national unity that was to be dominated by EAM's Political Committee of National Liberation (PEEA).

32. Here the speaker is referring to the fighting that broke out in Athens following the communist-led demonstration of 3 December 1944. Interview conducted in Athens, Greece, on 25 January 1994.

33. Interview in Athens, Greece, on 8 February 1994 with a former deputy who served under the Sophoulis government and later under Karamanlis and who had fought in the resistance as a member of EDES.

34. J. C. Loulis, "New Democracy: The New Face of Conservatism," in Penniman, ed., *Greece at the Polls*, p. 52. Emphasis in original.

35. On the military purges that began in 1935, see Thanos Veremis, *Hoi Epemvaseis tou Stratou*; and *The Military in Greek Politics*. On the purges that peaked in the Middle East, see Fleischer, "The 'Anomalies'."

36. On IDEA see Dimitris Charalambis, *Stratos kai Politike Exousia: He Dome tes Exousias sten Metemfyliake Ellada* (Army and Political Power: Organizing Power in Post–Civil War Greece) (Athens: Exantas, 1985).

37. On the post–civil war period, see Nicos Alivizatos, *Hoi Politikoi Thesmoi se Krise, 1922–1974: Opseis tes Ellenikes Emperias* (Political Institutions in Crisis, 1922–1974: Survey of the Greek Experience) (Athens: Themelio, 1983); "The Emergency Regime and Civil Liberties," in Iatrides, ed., *Greece in the 1940s*, p. 227; and Minas Samatas, "Greek McCarthyism: A Comparative Assessment of Greek Post–Civil War Repressive Anticommunism and the U.S. Truman-McCarthy Era," *Journal of the Hellenic Diaspora* 13:3–4 (Fall–Winter 1986), p. 41.

38. Alivizatos, *Hoi Politikoi Thesmoi se Krise*, p. 484; and Samatas, "Greek McCarthyism," p. 19.

39. Samatas, "Greek McCarthyism," p. 35.

40. Clogg, *A Short History of Modern Greece*, p. 168; Samatas, "Greek McCarthyism," p. 12; and Alivizatos, *Hoi Politikoi Thesmoi se Krise*, pp. 458–94.

41. Constantine Tsoucalas, *Kratos, Koinonia, Ergasia ste Metapolemike Ellada* (State, Society, Labor in Post–war Greece) (Athens: Themelio, 1986), p. 91.

42. By "enemy," the respondent is referring to the Axis occupiers.

43. Interview conducted in Athens, Greece, on 17 May 1994.

44. Interview conducted in Athens, Greece, on 29 March 1994.

45. See Samatas, "Greek McCarthyism."

46. Interview conducted in Athens, Greece, on 17 May 1994.

47. *Ta Nea* is a Greek left-of-center newspaper.

48. Interview conducted in Athens, Greece, on 8 February 1994.

49. Interview conducted in Athens, Greece, on 19 May 1994 with former Centrist deputy.

50. Interview in Athens, Greece, on 18 April 1994 with a Centrist deputy.

51. Interview conducted in Athens, Greece, on 14 February 1994 with a retired military officer.

52. From 1944–47 the Greek Communist Party was legal.

53. Interview conducted in Athens, Greece, on 3 February 1994 with a former centrist deputy.

54. Interview conducted in Athens, Greece, on 27 January 1994 with a former conservative deputy of the Liberal Party, the National Radical Union, and Nea Demokratia.

55. Interview conducted in Athens, Greece, on 7 April 1994 with former deputy of Nea Demokratia.

56. Nikos Zachariades was the Secretary General of the KKE. He spent the years of the occupation in German concentration camps.

57. Interview in Athens, Greece, on 17 March 1994 with a retired military officer who fought in EDES.

58. KYP is the Greek central intelligence agency.

59. Panayiotes Kanellopoulos (Narration to Nineta Kontrarou-Rassia), *He Zoe Mou: He Aletheia gia tis Krisimes Stigmes tes Istorias tou Ethnous apo to 1915–1980* (My Life: The Truth About the Critical Moments in the History of the Nation from 1915–1980) (Athens: Dion. Gialleles, 1985), p. 168.

60. Interview conducted in Athens, Greece, on 21 April 1994.

61. Maurice Genevoix, *The Greece of Karamanlis* (London: Doric Publications Ltd., 1973), p. 72. Emphasis in original.

62. "Building Formal Structures of Penetration: The United States in Greece, 1947–1948," in Iatrides, ed., *Greece in the 1940s*, p. 239.

63. "American Policy toward Greece, 1944–1949," in Iatrides, ed., *Greece in the 1940s*, p. 237.

64. For accounts of the repression that took place in the 1961 elections, see Nicolacopoulos, *Kommata kai Vouleutikes Ekloges*, pp. 255–81; and Jean Meynaud, *Rapport sur l'Abolition de la Democratie en Grèce* (Montreal: n.p., 1970), pp. 112–19. For the role of the army, see Charalambis, *Stratos kai Politike Exousia*; Andreas Lentakes, *Parakratikes Organoseis kai 21e Apriliou* (Parastate Organs and the 21st of April) (Athens: Ekd. Kastaniote, 1975), pp. 46–67; and Solon N. Gregoriades, *He Historia tes Diktatorias* (The History of the Dictatorship) (Athens: Kapopoulos, 1975), vol. 1, p. 14ff.

65. Clogg, *Parties and Elections in Greece*, p. 43.

66. See *Mavri Vivlos: To Chronikon tou Eklogikou Praxikopimatos tis 29/10/61* (Black Book: The Chronicle of the Electoral Coup of 29/10/61) (Athens, n.p., 1962), pp. 5, 8–9.

67. Woodhouse, *Modern Greece*, p. 284.

68. Theodore A. Couloumbis, "Conclusion," in Penniman, ed., *Greece at the Polls*, p. 187.

69. On this, see C. M. Woodhouse, *Karamanlis: The Restorer of Greek Democracy* (Oxford: Clarendon Press, 1982), p. 167.

70. Athenian (Rodis Roufos), *Inside the Colonels' Greece* (New York: W.W. Norton and Company Inc., 1972), p. 37.

71. George Mylonas, *Escape From Amorgos* (New York: Charles Scribner's Sons, 1974), pp. 82–83.

72. Karamanlis feared that a royal visit to Britain would provide an opportunity for protest against the Greek government. Specifically, his fear was that leftists, protesting the continued holding of prisoners charged with civil war–era crimes, would disrupt the royal visit and thereby embarrass the Greek government. In the event the king and queen did visit Britain and such protests did take place.

73. Woodhouse, *Modern Greece*, p. 288.

74. According to Richard Clogg, *A Concise History of Greece*, p. 161, Papandreou offered his resignation, never really expecting King Constantine to accept it. The king, however, apparently called his bluff.

75. *A Concise History of Greece*, p. 161.

76. *Facts on File*, v. 25 (1965), p. 264.

77. *Facts on File*, v. 25 (1965), p. 264.

78. See Woodhouse, *Modern Greece*, p. 288.

79. *Facts on File*, v. 25 (1965), p. 264.

80. *Facts on File*, v. 25 (1965), p. 264.

81. *Facts on File*, v. 25 (1965), p. 264.

82. *Facts on File*, v. 25 (1965), p. 264.

83. *Facts on File*, v. 25 (1965), p. 264.

84. *Facts on File*, v. 25 (1965), p. 311.

85. Stephanopoulos was a right-wing member of the Center Union.

86. *Facts on File*, v. 26 (1966), p. 279.

87. *Facts on File*, v. 27 (1967), p. 100.

88. D. George Kousoulas, "The Origins of the Greek Military Coup, April 1967," *Orbis* 13:1 (Spring 1969), p. 351.

89. Kousoulas, "The Origins of the Greek Military Coup," p. 355.

90. *Diati Eginai He Epanastase tes 21 Apriliou 1967* (Why the Revolution of 21 April 1967 Occurred) (Athens: Government Printing Office, 1968), pp. 81 and 95.

91. *Diati Eginai He Epanastase*, p. 48–49.

92. See *To Pistevo Mas* (Our Creed) (Athens: Greek Government Printing Office, 1968), vol. 1, pp. 10–15.

93. George A. Kourvetaris, "The Role of the Military in Greek Politics," *International Review of History and Political Science* 8:3 (August 1971), p. 106. See also relevant chapters in Kourvetaris, *Studies on Modern Greek Society and Politics*.

94. *Keesing's Contemporary Archives*, v. 16 (1967–68), p. 22025.

95. Kevin Andrews, *Greece in the Dark ... 1967–1974-* (Amsterdam: Adolf M. Hakkert, 1980), p. 232.

96. Athenian (Roufos), *Inside the Colonels' Greece*, pp. 142–43.

The Political Elites and the Processes...

...consta... national consensus. ... they wo... anchored in the ... ... of political ...
... if the ... general process of ... ... become ... the ... political cha...
... social and political ... ... of ... general process of ... ... its ... it ... must ...
... on the ... the ... government process ... ... by the ... by the ...

CHAPTER 3

Models of Democratic Transition and Consolidation Processes: Greece in Comparative Perspective

The extrication of the Greek military regime from power in July 1974 was brought about by developments within the armed forces, not by direct pressures from resistance groups, political parties, or the general public. An attempted coup by the Greek colonels against Archbishop Makarios, the president of Cyprus, on 15 July 1974, and the subsequent Turkish invasion of the island marked the formal end of the colonels' regime and launched the country's transition to democracy. Faced with the possibility of war, General Ioannides, the junta strongman, ordered a general mobilization of the Greek armed forces. The chaotic mobilization effort revealed the military's lack of preparedness to defend Greece against the possibility of war with Turkey, and prompted the military hierarchy to reassert traditional lines of authority and return political power to the hands of civilian elites. As stated in chapter 1, some common hypotheses of democratic consolidation suggest that the abruptness of the Greek transition (as power was transferred from military to civilian rule virtually overnight), the dominance of the transition process by a single partisan individual, and the absence of any successful negotiations between elites should have hindered Greece's prospects for a successful consolidation process. Nonetheless, Greek democracy became consolidated within a relatively short period of time.

This chapter will analyze Greece's transition and consolidation trajectories or "paths" in the light of a number of models of democratic consolidation that have been advanced in the theoretical literature.[1] In order to illustrate how transition trajectories relate to the existing theories of consolidation, I present four other cases—Spain, France, Portugal, and Italy—and contrast their experiences with that of Greece. As this chapter will illustrate, the Greek transition trajectory and consolidation process does not fit easily with most models of successful consolidation. Unlike in Spain, where all significant political elites met behind closed doors and ironed out compromises on the most divisive issues separating them, Greek elites remained unwilling to reach broad agreement on issues pertaining to the transition as well as the form of government the new democratic regime would take.[2] Moreover, rather than forming an inclusive transition government with representatives from all significant political parties, Constantine Karamanlis, the leader of the traditional right, dominated the process and made most decisions single-handedly.   These aberrant characteristics of Greece's transition trajectory as well as the rapidity with which it occurred led many to conclude that Greece's transition would be disturbingly similar to the highly complex and difficult Portuguese transition. Thankfully, this never materialized. The abrupt transition to democracy in Greece developed relatively smoothly into a stable and consolidated democratic regime.

ABRUPT, UNNEGOTIATED TRANSITIONS

In contrast to those all-too-rare transitions characterized by gradual and long-term processes of interelite negotiations—as in Spain—transition trajectories characterized by rapidity, abruptness, and dominance by a single partisan individual or group tend to be much more problematic. In such cases elite compromise on fundamental disagreements—an absolute must if democracy is to be perceived as "the only game in town"—is difficult to achieve. Transition outcomes are often biased in favor of one political group and its supporters, thereby leading opponents of the regime to adopt semi- or antisystem oppositional tactics that may threaten democratic consolidation and stability.

Many of these ostensibly "negative" features were manifest in the Portuguese and Greek transitions to democracy. Take the case of Portugal, where two transitions occurred. The first of these, because of radicalization and polarization partly resulting from the abrupt overthrow of its authoritarian regime, did *not* culminate in a democratic regime but instead installed a military clique in power. This, in turn, required a second transition—a real transition to democracy—that was severely complicated by the need to extricate the newly politicized military from power. To elaborate, the outstanding characteristic of the Portuguese transition is that it was initiated by an abrupt military *coup d'état* in 1974 and was thereafter dominated by leftist officers of the Armed Forces Movement who, in collaboration with the Portuguese Communist Party, took power after toppling the Salazar-Caetano regime.[3] The radical, revolutionary nature of the transition as well as its complete domination by a single partisan group contributed to a number of serious crises that seriously threatened the transition's prospects for successful democratization.

Initially, the revolutionaries institutionalized a substantial political role for the military by stipulating that the Assembly of the Armed Forces Movement, an unelected body of military officers, would have a role coequal with that of the newly formed Portuguese parliament.   Later, following the November 1975 countercoup that brought more moderate leftist officers to power, the military's role in political decision-making was somewhat reduced in that it was to no longer serve a legislative function in the Assembly of the Armed Forces Movement.

Instead, its political influence was institutionalized by the creation of the Council of the Revolution—a body created to judge the "constitutionality" of parliamentary acts. Through this mechanism, unelected military officers held considerable political power throughout the 1970s and early 1980s.

The Armed Forces Movement also made radical public policy decisions, initially announcing the nationalization of banks, insurance companies, and many industries, and promising the expropriation of great landed estates. Intent on carrying out a thoroughgoing economic and social revolution, the revolutionaries mobilized landless laborers in the latifundist south and radicalized workers in the industrial center who seized land and occupied farms, industries, and vacant homes on a massive scale, expropriating 1.2 million hectares of property. These actions were sanctioned by the new constitution, which included clauses assuring a transition to socialism and legitimizing state expropriation of the principal means of production. Assurances were also given that nationalizations were "irreversible conquests of the working class"[4]—that is, were to be incapable of reversal by any succeeding government. In short, the revolutionary and one-sided nature of the abrupt Portuguese transition path threatened to replace authoritarianism of the right with an authoritarianism of the left.

In response to the radicalism of the new regime, counter-revolutionary forces of conservative peasants and small property owners mobilized. During "the long hot summer of '75," small landholders attempted to stop the revolutionary momentum by taking matters into their own hands. Enraged that their traditional way of life was under attack, many peasants (particularly in the North) reacted by burning and sacking communist party offices. By August 1975, Portugal was at the brink of armed conflict between proponents of the revolution and those of resistance—all a result of a single partisan group effecting radical change without consideration of other political forces. Consequently, although Portuguese democracy eventually became consolidated by the end of the 1980s, the consolidation process involved undoing many of the excesses of the first Portuguese transition as well as ensuring that the military would fully extricate itself from politics and submit to civilian supremacy.

The Greek transition process was also abrupt and would, on the surface, seem to pose similar problems for eventual democratic consolidation. The rapidity with which it occurred—as all arrangements for the transfer of power were decided within a few hours between a very small group of participants—was a primary aberrant characteristic of the process. Unlike in Spain, where Suárez invited opposition elites into negotiations concerning basic economic, constitutional, and regime issues, the speed of the Greek transition did not allow for inclusive and protracted negotiations between elites of competing factions. Neither negotiations between former civilian elites who would now be returning to power nor negotiations between the outgoing military rulers and their successors occurred.

In short, unlike in Spain where the transition to democracy was initiated from within the authoritarian regime in meetings between the regime's leaders and the opposition in order to reach compromise on the most divisive issues confronting the nation, in Greece even civilian elites totally opposed to authoritarian rule refused to reach agreement on matters of importance with each other. Thus, the Greek colonels, rather than being extricated from power by a prolonged process of negotiations, were abruptly replaced with a civilian government—one, however, dominated by a single partisan leader without input from other democratic political forces. The following section will highlight Spain's transition to democracy in which extensive negotiations, or "settlements," between all significant political elites occurred.

ELITE SETTLEMENTS

According to Burton, Gunther, and Higley, the process of elite settlement may constitute the most advantageous route to a prompt and successful democratic consolidation.[5] As stated in chapter 1, democratic consolidation and stability implies an elite transformation from elite disunity[6] to consensual unity[7] as elites come to respect the norms and institutions of democracy and agree to play by the democratic rules of the game. One way this can occur is when previously warring elite factions deliberately reorganize their relations by secretly meeting to negotiate compromises on the basic set of rules of the emerging democratic regime. Such settlements are said to have two consequences: (1) they create peaceful competition in a climate of democratic stability in which the norms, rules, and procedures of restrained partisanship are respected by all, and (2) they lead to the creation of regimes in which "forcible power seizures no longer occur and are not widely expected."[8]

The Spanish democratic consolidation process has been characterized as the very model of such a rare elite transformation.[9] No sooner was Adolfo Suárez sworn into office in 1976 than he consciously and deliberately made contact with all opposition elites in an effort to iron out compromises on many fundamental disagreements. The inclusion of all nationwide parties—from the communists on the left to their former Franquist enemies on the right—into "the politics of consensus" forged mutually respectful patterns of elite interactions and led to overwhelming popular support for the new democratic regime.

The first attempt at an all-inclusive elite settlement in Spain was an effort by Suárez to reach a broad social pact with the left in order to deal with the severe economic crises Spain experienced in the 1970s. Private negotiations between the government, all other parliamentary parties, and the trade unions led to the signing of the Pact of Moncloa in September 1977. In this agreement the opposition agreed not to call into question Suárez's decisions to freeze salaries, reduce public spending, restrict credit, and increase taxes. In exchange, the government promised to carry out progressive tax reform, improve the social security system, reorganize the financial system, and initiate other political reforms.

More importantly, Suárez and the opposition also engaged in secret negotiations concerning fundamental constitutional and regime issues. In private, agreement was reached on basic constitutional provisions. For example, the parties of the right expressed a desire to have the monarchy institutionalized, requested an explicit recognition of the free-market economy, and maintained a preference for executive supremacy over parliament. The left accepted many of these propositions. It allowed the monarchy to be institutionalized so long as it would be a constitutional monarchy with limited and well-defined powers. It accepted a free-market economy but requested that government intervention occur when necessary. A strong, stable executive was tolerated as well, so long as the right guaranteed a greater equilibrium between government and parliament. The left also demanded and secured a progressive and detailed bill of rights.

Suárez's third effort to reach a settlement was his attempt to resolve the problem of Basque autonomy. Negotiations on this proved much more problematic, however. The Basque nationalists demanded the recognition of the Basque *fueros*, or historic rights, as taking precedence over the new constitution, and thus not open to debate or compromise. Suárez's UCD refused to accept this formulation, arguing that the *fueros* could only function "within the framework" of the Spanish constitution. This conflict went unresolved, with some Basque nationalists abstaining from the constitutional referendum and others actively opposing ratification. While the ultimate ratification of the Basque autonomy statute in 1979 served to reduce tensions, the continued campaign of ETA terrorism serves as a constant reminder of the underlying conflict still remaining. In short, unlike the economic, constitutional, and regime issues that were negotiated and settled, the unresolved issue of regional autonomy posed long-term difficulties for democratic consolidation and stability, often threatening to become a potential deconsolidating problem in the Basque region.[10]

Unlike in Spain, such an elite settlement did not take place during the transition to democracy in Greece. In fact, if observers of the Greek transition take a retrospective view of elite interaction during the seven years of dictatorial rule, they will find that even during the years of the dictatorship when elites were faced with a common enemy—the colonels—they were unable to bridge their ideological and partisan differences and unite in order to oust the authoritarian rulers. Efforts to achieve a settlement—one that would potentially overthrow the dictatorship and restore democracy—were repeatedly thwarted by the unwillingness and inability of elites to compromise.

Almost immediately after the colonels' coup was launched in April 1967, the leaders of the United Democratic Left (EDA) proposed the dissolution of all parties and the formation of a united antidictatorial front. Because both the Center Union and the right-wing National Radical Union (ERE) distrusted the left, the proposal was rejected immediately. Reminiscent of civil war animosities, internal party documents from the Center Union's wing in exile in Western Europe indicate that both the Center Union and ERE feared the EDA's call for unity was really an attempt to monopolize the antidictatorial struggle as the left had done during the Axis occupation of Greece. According to the external wing of the Center Union, "EDA wants ... to take over all [of the] anti-dictatorial struggle (peaceful and political) abroad and in Greece. They hope that gradually they will absorb all EK (Center Union) people and be ready, when [the] green light comes from Moscow, to be the only organization fighting the regime."[11]

Moreover, the fear that the left would somehow come to monopolize a violent resistance to the colonels also contributed to the fact that virtually all elites sought a political rather than a revolutionary solution to the dictatorship. As one participant exclaimed, "We did not think that a popular revolution could take place—but even if it could occur, we did not want it, because we would not control it; others would."[12] Karamanlis, too, wanted to avoid a popular revolutionary uprising, fearing that an insurrection might lead to civil war and a communist takeover.[13] Even Mikis Theodorakis, a deputy of EDA and leader of the leftist resistance organization Patriotic Front (PAM),[14] believed that there were two solutions to the dictatorship—the first being violent resistance and the second being "the formation of a national front … to lead the country back to parliamentary democracy."[15] However, even he argued that one could "not consider it possible to contemplate the first solution before we have exhausted all the possibilities for overthrowing the dictatorship *without* bloodshed on the basis of the second solution."[16]

A second failed attempt at negotiating unity among all Greek antidictatorial forces was the proposed "Karamanlis Solution" to the dictatorship. This "solution," which was widely accepted and supported by the right, the center, and the left, called for the return of Constantine Karamanlis to Greece to head a government of national unity. The general belief, according to Stephen W. Rousseas, a participant in those events, was that the United States would be willing to force the junta out of power if it were guaranteed that political extremists would be kept under control.[17] Thus, as early as 1967, immediately after the colonels' seizure of power, many saw the return of Karamanlis as the only feasible option for democratization. The Center Union, in particular, agreed to this solution provided certain conditions were met: (1) all political prisoners were to be released unconditionally, (2) no political prisoner was to be denied his or her civil or political rights, and (3) all former political prisoners would be free in the postcoup period to participate fully in the democratic process. If these conditions were met, the Center Union (and Andreas Papandreou, in particular) guaranteed that the EK would not raise the issue of whether the nation should remain a constitutional monarchy or become a republic, nor that of removing Greece from NATO.[18]

Over time, Theodorakis also came to embrace the Karamanlis Solution. Initially, in September 1969, Theodorakis simply called for a "conservative" solution to the dictatorship: "There is still the possibility of overthrowing the dictatorship from within and forming a government of pro-American politicians ([K]aramanlis, Mavros, Mitsotakis, etc.). … By accepting such a solution … [the Americans] would … permit only a very slender measure of liberty … This solution would nonetheless in my view be an important step forward."[19] By 1970, however, this "conservative solution" had explicitly become the Karamanlis Solution for Theodorakis as a smuggled letter from him to Karamanlis indicates: "By taking on the leadership of this struggle," wrote Theodorakis to Karamanlis, "you will have deserved well of the Nation. … I am at your service."[20]

Such informal communication took place throughout the seven years of dictatorial rule between political elites of all parties, but bore no fruit. In 1970, with the assistance of the Norwegian Committee for Democracy in Greece,[21] a rather more formalized effort to adopt a democratization plan took place. Under this plan all parties would unite under one program with one objective—to rid Greece of the colonels. If the plan was to succeed, it was understood that all differences would have to be set aside and all efforts would have to unite for this goal. Talks were started with Karamanlis in Paris as well as Kanellopoulos and Mavros in Greece. Theodorakis, George Mylonas (a former Center Union minister), Constantine Mitsotakis (one of the more prominent Center Union "apostates"), Andreas Papandreou (whose father had died in 1968), Kostas Koliyiannis (Secretary General of the Greek Communist Party in Eastern Europe), a Greek colonel, a Greek bishop, as well as King Constantine were approached. It was finally agreed that this group, minus the king—who supported the plan but could not come out publicly in favor of it—would meet in London or Oslo to "map out a unified program and *perhaps* set up a government in exile."[22]

Rousseas indicates that "[e]veryone was in tentative agreement. The only holdout was Papandreou."[23] It appears that while Papandreou did not reject the plan outright, he was against the Karamanlis Solution and against cooperation with the king and right-wing conservatives. Moreover, when Kanellopoulos and Mavros were informed that Andreas Papandreou had refused to participate, they too withdrew saying, "that if Papandreou were not in the plan, they could not expose themselves."[24]

Why did Papandreou refuse to participate in the Norwegian plan for the return of Greek democracy? It appears that many old animosities contributed to his decision. First, he opposed cooperation with the right. On the one hand, Kanellopoulos had been among those deputies before the coup who were "trying to strip Papandreou of his parliamentary immunity and send him to jail on ... charges of conspiracy over ... *Aspida*."[25] Mitsotakis, on the other hand, was one of the forty-five "apostates," and when the Center Union refused to allow the "apostates" to sign a draft declaration of unity during the dictatorship, the negotiations broke down. Papandreou was against cooperation with the king as well. In fact, when international mediator Mogens Camre told him that cooperation with King Constantine was imperative ("apparently there is no choice, because all the others—even the communists—are for collaboration with the king."[26]), Papandreou responded angrily: "[A] great liberation struggle calls for a vision. And visions are seldom incorporated in minimum programs—especially if such [a] program is to include the KING!"[27] Finally, Papandreou was vehemently opposed to the return of Constantine Karamanlis to head the national unity government. "The probability was thought to be very high that a [K]aramanlis solution might very well banish Papandreou from active participation in post-coup political life."[28]

Thus, even when Andreas Papandreou was being held in prison by the colonels for his alleged participation in the *Aspida* conspiracy, and was therefore most willing to accept a Karamanlis Solution, negotiations concerning the return of Karamanlis to Greece were approached cautiously for fear of hurting Papandreou politically. As an internal Center Union party document noted: "Andreas must be safe at any expense ... he should [never] be eliminated politically. He is the symbol of our fight. Without Andreas politically strong, the outcome of our struggle will be doubtful. He should be very careful under what conditions he will accept any release from prison."[29] The cautiousness with which negotiations were to take place is also clear in a letter written by Margaret Papandreou[30] on 27 August 1967 to a Papandreou representative outside of Greece. In this letter, she indicates that, in communicating with Karamanlis, the representative should present himself as someone *close* to Andreas Papandreou, but *not* as his official representative:

Karamanlis ... could be acceptable to our forces if he replaces the junta, gives amnesty and keeps the palace under control. There should be contact with him. ... Think of a way to do this. ... Takis [Andreas Papandreou] himself is positive toward this notion because I have talked to him—under certain restraints and conditions, of course. The country simply must get rid of rule by the military! ... [O]n the Karamanlis contact—you cannot ... go as representatives of Takis but as those close to him who feel you know him well enough to guess his thinking.[31]

By the autumn of 1967, when the Greek press went public with news of the Karamanlis Solution and announced that George Papandreou had accepted it, the Papandreous appear to have grown increasingly apprehensive. One of their representatives indicates this in October 1967: "If there is any future coordination to be done with Karamanlis then it has to take place in Athens, between one of his men in Greece and one of our lawyers. ... [W]e can no longer be accused that we run after him."[32] Soon thereafter, by November of 1967, Margaret Papandreou indicates that no further discussions were to take place:

One more item—the so-called Karamanlis solution. When I initially wrote to you I said merely to have a contact and that Andreas would not be against such a possible "way out" of the morass. Since then it has grown into something bigger—as if Andreas were supporting solely such a solution. He can hardly be a backer of Karamanlis. ... By this time the notion seems a bit outdated, partially because of his own weaknesses, lack of courage and indecision. I think he missed his boat some time back—and I think we can no longer show him interest.[33]

Thus, the Karamanlis Solution was shelved by the Papandreous, partly out of a fear that Andreas Papandreou would be eclipsed by Karamanlis. Ironically enough, then, political maneuvering of the kind usually witnessed between elites in a *democratic* regime precluded agreement in opposition to Greece's nondemocratic, military regime.

Respondents indicated, moreover, that this was not the only negotiation attempt to be frustrated by Andreas Papandreou. In June 1968 Papandreou founded a resistance organization, the Panhellenic Liberation Movement (PAK) and, according to one person's appraisal, "set about assiduously undermining other anti-junta groups."[34] For example, when the Freedom Front (MEL), the resistance organization of ERE, proposed the formation of a center-right government in exile with Kanellopoulos as constitutional prime minister, supporters of the Andreas Papandreou center-left faction of the Center Union believed such an agreement would be politically detrimental for Papandreou, for even Kanellopoulos "would outrank him since he would have to be regarded as the constitutional prime minister of Greece."[35] As Stephen Rousseas, a Papandreou supporter, argued at the time, "With Eleni Vlachou in London and Karamanlis in Paris, Andreas could very well have the rug pulled out from under him."[36]

Cooperative efforts were also made by the leaders of a number of other resistance organizations to unify their resistance efforts. In November 1967 an agreement was signed between Democratic Defense, a resistance organization composed primarily of individuals with center-left orientations, and the leftist Patriotic Front. These two resistance organizations agreed to create a Coordinating Bureau of antidictatorial struggle to be composed of representatives from both groups. They also published a statement proposing a number of common goals: the dissolution and removal of the junta from power, the formation of a government comprised of all political forces and resistance organizations, the release of political prisoners, the full restoration of liberty and human rights, and the holding of free elections.[37] When they attempted to elicit cooperation from Papandreou's PAK, however, negotiations broke down. In a March 1968 statement, Papandreou argued that "PAK rejects unconditionally any behind-the-scenes agreements or arrangements among political leaders ... which will to any extent restrict the freedom of the Greek people to determine their future."[38] Many have argued, however, that partisan interests were really to blame for Papandreou's unwillingness to cooperate with others. As one observer commented, "[Papandreou's] favoured tactic was to enter alliances but then work to discredit his supposed colleagues so that anti-junta opposition became synonymous with him personally."[39]

After many such attempts to unify the various resistance groups, a National Resistance Council was finally formed outside of Greece in 1971, composed of the Free Greeks (largely an organization of officers), the Defenders of Freedom (an organization of the right), Democratic Defense and the Patriotic Front. Andreas Papandreou's PAK refused to join the Council, however, arguing that the Council's program did not provide for a plebiscite on the monarchy.[40]

As was the case with the individual resistance organizations, the Council remained largely uninfluential. Members did not always attend meetings, resistance activities often did not occur as scheduled, and squabbling and recriminations characterized inter- as well as intragroup relations in the various resistance movements. In short, "there seemed to be lots of talk and little real action."[41]

In many ways political considerations frustrated attempts at negotiating a solution to the dictatorship. Papandreou was not the only politician to impede such efforts, however; most elites were skeptical and unwilling to reach compromise at one time or an other, apparently placing tactical expediency over more long-term considerations. Indicative of elite disunity was the fact that intraparty divisions were often as pronounced as interparty divisions as disagreements broke out between members of the same party on numerous issues. The Center Union's exiled wing, for example, was disorganized and without a universally accepted leader. It was also divided into two groups. One of the wings was hostile toward

Andreas Papandreou and was willing to collaborate with EDA as well as accept the king, while the other, the pro-Andreas Papandreou faction, was not. ERE was also divided between those members who were pro-Karamanlis and those who were against his return. As one international mediator involved in promoting unity among Greek elites expressed in private correspondence: "As far as I know the moderate wing of ERE and especially Kanellopoulos hate Karamanlis."[42] Finally, in no political camp was division more pronounced than within the left. The revisionist Eurocommunists did not question (at least publicly) the future of the monarchy and the return of Karamanlis, while the dogmatic Marxist-Leninists were initially intransigent on these issues.

Interparty divisions and disagreements also contributed to the lack of an elite settlement or pact in Greece. The monarchy issue is but one example. Internal party documents from the pro-Andreas Papandreou faction of the exiled Center Union indicate that some elites' unwillingness to reach an agreement on the monarchy issue was often motivated by partisan and tactical concerns. For example, as previously stated, while many Greek elites were willing to accept cooperation with King Constantine if that meant a solution to the dictatorship, many Center Union deputies' refusal to do so was tactical in nature: "If we have made clear that the King is responsible for everything … we may say—[at the] negotiating table—that in spite of what [the] King did in the past, we may [allow] him as a sacrifice on our behalf to stay in exchange [for] a full democracy without restrictions. [At] the negotiating table the King must be extremely weak."[43]

There was also disagreement as to whether cooperation with the communists was possible. In an interview given by Constantine Mitsotakis in 1969, he indicated that cooperation of all elites under the framework of the Karamanlis Solution was acceptable, so long as the communists remained excluded: "[I]n my opinion, the large majority of the Greek political elite today converges on one proposal. And that proposal is that after the junta leaves from government, a national unity government ought to be formed under the leadership of Karamanlis which ought to take on representatives … of all political tendencies, except for the communists."[44]

Finally, the issue of whether cooperation with Andreas Papandreou should occur contributed to interparty disagreements. On 16 June 1969, for example, Kanellopoulos expressed doubts whether cooperation was possible with Papandreou so long as he attacked the Americans. At about this same time, Karamanlis, too, conveyed reservations "about Andreas Papandreou, with whom he had no common ground."[45] Later, in October 1972, when a group of lower-ranking party members from ERE and the EK, tired of what they perceived to be fruitless interelite discussions, decided to come together and issue a joint declaration stating that past animosities between their parties must cease and announcing that they would support any initiative taken by Karamanlis so long as he returned to Greece and took control, both Kanellopoulos and Mavros were displeased, discouraging members of their respective parties from signing the pronouncement. This was despite the fact that they too had been involved in negotiating a Karamanlis Solution to the dictatorship. Hearing of this,

Karamanlis—who had, from the beginning, been skeptical of having his name associated publicly with the Solution and "who had stood aloof from moves to concert a united political opposition"[46]—published a statement on 7 November dissassociating himself from the declaration in his support.

In sum, many attempts at negotiation took place during the years of the dictatorship. Contacts were made between low- and high-ranking party members and resistance organizations both within Greece and abroad. Often, these formal and informal talks were mediated by prominent international figures, among whom were Einer Gerhardsen, a Norwegian politician with more than forty years in public life; Einor Fodre, a Norwegian Labor Party parliamentarian and Chairperson of the Norwegian Committee for Democracy in Greece; Mogens Camre, a deputy of the Social Democratic Party of Denmark and a close friend of Andreas Papandreou; Sir Hugh Green, the head of the London-based European Atlantic Committee on Greece; and Max van der Stoehl, the foreign secretary of the Netherlands. Despite such efforts, no successful negotiations took place as the ability and/or willingness of elites to compromise was frustrated by partisan interests, mistrust of one's opponents, historical animosities, and ideological rigidity. Thus, while unity among the various antidictatorial forces was, in theory, universally advocated by virtually all elites, suspicion that one group would come to dominate all others militated against even minimal formal unity. The Center Union's position on this issue appears to be typical of all political parties: "Our line: ... We recognize as the only leaders George and Andreas (Papandreou). ... [We] call all Greeks to participate in a very real national front on a fair basis (EK 5 - ERE 3 - EDA 2).[47] We will be fair and sincere. We will not try to manoeuver against anyone but we are not so stupid to be taken over by anyone also."[48] As this statement indicates, the imperative of unity among all antidictatorial forces was virtually universally recognized. Since no group would accept the leadership of any other group, however, the calls for unity did virtually nothing to unite the various antidictatorial groups.

This apparent unwillingness of elites to compromise and unite frustrated many of the international observers and mediators who had become participants in the negotiations. Einor Fodre was reportedly disgusted by the inability of Greek elites to compromise with each other:

The most rational [options] ... in this situation [are] the efforts to join the Greek people—join the people in their struggle against the junta. ... What is irrational ... is the way a lot of the old politicians behave—still talking about their own party, still unwilling to discuss whether the communists should be included in the new democracy, and to a great extent still relying on the help of the liberal opposition within the United States and the fantastic idea that Scandinavia should liberate Greece. All this is trash. A rational attitude is what I have characterized earlier—the idea that the liberation of Greece is their own task, and the only way they can do it is to join [efforts].[49]

Mogens Camre, who was also active in behind-the-scenes negotiations with deputies from all parties, revealed his despair in September 1971: "I must admit that I have given up the hope of uniting these groups. And this of course may be due to the fact that they cannot unite. There are [such] big difficulties, there are [such] big differences that even the colonels cannot bring them together."[50] Finally, Carl Barkman, the Dutch Ambassador to Greece from 1969–75, writes in his diary on 11 June 1974: "One wonders what would be needed to produce some sort of unity of purpose in Greece; they are about the most individualistic and divided people I have known."[51]

This unwillingness of Greek elites to enter into successful negotiations during the dictatorship in order to bring about the downfall of a common enemy—the colonels' regime—was, theoretically, a potentially problematic characteristic of the Greek transition process. Even though Greece might have seemed a prime case for a settlement—since both its regime type (an authoritarian nonhierarchical military regime rather than a sultanistic, totalitarian or post-totalitarian regime) as well as its elite patterns (characterized by a multiplicity of well-articulated elites, all in open opposition to the colonels) were conducive to democratic consolidation[52]—elite actors failed to cooperate and reach agreement. Not surprisingly, objective observers of this situation in the late 1960s and early 1970s concluded that the prospects for successful democratization were extremely poor.

Moreover, elite cooperation was not a characteristic of the transition to democracy either. As chapter 7 on the Greek military illustrates, its failed coup attempt in Cyprus, the subsequent Turkish invasion of the island, and the possibility of war with Turkey forced the Greek military hierarchy to admit it was ill-prepared to defend Greece against the possibility of war, stepping down from power on its own account. Humiliated by the nonhierarchical military regime's actions, the President, former Lieutenant General, Phaedon Ghizikis, called for an emergency meeting in the parliament building to arrange for a transfer of power to civilians. This meeting was not inclusive of all elites: A conscious decision was made to exclude the left and center-left and invite only certain representatives of the right and center-right. As such, Ghizikis summoned four military officers,[53] four former premiers of the right and center-right,[54] three former ministers of government (also of the right and center-right),[55] and George Mavros, the leader of the Center Union, to the meeting. In fact, three of the eight civilians were protagonists in the 1965 royal intervention in politics that split the Center Union Party, eventually leading to the colonels' dictatorship; a fourth civilian had been chosen in 1973 by junta chief George Papdopoulos himself to head liberalization efforts that were brought to an end by the Polytechnic student uprising; two others were prominent members of ERE; and a seventh was a respected conservative banker. Only Mavros represented the moderate wing of the Center Union.[56]

At this meeting several suggestions were made concerning the choice of a prime minister to lead the transition government. General Grigorios Bonanos, chief of the armed forces, suggested Petros Garoufalias—a man close to King Constantine—as prime minister; Spyros Markezinis, a conservative politician who briefly served as premier in 1973 under the colonels, proposed Christianos Xanthopoulos-Palamas, a minister of foreign affairs in his short-lived 1973 government; while former minister of the right, Evangelos Averoff-Tossizza, proposed Constantine Karamanlis. Wishing to make a clean break with the past, the first two candidates were immediately rejected by Kanellopoulos and Mavros.[57] Ghizikis also ruled out the Karamanlis suggestion, arguing that Karamanlis had been in Paris for more than ten years and that locating him would be difficult. Finally, everyone present agreed that Panayiotes Kanellopoulos, the leader of the National Radical Union since Karamanlis' departure to Paris in 1963, should lead a transitional coalition government and that George Mavros, leader of the Center Union since George Papandreou's death, should serve as his deputy prime minister and minister of foreign affairs. It was further agreed that after a brief adjournment of three hours, the group would reassemble so that the new government could be sworn into office.[58]

But even this agreement—that a Kanellopoulos-Mavros government would be sworn into office in a matter of hours—was broken as a smaller group decided in the interim that Karamanlis should return instead. Averoff, who had not left the parliament building during the recess, convinced President Ghizikis and the service chiefs that Karamanlis was the best person to lead the transition. Without informing the others they telephoned Karamanlis in Paris, who agreed to return to Greece immediately to head the transition government. When Kanellopoulos and Mavros returned to be sworn into office, they were told that Karamanlis had been contacted and that he was on his way to Greece.[59] Based on these facts alone, objective observers of Greece's abrupt and one-sided transition to democracy might have expected in 1974 a return to politics characterized by the deep crises, partisan divisions, rancor, emotionalism, and demagoguery characteristic of precoup Greek politics.

The final aberrant characteristic of the Greek transition is the fact that Constantine Karamanlis—a single partisan individual accused of being anticommunist and, even, antidemocratic in the precoup period—dominated the entire transition process and enjoyed virtually unlimited latitude in making all decisions. He, for example, had complete control over the membership of his 1974 transitional Government of National Unity, in which the left was virtually unrepresented. Instead of being inclusive, an early criticism launched against this government was that it was not in reality a Government of National Unity. Neither Andreas Papandreou, EDA, nor the communists were represented. And while Karamanlis included several popular politicians from outside the ranks of the traditional right—individuals who had suffered persecution and imprisonment under the junta (such as centrists George Mangakis and Ioannes Pesmazoglou)—he went no further than the center-left (appointing Charalambos Protopappas from the Greek Socialist Union) in making his final appointments.

Furthermore, interviews with leading members of the National Unity Government reveal that Karamanlis made the most important decisions single-handedly during the entire transition. As one deputy exclaimed when asked whether anyone set restraints on what Karamanlis could or could not do in 1974, "Who could set restraints? Karamanlis was omnipotent when he came!"[60]

It is interesting to note that the way in which Karamanlis dominated decision-making during the transition appears to be consistent with his traditional decision-making style—forceful to the point of being authoritarian. A preliminary analysis of his leadership style indicates that Karamanlis had always kept most of his thoughts to himself, very rarely revealing them to even his closest collaborators. Konstantinos Tsatsos, for example, claims that Karamanlis would (1) only discuss decisions with his closest collaborators and ministers; (2) only if it was absolutely necessary; and (3) "only when it was time to carry them out, when he had already crystallized a decision as to what had to be done."[61] Moreover, when Karamanlis would chair a meeting, he would *listen* to everyone's points of view, but never reveal his own thoughts on the matter being discussed. And when he made a decision as to the appropriate action to be taken, he made it by himself—even though it was often contrary to the recommendations of the specialists he had invited to the meeting.[62]

Moreover, Karamanlis himself admitted that his style of decision-making consisted of a *conscious* effort to exclude as many people as possible from the process:

It is natural but also usual for the distinguished politician to keep a distance between himself and his contemporaries. Natural due to his superiority and useful because his distance protects him from the habits of political weakness which familiarity leads to, such as favoritism, flattery, etc. ... The natural result of distance is loneliness. But as a counterweight it has the increase in authority and the imposition of the leader, which are necessary for the person who governs. In my opinion the ability of a leader to impose himself is a natural virtue.[63]

Thus, when asked about the transition to democracy, Karamanlis openly acknowledged that he virtually monopolized the decision-making process. Apparently, he believed that if he were to engage in negotiations and compromise during this crucial period of Greek politics, as did Suárez in Spain, it would likely have contributed to unnecessary delay, stalemate, and even immobilism, endangering the transition process: "Alas, if we had fallen into discussions, bargaining, personal ambitions! ... [I]f [I] waited for each one to submit his own plan ... [i]f I had not acted so quickly and with a decisive rhythm, the game would have been lost. I would have drowned in our country's usual bargaining, in the compromises and the traps. ... Hesitations during such situations are equivalent to catastrophe."[64] Thus, unlike his counterpart in Spain who viewed compromise as fundamental to a successful transition trajectory, Karamanlis was suspect of and even hostile to a similar process occurring in Greece.

In short, Karamanlis avoided negotiations with members of the opposition during the transition to democracy. Instead, he decided to make all important decisions uninfluenced by others. Upon taking office in July of 1974, he decided to free political prisoners, to proclaim a general amnesty for political crimes, and to declare that civil war and related restrictive legislation were no longer in force. Later, in September 1974, it was he alone who resolved to legalize the Communist Party, making it possible for communists and other leftist forces to compete freely for political office for the first time since 1947. It was also he who decided, without consulting Panayiotes Kanellopoulos (leader of ERE and constitutional prime minister in 1967 when the coup was launched) or holding any deliberations with former ERE notables, to dissolve ERE and create in its place on 28 September 1974 a new party of the right, *Nea Demokratia*. Finally, he alone chose the date of the first post-junta elections and decided to call a referendum on the monarchy, ordering his party—which had within its ranks many deputies who favored the restoration of the king—to take a publicly neutral stance on the issue.

Not surprisingly, members of the opposition severely criticized Karamanlis' heavy-handed style. Concerning the date chosen for the first post-junta elections, Andreas Papandreou maintained that it would be a fallacy to believe that free elections could take place so long as a purge of the state machinery did not occur first. Ioannis Zigdis, a prominent member of the Center Union, accused Karamanlis of "neo-Caesarism," contending that such an early election date was "a crime against the nation" and predicting that Karamanlis was about to launch "a parliamentary dictatorship."[65] Despite such accusations, Karamanlis remained unpersuaded. The elections were held on 17 November 1974 as he had originally scheduled.[66]

A second decision—to hold the referendum on the monarchy after, rather than before, the national elections—also frustrated opposition parties. The left accused Karamanlis of attempting to deliberately defer the issue for fear of splitting the conservative vote. Andreas Papandreou went so far as to accuse him of having already made plans for the return of the king after carrying out a right-wing "electoral coup."[67] Again, however, despite opposition criticism, he refused to be influenced. The referendum on the monarchy was also held in early December, as scheduled by Karamanlis.

Most importantly, Karamanlis also dominated the constitutional-drafting process. The opposition was not invited to contribute to the process of drafting the new constitution. Instead, the government presented its own draft—apparently the product of Karamanlis and his three or so closest advisors (Konstantinos Papakonstantinou, Konstantinos Stefanakis, and, especially, Konstantinos Tsatsos)—to parliament and limited parliamentary debate on the constitution to three months, an extremely brief debate for such a critical regime issue.

No sooner did the Karamanlis government release the 112 articles of the draft constitution than the opposition's forceful criticisms began. The center (renamed the Center Union-New Forces, [EDIK]) issued a statement on 24 December 1974, describing the proposed form of government as "despotic and illiberal," and maintained that the role envisaged for the president of the republic would make him "not a regulator but a ruler of political developments."[68] George Mavros, leader of EDIK, also contended that the constitution had been drafted "to fit the requirements of a single person—the leader of the majority party, Premier Constantine Karamanlis."[69] Andreas Papandreou maintained that the aim of the draft constitution was the establishment of "a totalitarian regime under a parliamentary mantle,"[70] while Charilaos Florakis, leader of the Greek Communist Party, called for the "decisive rejection of the attempt of an anti-democratic, despotic, power" and its replacement by "a constitution that will rule out anything which is fascist, tyrannical, anachronistic and reactionary."[71] Even the press complained that "the draft articles concerning the rights of trade unions and the press were similar to those which had been included in the constitution promulgated by the Papadopoulos Government in 1968."[72]

Apparently taking some of these criticisms into consideration, Karamanlis amended several articles of the draft constitution before submitting it to parliament. There it was considered by two special committees whose composition reflected the relative strength of the various parties in parliament—thereby securing ND a majority, given its 54.5 percent of the vote in the 1974 elections. Karamanlis amended several constitutional articles having to do with the administration of higher education, personal liberties, individual rights, freedom of the press, the minimum voting age, and the normal term of parliament. These revisions notwithstanding, the basic features of the proposed government structure remained—to the opposition's disappointment—firmly intact.

Subsequently, the opposition objected that the government had rejected most amendments proposed by members of the opposition in committee. It also maintained that despite the fact that only one-half of the proposed articles were examined by the time the three-month government-imposed deadline was up, the government rigidly refused to extend its deadline past 27 March 1975. Parliamentary deputies also indicated in interviews that even when concessions were made by the government, the articles on which such concessions were granted were of wholly secondary importance. Karamanlis, relying upon the advice and expertise of his small circle of "consultant-friends," had the final word over the draft that was finally presented to parliament for a vote. As one parliamentary deputy put it: "Committees existed. The legislative branch functioned back then. Certainly, the legislative branch functioned. But the articles were coming straight from Mr. Karamanlis' personal advisors. Let's not fool ourselves. ... No one said that the legislative branch did not function. ... But from that point on, the architect of the constitution was Karamanlis. Let's not fool ourselves!"[73]

The new constitution was adopted by the Greek parliament on 7 June 1975, on the votes of all *Nea Demokratia* deputies. All eighty-four opposition deputies abstained from the vote, however, walking out of the debate on 21 May and refusing to attend most of the subsequent sessions. The opposition also boycotted the signing ceremony of the constitution on 9 June. At a press conference arranged to coincide with the ceremony, Papandreou denounced the new constitution as "totalitarian" and "no better than the constitution of dictator Papadopoulos." He also stated that should his party attain power, it would "dissolve Parliament and call for the election of a constituent assembly to produce a constitution based on the people's sovereignty."[74] On the same day George Mavros also denounced the constitution as "reactionary" and criticized its "failure to provide an effective safeguard for the democratic form of government against those nostalgic for monarchy and dictatorship." Like Papandreou, he pledged that his party would work toward "the establishment of a true parliamentary democracy which [would] safeguard the people's sovereignty."[75]

The actions and rhetoric of the opposition during the entire constitutional engineering process, signaled to many a possible return to the old-style politics characteristic of the precoup period. Party relations became extremely conflictual, and highly charged debates with populist rhetoric and impassioned exchanges frequently took place.[76] Karamanlis maintained that the opposition's boycott of the final stages of the constitutional debate indicated "a lack of respect for the basic rule of democracy" and maintained that "whoever defeats this principle defeats democracy."[77] Thus, from a number of perspectives, the prospects for democratic consolidation and stability did not appear promising in 1975. Instead, based on the "facts" of the Greek case, one would have expected its transition to democracy to be more like the chaotic, polarized, and tumultuous Portuguese transition and less like the peaceful, cooperative transition in Spain. And yet, democratic consolidation occurred relatively quickly in Greece. How this might have occurred in the absence of interelite negotiations will be discussed below.

ELITE CONVERGENCE

As previously stated, one method by which elite consensual unity is achieved is through an elite settlement. This was the process by which democratic consolidation was achieved in Spain but clearly not in Greece or Portugal. By all accounts the elite settlement path to democratic consolidation is an extremely rare event. Higley and Burton estimate that over the course of the last three hundred years, the world has seen approximately twelve settlements that "tamed" politics and led to democratic consolidation.[78] Since settlements are rare events, highly unlikely to occur, it is even more crucial to uncover the process by which "politics are tamed and cease being a deadly, warlike affair"[79] via a second, more common, path to democratic consolidation—the two-step process of elite convergence.[80] In step one of this process, some of the opposing factions of a disunified elite enter into a broad electoral coalition when they come to realize that, in so doing, they can mobilize a reliable majority of votes, win elections repeatedly, and, thereby, protect their interests by dominating government. The second step of this process occurs when the opposition, tired of losing elections, realizes that the only way it can emerge from seemingly permanent opposition status is to beat the dominant coalition at its own game by abandoning antisystem or semiloyal stances and acknowledging democratic institutions and rules. Despite its more common occurrence, this process of democratic consolidation tends to be relatively more difficult and protracted than the elite settlement model, usually requiring many more years to complete.

France's consolidation trajectory is said to be a paradigmatic example of this successful, albeit lengthier, processes of democratic consolidation—beginning with the founding of the Fifth Republic and culminating with the successful "cohabitation" of 1986–88 when parliament was controlled by the center-right, while the presidency was held by socialist François Mitterrand.[81] Until this time modern French politics had been characterized by deep elite disunity, generally resulting in repeated political crises and governmental instability. Constant power struggles between feuding elite factions as well as the presence of significant antisystem parties and movements on both extremes of the political spectrum contributed to widespread popular dissatisfaction with both the Third and Fourth

Republics. In the 1950s, for example, nearly 50 percent of seats in the National Assembly were held by such antisystem parties as the Stalinist *Parti communiste français* (PCF), the Poujadist movement, as well as the conservative supporters of General Charles de Gaulle—all withholding their support from the regime.[82] This being the case, governments could only be formed if virtually all other parties in the assembly agreed to participate in extremely broad coalitions. The precarious nature of these coalitions—composed of such ideologically and programmatically incompatible bedfellows as conservatives, Socialists (SFIO), anticlerical Radical Socialists, and the Catholic *Mouvement républicain populaire* (MRP)—led to governments that on average survived no longer than eight months.

The 1958 Algerian Crisis, which threatened the very integrity of the French state, was a conversion for French elites. It was then that previously disorganized right and center elite factions were brought together for the first time under the leadership of Charles de Gaulle. The period between de Gaulle's return to power in 1958 and the winning of an absolute majority by the pro-Gaullist coalition, the *Union pour la nouvelle républic* (UNR), in November 1962 marked the first step in the elite convergence model. It was at this time that previously antagonistic rightist and centrist elite factions realized that their electoral interest could best be protected by cooperating in elections against the left. Thus, they proceeded to form a center-right coalition that dominated French politics for the next two decades.

It was over the next twenty years that the second step of the elite convergence process developed. De Gaulle's leftist opponents—socialists and communist party leaders, many trade union officials, and prominent leftist intellectuals and celebrities—began to moderate their programmatic and ideological positions in order to win elections and enter government. The PCF, in particular, underwent the most significant change. It abandoned such radical Marxist-Leninist tenants as the "dictatorship of the proletariat" and transformed itself into a Eurocommunist party, accepting the legitimacy of democratic institutions and rules of the game and agreeing to participate fully in democratic, parliamentary government. Concluding that only an explicit break with their former antisystem stance would give them a majority of French votes, the communists formalized their commitment to democracy in the Common Government Program of 1972 in which they explicitly agreed to share posts with the socialists should the left be voted into government. When, in 1981, the socialists, displacing the communists as the largest party on the left, won both the presidency and an absolute majority in the National Assembly, socialist President François Mitterrand proceeded to implement many socialist policies, including significant nationalization of banks and industries. His policies were largely a failure, however, and, wishing to avoid electoral defeat in 1984, the socialists quickly moderated their own programmatic and ideological positions, moving from maximalist socialism to moderate social democracy. With this, the second step of the elite convergence model was complete.

This path to consensual unity also appears to fit the Italian consolidation process despite the fact that Italy experienced the most protracted and difficult consolidation process of all the Southern European countries.[83] One study has even gone as far as to conclude that while the transition to democracy was completed in

Italy in the 1940s, full democratic consolidation did not occur until the mid- to late 1970s.[84]

Briefly, the first stage in the two-step process occurred in the late 1940s and early 1950s in Italy. It was at this time that the Christian Democratic Party (DC) established itself as the dominant political force by securing an absolute majority of seats in the Chamber of Deputies in the 1948 elections. Similar to the role played by de Gaulle and his supporters in France, the Italian Christian Democrats were successful in securing the allegiance and support of various social groups on the center and right of the political spectrum who had previously been supporters of fascism.[85] By attracting center and rightist votes, the Christian Democrats came to dominate Italian politics for a decade while socialists and communists were excluded at the national level altogether.

With the passage of time, however, the parties of the left gradually abandoned their extreme ideological and programmatic positions and moved closer to the center of the political spectrum. The first important step in this process was the "opening to the left"—initiated by none other than the governing Christian Democrats—who incorporated the socialists into the governing coalition in 1963. This was later followed by the full incorporation of the communists into the democratic game. Faced with the near-total domination of political power by the DC and its coalition partners, and recognizing that moderation was the only ticket to government, the Communist Party of Italy (PCI) agreed in 1976 to lend support in parliament to the Christian Democratic minority government in exchange for important government posts (e.g., speaker of the Chamber of Deputies and the chairmanship of some legislative committees). Thus, by the end of the 1970s, the communists too had unquestionably demonstrated their loyalty to the democratic regime and, in turn, were accepted as loyal democratic contenders by the other parliamentary parties. In this way elite convergence was complete and democracy consolidated at the elite level.

It is important to note, however, that progress toward democratic consolidation was slow and often difficult in Italy. Social and political unrest in the 1960s and 1970s reached crisis proportions and culminated in turbulent mass mobilizations. Serious outbreaks of terrorist violence by both the extreme left and the extreme right were common features of Italian political life in the late 1970s. Additionally, survey data collected as late as 1985[86] indicate that at the mass level, attitudinal support for the regime remained relatively low, as many citizens expressed cynicism about political parties and governing elites. According to many observers this lingering mistrust and dissatisfaction was the primary explanation for the 1994 electoral earthquake—the most dramatic party system realignment in modern European history.[87]

In sum, the two-step elite convergence model was successful in bringing about democratic consolidation and stability in France and Italy. Unlike in Spain, where democratic consolidation occurred relatively quickly, however, a lengthy twenty-year span was necessary for the achievement of elite convergence in France. A protracted period of two decades was required for French elites to realize that, given the changed rules of the game of the Fifth Republic, moderation of ideological and programmatic stances was necessary if they were to win elections and enter government. As in France, Italy's progress toward democratic consolidation via elite convergence was also lengthy but also more difficult. The case of Italy emphasizes that elite convergence does not always unfold in a neat, unilinear path. Indeed, a protracted process of elite convergence may also be troubled by a number of difficulties and setbacks (e.g., mass disenchantment with the political system, mobilization, and terrorist violence) that may threaten democratic stability and consolidation.

With these cases in mind, the following chapters will analyze the case of Greece from the perspective of the elite convergence model. As will be shown, despite a number of aberrant features of its transition, Greece eventually became a consolidated democracy—largely through elite convergence. Thus, the focus below will be on explaining how successful consolidation occurred in spite of such numerous "obstacles" that complicated the path to a consolidation and that today continue to negatively affect the quality of Greek democracy.

NOTES

1. On democratization paths, see Juan J. Linz and Alfred Stepan, *Problems of Democratic Transition and Consolidation: Southern Europe, South America, and Post-Communist Europe* (Baltimore: The Johns Hopkins University Press, 1996); and "Toward Consolidated Democracies," *Journal of Democracy* 7:2 (April 1996), pp. 14–33.

2. Moreover, while the colonels' regime was not monistic (neither sultanistic, totalitarian, nor post-totalitarian) and was opposed by a heterogeneous group of elites, representing the entire span of the political spectrum, negotiations (the two- and four-player games usually thought to be necessary for a successful democratization effort) failed in Greece. For a theoretical discussion of this, see Linz and Stepan, *Problems of Democratic Transition*; and "Towards Consolidated Democracies."

3. On the transition to democracy in Portugal, see Kenneth Maxwell, "Regime Overthrow and the Prospects for Democratic Transition in Portugal," in Guillermo O'Donnell, Philippe C. Schmitter, and Laurence Whitehead, eds., *Transitions from Authoritarian Rule: Southern Europe* (Baltimore: Johns Hopkins University Press, 1986). On democratic consolidation there, see Lawrence S. Graham, "Redefining the Portuguese Transition to Democracy," in John Higley and Richard Gunther, eds. *Elites and Democratic Consolidation in Latin America and Southern Europe* (Cambridge: Cambridge University Press, 1992); and Richard Gunther, P. Nikiforos Diamandourous, and Hans-Jürgen Puhle, "Introduction," in Richard Gunther, P. Nikiforos Diamandouros, and Hans-Jürgen Puhle, eds. *The Politics of Democratic Consolidation: Southern Europe in Comparative Perspective* (Baltimore: Johns Hopkins University Press, 1995), pp. 26–29.

4. Article 38, quoted in Gunther et al., "Introduction," p. 28.

5. "Introduction: Elite Transformations and Democratic Regimes," in Higley and Gunther, eds., *Elites and Democratic Consolidation* (Cambridge: Cambridge University Press, 1992). See also Michael G. Burton and John Higley, "Elite Settlements," *American Sociological Review* 52:3 (June 1987), pp. 295–307; "The Elite Variable in Democratic Transitions and Breakdowns," *American Sociological Review* 54:1 (February 1989), pp. 17–32; John Higley, Michael G. Burton, and G. Lowell Field, "In Defense of Elite Theory: A Reply to Cammack," *American Sociological Review* 55:3 (June 1990), pp. 421–26; and John Higley and Michael Burton, "Elite Settlements and the Taming of Politics," *Government and Opposition* 33:1 (Winter 1998), pp. 98–115.

6. A disunified elite group is said to consist of elites who distrust one another, perceive political outcomes in zero-sum terms, and engage in unrestricted and often violent struggles for dominance.

7. A consensually unified elite is characterized by open communication channels between elites, the perception of politics in positive-sum terms, as well as an underlying consensus about rules of the game and political institutions.

8. Burton and Higley, "Elite Settlements," p. 295. See, also, Higley and Burton, "Elite Settlements and the Taming of Politics."

9. On the transition to democracy in Spain, see José María Maravall and Julián Santamaría, "Political Change in Spain and the Prospects for Democracy," in O'Donnell et al., eds., *Transitions from Authoritarian Rule: Southern Europe*. On democratic consolidation, see Richard Gunther, "Spain: The Very Model of the Modern Elite Settlement," in Higley and Gunther, eds., *Elites and Democratic Consolidation*; and Gunther et al., "Introduction," pp. 21–22.

10. Gunther, "Spain," pp. 62–64.

11. Internal party document of the pro-Andreas Papandreou faction of the exiled wing of the Center Union titled, "Report 1: Political Situation," Stephen Rousseas Archives, Butler Library, Columbia University, NY.

12. Nikos D. Delepetros, *Apofasisa Na Mileso* (I Decided to Speak) (Athens: Estia, 1988), p. 307. Delepetros was a member of the central committee of the Social Democratic Party (George Papandreou, leader) and of the Liberal Party (George Papandreou and Sophocles Venizelos, leaders). During the dictatorship he lived in Paris and edited the resistance newspapers, *Eleuthere kai Demokratike Ellada* (Free and Democratic Greece), using the pen name Nikiforos Demokrates. He was also coeditor, with Konstantinos Mitsotakis and Takis Lambrias, of the "Greek Report."

13. Potes Paraskevopoulos, *Ho Karamanlis sta Chronia 1974–1985* (Karamanlis in the Years 1974–1985) (Athens: O Typos, n.d.), p. 10.

14. The Patriotic Front (PAM) was a leftist resistance group to the colonels.

15. Stephen W. Rousseas, "Memoire on the 'Second Solution'," *Journal of the Hellenic Diaspora* 2:1 (January 1975), pp. 31–32. Rousseas was an American academic who was a close personal friend of the Papandreous at the time of the dictatorship.

16. Rousseas, "Memoire," pp. 31–32. Emphasis added.

17. Rousseas, "Memoire," p. 22.

18. Rousseas, "Memoire," p. 25.

19. Rousseas, "Memoire," p. 32.

20. Rousseas, "Memoire," p. 32.

21. This antidictatorial Norwegian Committee devised a plan whereby Greece was to adopt the same strategy used by Norway in 1944 to free itself from German occupation. Under this plan, during the German occupation of Norway all parties set aside their differences and united under one program with one sole objective—to rid Norway of the Germans.

22. Rousseas, "Memoire," p. 33. Emphasis in original.

23. Rousseas, "Memoire," p. 33.

24. Rousseas, "Memoire," p. 34.

25. Rousseas, "Memoire," p. 34.

26. Personal correspondence to Andreas Papandreou from Mogens Camre, who was involved in negotiations to unify the Greek national elite, dated 20 November 1970, Rousseas Archives.

27. Personal correspondence from Andreas Papandreou to Mogens Camre, dated 25 November 1970, Rousseas Archives.

28. Rousseas, "Memoire," p. 34.

29. Internal document of the exiled wing of the Center Union in Western Europe, "A report detailing the political situation in Western Europe some 45 days after the coup was launched," Rousseas Archives.

30. Margaret Papandreou was the wife of Andreas Papandreou at that time.

31. Letter smuggled out of Greece by Margaret Papandreou to Stephen Rousseas, dated 27 August 1967, Rousseas Archives.

32. Personal correspondence of a first cousin of Andreas Papandreou, dated 30 October 1967, Rousseas Archives.

33. Personal correspondence of Margaret Papandreou, dated 27 November 1967, Rousseas Archives.

34. Peter Murtagh, *The Rape of Greece: The King, the Colonels, and the Resistance* (London: Simon and Schuster, 1994), p. 207.

35. Personal correspondence of Stephen Rousseas, a close participant in the negotiations, dated 23 June 1968, Rousseas Archives.

36. Personal correspondence of Stephen Roussea, dated 23 June 1968, Rousseas Archives. Eleni Vlachou, owner of two major conservative dailies and a weekly periodical, refused to issue her newspapers under conditions of press censorship during the dictatorship. She was placed under house arrest but escaped to London.

37. These common goals were taken from the "First Agreement Between Democratic Defense and Patriotic Front," published in the underground press in February 1968.

38. Statement by Andreas G. Papandreou on the Nature and Activities of the Panhellenic Liberation Movement (PAK), March 1968, Rousseas Archives.

39. Murtagh, *The Rape of Greece*, p. 207.

40. C. M. Woodhouse, *The Rise and Fall of the Greek Colonels* (New York: Franklin Watts, 1985).

41. Murtagh, *The Rape of Greece*, p. 172.

42. Personal correspondence of Mogens Camre, dated 20 October 1967, Rousseas Archives.

43. "Report 1, Political Situation."

44. Interview with Constantine Mitsotakis in late 1969 with the *Free Voice of Greece* radio broadcast (New York, NY), although the interview never aired.

45. Woodhouse, *Karamanlis*, pp. 191–92.

46. Richard Clogg, *Parties and Elections in Greece: The Search for Legitimacy* (London: C. Hurst and Co. Ltd., 1987), p. 152.

47. According to this document the Center Union was proposing a national front based on EK, ERE, and EDA membership. The number of EK members, however, would clearly outnumber those of the other two parties, as the ratio 5:3:2 indicates.

48. "Report 1, Political Situation."

49. Interview given to *The Free Voice of Greece* radio broadcast after the expulsion of Greece from the European Council in December 1969.

50. Interview aired in September 1971 on *The Free Voice of Greece* radio broadcast.

51. Carl Barkman, *Ambassador in Athens, 1969–1975: The Evolution from Military Dictatorship to Democracy in Greece* (London: The Merlin Press, 1989), p. 168.

52. Linz and Stepan, *Problems of Democratic Transition*; and "Toward Consolidated Democracies."

53. The four military officials, one from each branch of the armed forces, included General Grigorios Bonanos, Lieutenant General Andreas Galatsanos, Vice Admiral Petros Arapakis, and Air Marshal Alexander Papanikolaou.

54. The four former premiers were George Athanasiades-Novas, Spyros Markezinis, Stephanos Stephanopoulos, and Panayiotes Kanellopoulos.

55. The three ministers included Evangelos Averoff-Tossizza, Petros Garoufalias, and Xenophon Zolatas.

56. P. Nikiforos Diamandouros, "Regime Change and the Prospects for Democracy in Greece: 1974–1983," in O'Donnell et al., eds., *Transitions from Authoritarian Rule: Southern Europe*, pp. 156–57.

57. Petros Garoufalias was largely rejected because of his complicity in the Center Union's demise (brought on by his refusal to purge the military as ordered by George Papandreou). Christianos Xanthopoulos-Palamas was likewise rejected because of his participation in the short-lived civilian government of 1973 under military rule.

58. For a discussion of these events, see Stavros P. Psychares, *Ta Paraskenia tes Allaghes* (Behind the Scenes of the Transition) (Athens: Ekdoseis Papazese, 1975); Spyridon V. Markezinis, *Anamneseis* (Reminiscences) (Athens: Ekdoseis Sp. V. Markezine A.E., 1979), pp. 541–80; P. Nikiforos Diamandouros, "Transition to, and Consolidation of, Democratic Politics in Greece, 1974–1983: A Tentative Assessment," in Geoffrey Pridham, ed., *The New Mediterranean Democracies: Regime Transition in Spain, Greece and Portugal* (London: Frank Cass, 1984); and Harry J. Psomiades, "Greece: From the Colonels' Rule to Democracy," in John H. Herz, ed., *From Dictatorship to Democracy: Coping with the Legacies of Authoritarianism and Totalitarianism* (Westport, CT: Greenwood Press, 1982).

59. On the decision to have Karamanlis return to Greece, see Psychares, *He Allaghe*, pp. 140–49, 156–60, 189–91, and 210–12.

60. Interview conducted in Athens, Greece on 25 January 1994 with a former ERE and ND deputy.

61. Konstantinos Tsatsos, *Ho Agnostos Karamanlis: Mia Prosopografia* (The Unknown Karamanlis: A Personal Account) (Athens: Ekdotike Athenon A.E., 1989), p. 26.

62. Tsatsos, *Ho Agnostos Karamanlis*, p. 77.

63. Quoted in Paulos N. Tzermias, *He Politike Skepse tou Konstantinou Karamanli: Mia Anichneuse* (The Political Thought of Constantine Karamanlis: An Investigation) (Athens: Hellenike Euroekthotike, 1990), p. 170.

64. Takis Lambrias, *Ste Skia Enos Megalou: Meletontas 25 Chronia ton Karamanli* (In the Shadow of a Great One: 25 Years of Studying Karamanlis) (Athens: Morfotike Estia, 1989), pp. 265, 267.

65. *Keesing's Contemporary Archives*, v. 20 (1974), pp. 26781–82.

66. *Nea Demokratia* emerged victorious in those elections, receiving 54.5 percent of the national vote. In contrast, the Center Union won 20.5 percent, PASOK 13.6 percent, and the United Left 9.5 percent of the vote.

67. *Keesing's Contemporary Archives*, v. 20 (1974), p. 26782.

68. *Keesing's Contemporary Archives*, v. 21 (1975), p. 27088.

69. *Facts on File*, v. 34 (1974), p. 1095.

70. *Keesing's Contemporary Archives*, v. 21 (1975), p. 27988.

71. *Keesing's Contemporary Archives*, v. 21 (1975), p. 27088.

72. *Keesing's Contemporary Archives*, v. 21 (1975), p. 27088.

73. Interview in Athens, Greece, on 10 December 1993 with a former deputy of ND.

74. *Keesing's Contemporary Archives*, v. 21 (1975), p. 27456.

75. *Keesing's Contemporary Archives*, v. 21 (1975), p. 27456.

76. Kevin Featherstone, "Political Parties and Democratic Consolidation in Greece," in Geoffrey Pridham, ed., *Securing Democracy: Political Parties and Democratic Consolidation in Southern Europe* (London and New York: Routledge, 1990), p. 189.

77. *Keesing's Contemporary Archives*, v. 21 (1975), p. 27456.

78. Higley and Burton, "Elite Settlements and the Taming of Politics," p. 113.

79. Higely and Burton, "Elite Settlements and the Taming of Politics," p. 98.

80. Burton et al., "Introduction."

81. On this interpretation of democratic consolidation in France, see Burton et al., "Introduction," pp. 25-30; G. Lowell Field and John Higley, "Imperfectly Unified Elites: The Cases of Italy and France," in R. Tomasson, ed., *Comparative Studies in Sociology* (Greenwich, CT: JAI Press, 1978).

82. On these antisystem parties, see Martin Harrison, ed., *French Politics* (Lexington, MA: Heath, 1969), pp. 24–28; and William Safran, *The French Polity*, Second Edition (New York: Longman, 1985), p. 68.

83. On the transition to democracy in Italy, see Gianfranco Pasquino, "The Demise of the First Fascist Regime and Italy's Transition to Democracy: 1943–1948," in O'Donnell et al., eds., *Transition from Authoritarian Rule: Southern Europe*. On democratic consolidation, see Maurizio Cotta, "Unification and Democratic Consolidation in Italy: An Historical Overview," in Higley and Gunther, eds., *Elites and Democratic Consolidation*; Leonardo Morlino, "Political Parties and Democratic Consolidation in Southern Europe," in Gunther et al., eds., *The Politics of Democratic Consolidation*; and Gunther et al., "Introduction," pp. 22–26.

84. This argument is made by Cotta, "Elite Unification and Democratic Consolidation in Italy."

85. See Morlino, "Political Parties and Democratic Consolidation."

86. See Leonardo Morlino and José R. Montero, "Legitimacy and Democracy in Southern Europe," in Gunther et al., *The Politics of Democratic Consolidation*.

87. On recent Italian party system realignments, see Leonardo Morlino, "Crisis of Parties and Change of Party System in Italy," *Party Politics* 2:1(1996), pp. 5–30; and Stephano Bartolini and Roberto D'Alimonte, "Plurality Competition and Party Realignment in Italy: The 1994 Parliamentary Elections," *European Journal of Political Research* 29:1 (January 1996), pp. 105–42.

CHAPTER 4 _____

Contagion from the Right:
Conservative Moderation in Greece

One of the most decisive factors contributing to democratic consolidation and stability in post-junta Greece was the appearance in 1974 of a moderate and modernizing right. Had *Nea Demokratia* (ND) maintained the precoup right's traditional commitment to zealous anticommunism and its attachment to the unpopular and divisive monarchy, Greece's new democracy may have been stillborn from the start. Significant political groups and their supporters would have been effectively denied personal liberties, and ideological cleavages based on the politics of the pre-junta years would have fostered feelings of regime illegitimacy among large sectors of the Greek population. The post-1974 attempt at democratization would thus have been seriously threatened. As the existing literature on the Greek transition shows, however, it was none other than the leader of the precoup right, Constantine Karamanlis, who legalized the Communist Party, did away with all the restrictive post–civil war legislation, held an impeccably fair referendum on the monarchy, modernized the right by founding his own party, *Nea Demokratia*, and drafted one of the most liberal democratic constitutions Greece had ever seen. Such moderate actions by a leader often held to have been culpable in the precoup parastate are curious indeed.

The question of why the right decided to democratize the post–civil war political system is almost completely unexplored in existing studies of the Greek transition, leaving unanswered the most interesting and theoretically critical questions: Why such a radical change? What were Karamanlis' motivations behind this reform? And why was the right wing of the political spectrum willing to moderate in 1974 given that it had refused to do so earlier? It is clear that the historical facts of the case as presented in the transitions literature on Greece are not enough to answer these questions. What is required instead is a critical assessment of the right's moderation.

Current perspectives on democratic consolidation are also not able to account for the unique characteristics of the Greek case: the role played by a single, dominant political leader acting without reference to a highly partisan political opposition, the lack of cooperative consensual agreements aimed at resolving fundamental divisions between opposing groups, and the lack of ideological and programmatic moderation stemming from electoral motivations. As previously stated, most emerging theories of democratic consolidation emphasize interelite negotiations ("pacts" or "settlements") that are argued to be key to the stability and survival of democratic regimes. These theories contend that such settlements, hammered out in face-to-face, private negotiations may constitute the most direct and rapid route to consolidated democracy that is available in today's world.[1]

As has been shown, however, a settlement or pact was never achieved in Greece. On the contrary, agreement was blocked by a combination of partisan political concerns, old animosities, suspicions, and personal rivalries on the part of opposing elites who refused to reach even a minimal consensus and collaborate. In the face of such disunity and factionalism, the prospects for democratic consolidation appeared poor. Much to scholarly surprise, however, a general consensus—albeit a very loose and informal one—desiring a return to procedural democracy emerged among all significant political elites during the junta years. This diffuse support for democracy as well as a general "understanding" that Karamanlis was the most capable person to bring it about, enabled him to monopolize the transition and consolidation processes without any significant opposition to his power.

In the absence of a settlement, elite consensus was forged through the two-step process of convergence. Karamanlis' decisions in 1974 to legalize the KKE, to hold a referendum on the monarchy, and to modernize the right wing of the political spectrum are indicative of such convergence. His *motivations* for moderation do not fully fit the elite convergence model, however. The model holds that the decision of opposition elites to enter into sustained, peaceful collaboration in electoral politics and to moderate their positions and behavior toward conformity with the rules of the new democratic regime is driven by a desire to win parliamentary elections and dominate government. Since both Karamanlis and *Nea Demokratia* maintained an unquestionably dominant position during the entire transition, however, and since *Nea Demokratia* received a resounding majority in the elections of November 1974, Karamanlis' primary motivations were clearly not electoral. Rather, moderation in the case of the Greek right was primarily triggered by the knowledge that the only way to normalize Greek politics and social relations, the only way to overcome the hatreds and fears of the post–civil war period—indeed, the only way to assure that democratic consolidation and stability would be achieved—would be through moderation. This, in turn, would lead to consensual unity among elites and between their respective social groups. Thus, the convergence that took place on the part of the right in post-junta Greece—as with the Spanish right under Adolfo Suárez—was a conscious and deliberate effort to forge national reconciliation, do away with the destabilizing schisms of post–civil war politics, and consciously and deliberately ensure democratic stability and consolidation. Contrary to theoretical expectations, electoral motivations clearly took a backseat to a concern for democratic stability.

Moreover, Karamanlis' moderation and the process of elite convergence began *prior* to the transition to democracy—indeed, prior to the dictatorship itself. As will be illustrated in this chapter, certain segments of the parliamentary right began to increasingly, albeit slowly, moderate their positions as the passions of the civil war receded into history.

In analyzing the right's convergence, this chapter maintains that an interaction of factors—the elite variable (i.e., the decisions and actions of Constantine Karamanlis and others) *as well as* the cumulative process of political learning brought about by the passing of time, generational change, and the negative experience of dictatorship contributed to democratic consolidation in Greece. Specifically, political learning facilitated programmatic and ideological moderation, thereby bringing about the successful resolution of a number of long-standing divisive cleavages—cleavages that had to be resolved if democratic consolidation were to result. This chapter on the Greek right thus demonstrates how political learning contributed to Karamanlis and the right's modernization, which itself was critical to democratic stability and consolidation.

While the analysis in this chapter is decisively elite-centered—focusing primarily on the decisions and behavior of Karamanlis—it attempts to move beyond the most common approach in the literature on Greece, which considers the role played by Karamanlis irrespective of more contextual, environmental factors. A wholly elite-centered approach ignores the fact that Karamanlis' actions were also shaped by structural-historical constraints as well as by changes within the environment in which he acted.[2] By the early 1970s the Greek Civil War was quickly receding into the annals of history. The Cold War atmosphere was also thawing in a period of East-West *détente,* and with it the perceived threat of communist takeover was reduced. To put it simply, times had changed. As interviews have shown, had Karamanlis attempted to carry out the 1974 reforms in the climate of the 1950s, they would have doubtlessly ended in failure. Thus, with the passing of time, both Karamanlis and the environment changed. As I will argue, both transformations were necessary for democratic stability and consolidation to occur.

THE PROBLEM THAT NEVER WAS: KARAMANLIS' DOMINANCE OF THE TRANSITION AND CONSOLIDATION PROCESSES

As argued in chapter 3, unlike Aldolfo Suárez who engaged in extensive face-to-face negotiations and subsequent compromise with all significant political elites in Spain, Constantine Karamanlis dominated the entire Greek transition and consolidation processes by controlling all decision-making concerning the rules and institutions of the new regime. As P. Nikiforos Diamandouros maintains, "What, above all, characterized Karamanlis's strategy . . . was his studied attempt to minimize commitments to collective and individual actors, to personalize crisis management, [and] to maximize his freedom of movement."[3] Much of the literature on democratic consolidation contends, however, that democratization paths characterized by such absolute control on the part of a single partisan individual (or group) are likely to prove problematic. This stems from the likelihood that such personalistic, individual control will inherently bias the transition and consolidation processes in favor of one group over another, tainting these processes with a partisan, majoritarian bent.[4] The ultimate danger is that the opposition, resenting such domination, could come to reject the newly established regime, its rules of the game, and its institutions, and, in the extreme case, could engage in extra-parliamentary forms of political protest.

If we consider Karamanlis' control of the transition process in light of the fact that he was the leading figure of the precoup parliamentary right—a right that had dominated that semidemocratic period of Greek politics—his control of the transition becomes even more anomalous and the prospects for consolidation seemingly even poorer. Yet Karamanlis did control the entire transition process in Greece, and, contrary to theory, democratic stability and consolidation resulted. What was it about this apparently anomalous situation that might help explain why Karamanlis' control of the process did not hinder democratic consolidation but instead *contributed* to it?

The answer appears to be two-fold: First, Karamanlis was acceptable to virtually all Greeks by 1974 and, second, he attempted to act as a national rather than a purely partisan leader. This was true for a number of reasons. After the fall of the colonels, there was such widespread diffuse support for democracy among Greeks that virtually any democratic alternative to the junta was perceived as acceptable. Moreover, most people perceived Karamanlis as having unmatched authority and prestige (having enjoyed a long and successful premiership from 1955 to 1963) and, therefore, as being the politician most capable of leading a successful transition. This, coupled with the conviction of most deputies that only a man of the right could peacefully secure the military's extrication from power, explains why there was virtually no real opposition to Karamanlis in 1974 and why he was able to dominate the entire transition process. In sum, his authority to make decisions went virtually unchallenged: everyone, including the opposition, essentially accepted every decision made by Karamanlis during the fragile period of the transition from authoritarian to democratic rule.[5]

Put simply, by 1974 elites committed to the restoration of full procedural democracy were willing to accept Karamanlis' dominance of the transition process so long as democracy would be restored in Greece. In fact, there was such broad support—indeed a demand—for democracy that the entire civilian political elite was willing to accept virtually *any* new regime under *any* effective leadership so long as it would guarantee the full civil and political rights of all Greek citizens and preclude the reintroduction of another authoritarian regime. In the words of one prominent leftist during the dictatorship: "At this time, I do not care about political differences. I only see one enemy—the dictatorship—and I have only one objective aim, its overthrow."[6]

Interviews with deputies of all political parties revealed that by 1974 there was no real opposition to Karamanlis leading the National Unity Government, and the general perception appears to have been that "everyone generally wanted him."[7] A former deputy of *Nea Demokratia* argued:

[W]e had decided that the only solution was the return of Karamanlis. We decided to . . . tell him that "the Greek people are waiting for you to come back to Greece to establish order and to bring back true democracy to our country" . . . All the parties of that period found this to be a way out of the impasse. And even if they didn't really want Karamanlis, . . . since he had been abroad for so many years, they believed that he was coming here not as a party man but as a man who would guarantee democracy and who would be able to bring back peace, progress, and true democracy to Greece.[8]

Karamanlis was also acceptable to deputies of all political persuasions because he was believed to be a man of great prestige, a dynamic leader of great authority and popularity who "dwarfed" every other politician. As a result he was seen as the most capable person to lead the transition from authoritarian to democratic rule. One scholar argued that "despite all the past calumnies against him, most Greeks still believed he was the one politician they could take seriously and even trust. ... In spite of all his past errors and shortcomings when in power, Karamanlis in the view of many Greeks was still the politician who said less and did more in eight years [1955–63] for the reconstruction of their country than any other."[9] As another person—someone who advocated the "Karamanlis Solution" to the dictatorship—expressed years later: "We believed that only Karamanlis with his tremendous authority would be able to succeed in [achieving] a bloodless transition from dictatorship to democracy."[10]

Even Karamanlis' "political opponents esteemed and respected him."[11] Both Mikis Theodorakis, a prominent leftist, and Elias Iliou, the leader of EDA, spoke approvingly of Karamanlis and supported him. And although Iliou criticized Karamanlis for not including members of the left in his Government of National Unity, he nevertheless publicly expressed that the government was an important part of the democratization process: "The formation of a civilian government ... constitutes under any circumstances a very positive step. ... That is why we welcome the transition as a great positive step, as an opening towards democracy."[12] Even the General Secretary of the Greek Communist Party–Interior (KKE-I), Charalambos Drakopoulos, announced on 28 July 1974: "The fall of the dictatorial regime and the formation of a civilian government by Constantine Karamanlis are important events for the country and they constitute an important first step towards the restoration of democracy."[13]

Another factor that made Karamanlis acceptable to the vast majority of Greek citizens and to the political leadership of the country was that he belonged to the right—to "the establishment." A widespread belief existed both in Greece and abroad that only a conservative politician would be able to oust the dictators without bloodshed. A conservative deputy describes the decision to call back Karamanlis in these terms:

[E]veryone, even the left, the communists, saw that only Karamanlis could [oppose] ... the dictatorship because the conservative *parataxi* (camp) ... would not accept just anybody. If Andreas Papandreou had come, for example, to be leader, they would have placed themselves on the side of the dictators. ... The one who was able to hit them had to be a leader who belonged to the conservative *parataxi*. And for this reason, everyone revolved around the central axis of Karamanlis.[14]

Indeed, George Rallis, who would later become leader of ND, also emphasizes Karamanlis' influence in the army as early as September 1970: "I expressed to [Karamanlis] the need to return as soon as possible to Athens, not only because he has popular trust, but also because he can influence the army."[15]

Even the opposition believed that Karamanlis held influence over the army and would therefore be the best person to lead the transition. As a centrist deputy put it: "We believed that he was the only person who could guarantee to the junta that it could depart without consequences. ... We could tell them that Karamanlis would be the guarantor. ... [T]his is how we truly believed we could pass politically from the junta to democracy bloodlessly and without the country having to pay a high price."[16] And Evangelos Averoff, the man who convinced Ghizikis and the service chiefs that Karamanlis—not Kanellopoulos or Mavros—was the best person to lead the transition, reveals: "I ... thought at the time that Karamanlis would be a more viable option in leading the country back to democracy. For one thing, Karamanlis would be able to rally the Greek people; more importantly, however, he was the sole leader that the military would obey."[17]

In short, the fact that the Greek opposition was willing to accept Karamanlis' leadership greatly facilitated the transition. Despite this willingness, however, Karamanlis, once in control, could have acted in a highly partisan manner, thereby alienating the opposition, hindering elite consensual unity, and endangering consolidation. This did not happen. As previously stated, Karamanlis behaved in ways conducive to democratic consolidation, further facilitating a successful transition path.

Karamanlis' motivation to act in the interest of democratic stability and consolidation—indeed, in the national interest—appears to have been reinforced by a sense of political mission that he should return to Greece as a national rather than as a strictly party leader. In fact, biographical evidence indicates that from an early age Karamanlis possessed what Gianfranco Pasquino argues imbues most leaders of transitions to democracy—a sense of Weberian vocation, mission, *Bewährung*,[18] or, as Karamanlis' biographers put it, a messianic self-image. A number of anecdotes indicate Karamanlis' disposition toward a messianic style of leadership. His sense of mission appears, for example, in a letter he wrote to a friend in 1945: "Do you know what the essence of politics is for me? The desire and the capability to sacrifice one's self for your country. When you have this power you may be useful to your country and to your time."[19] This messianic self-image became even more evident in 1966 when he replied to speculations about whether he would return to Greece from self-imposed exile: "If Greece needs me, I will not refuse my services. ... [However,] so long as I do not believe that I have a mission, I do not intend to return."[20] Significantly, Constantine Tsatsos, a close collaborator and personal friend of Karamanlis, also illustrates the leader's sense of political mission by revealing that Karamanlis never really aspired to be a narrow partisan leader but rather a national leader. As Tsatsos maintains,

Karamanlis performed the role of party leader because it was required of him: "[H]e would [have been] fortunate if he could [have] govern[ed] without leading a party," and if he founded two parties—ERE and ND—it is because such institutions are indispensable to democratic government.[21] Pavlos Tzermias further corroborates this argument: Karamanlis did not want his name connected with ERE in 1974 because, by his own account, he aspired to become "*ethnarches*" (a "leader of the nation").[22]

Thus, a number of factors—the widespread diffuse support for democracy that existed in 1974, the fact that most people believed Karamanlis to have unmatched authority and prestige, the belief that only a man of the right could peacefully secure the military's extrication, as well as the fact that Karamanlis acted from the beginning as a national rather than a purely partisan leader of the right—offer an explanation as to why Karamanlis' dominance of the transition was widely accepted by all democratic political forces and thus did not present an immediate obstacle to the consolidation process. However, more critical is how Karamanlis *used* his dominant position over the longer-term—that is, whether, over the course of his premiership, his actions facilitated or hindered the establishment and consolidation of post-junta Greek democracy. As will be shown in the next section, Karamanlis' fundamental importance to the consolidation of Greek democracy lies in his willingness to use his position of unchallenged leadership to modernize the Greek right and bring about fundamental democratic reforms to the reemergent democratic polity.

THE RIGHT'S MODERATION

Perhaps the most significant contribution Karamanlis made to democratic consolidation was his effort to modernize his party of the right. While Karamanlis could have chosen to allow the party to maintain the traditional right's hallmark features—its anticommunism, strongly pro-American and pro-NATO stance, attachment to the monarchy, and conservative social and economic positions—he returned to Greece apparently intent on modernizing it both ideologically and organizationally. To this end Karamanlis founded a new party to replace his old National Radical Union (ERE), choosing to name it *Nea Demokratia*, or New Democracy. *Nea Demokratia* "was to be composed not only of experienced and sound political forces, but also of progressive and radical ones. ... It was dedicated to serving the 'true' interests of the nation, which could not be categorized in terms of 'the misleading labels of Right, Centre, and Left'."[23]

The right provided evidence of modernization by its drafting of the new democratic constitution. By most accounts the constitution was one of the most progressive constitutions Greece had ever seen. Formal provisions for civil and human rights as well as for social welfare, gender equality, and environmental protection were formally included in the constitution that was ratified by *Nea Demokratia's* parliamentary majority in July 1975.[24]

The most dramatic break with the right's precoup past, however, was Karamanlis' decision to integrate the far left into the political system by legalizing

the Marxist-Leninist Greek Communist Party (KKE)—illegal since 1947—and the
Eurocommunist Greek Communist Party–Interior (KKE-I) that had split from the
KKE in 1968. Through legislative acts of his Government of National Unity,
Karamanlis officially put an end to all restrictive civil war–era legislation and
restored Greek nationality to communists returning from exile. The importance of
these changes cannot be overemphasized. Had Karamanlis maintained the right's
traditional anticommunist stance, keeping the party outlawed, a portion of the
electorate would have continued to be alienated from the new regime, calling into
question its legitimacy, its constitution, and its rules of the game. Instead, the
right's abandonment of simplistic anticommunism contributed significantly to
consolidation by effectively bringing to end the hatreds, animosities, and fears of
the repressive post–civil war years and thereby facilitating national reconciliation
between previously warring enemies.

Karamanlis did not stop, though, with the integration of the left into public life.
He also returned to Greece, foreseeing no role for the monarchy in post-junta
Greek politics. In December 1974 he conducted a referendum on the monarchy's
future, personally abstaining from a public position on the issue and ordering his
parliamentary deputies to do likewise. Unlike the previous referenda on the
monarchy (1920, 1924, 1935, 1946, and 1973), which had been manipulated either
for or against the king and which, as a result, were repeatedly challenged as
fraudulent, the 1974 referendum was universally recognized as fair and legitimate.
It resulted in the adoption of a parliamentary presidential republic (an "uncrowned
democracy") by a vote of 69 to 31 percent.

This impeccable referendum as well as Karamanlis' neutral stance on the issue
appears to have permanently settled this once divisive and destabilizing regime
issue—this despite the fact that some of the most prominent members of the right
(e.g., future party leaders Miltiades Evert and George Rallis) voted for the return
of the monarchy. A 1995 statement by President Kostis Stephanopoulos—who had
himself voted in support of the monarchy—is evidence that this once divisive and
conflictual issue had been put to rest: "[The monarchy is] finished once and for all.
… The referendum was conducted perfectly and the result was absolutely fair. …
Everyone must realize that it put an end, once and for all, to the cancerous
controversy over the monarchy."[25]

EXPLAINING CONSERVATIVE CHANGE

What were Karamanlis' motivations behind such decisions? Why would a
formally "authoritarian" leader of a formally "antidemocratic" right return to
Greece apparently intent on fully democratizing the post–civil war political system?
The answer appears to be that although Karamanlis was a partisan leader of the
right, he returned to Greece fully aware of the deep political problems and schisms
that had historically plagued Greek politics, realizing that it was necessary to reach
closure if democratic consolidation was to occur. Thus, Karamanlis (and the right)
underwent a process of political learning in which three factors—the passing of

time, the experience of authoritarian rule, and generational change—played key roles in bringing about the right's modernization.

The Passing of Time

The passing of time, or increased distance from the civil war years, greatly facilitated the right's moderation and its acceptance of Karamanlis' decision to bring about an end to the repressive civil war–era legislation. In order to understand the right's post-1974 moderation *vis-à-vis* the left, however, one must first comprehend the position of the nationalist forces *vis-à-vis* the outlawing of the Communist Party, the legal and illegal set of repressive anticommunist measures designed to exclude the left from public life, and the support they offered to the largely unpopular monarchy during the post–civil war period. Specifically, a number of respondents maintained that these earlier positions of the right (and some centrists) must be analyzed within the historical context of the late fifties and early sixties. The dominant mentality of that period, they argued, led to a deep schism requiring the passage of several repressive decades and particularly seven years of dictatorial rule before it could be healed. Conservatives argued that to understand the repressiveness of the post–civil war state and the lifting of these measures in 1974, both periods must be examined within their own historical/environmental contexts. Constantine Tsatsos argues that during the precoup period, for example, Karamanlis "governed at a time which was still charged by the deep passions and psychological traumas which had been brought on by a bloody civil war and that he was obliged to balance situations in order to protect the security and peace of the country and ... democracy [as well]."[26]

According to most rightists, legalization of the Communist Party would have been incomprehensible in the 1950s and 1960s due to the deep psychological wounds left by the Greek Civil War. As Panayiotes Kanellopoulos argued:

The thought (of legalizing the KKE) was not yet ripe. In 1951 and 1952 various governments were formed—all of them centrist. The government of Plastiras—and he himself personally—might have desired to abolish the constitutional act which made the functioning of the Communist Party illegal, but the psychological side-effects which the Civil War had provoked were such that it could not have been done then. And not only then, but later also, it was a very difficult thing. [27]

What was difficult—indeed impossible—in the early 1950s, however, became possible over time. Specifically, the further the civil war receded into history and in a climate of increasing security, communist persecutions became increasingly less extensive and brutal. Successive governments—the center under Plastiras and the right under both Papagos and Karamanlis—released many civil war prisoners held in camps and prisons. According to David Close, political prisoners in detention camps and jails were reported to number 17,089 in January 1952, 5,396 in November 1955, and 1,655 in March 1962. By 1967, however, virtually no one remained in jail, and at most only a few hundred were left in detention.[28] The picture, then, is one of progressive, albeit gradual, liberalization as the civil war receded into the past.

Accordingly, Karamanlis himself had gradually yet increasingly begun to moderate during his precoup tenure in office. A former deputy of the United Democratic Left (EDA) indicated in an interview that Karamanlis had indeed begun to moderate his positions on a number of issues long before the dictatorship was launched: "The longer Karamanlis remained in government, and as he began to have disagreements with the palace, he started to become more democratic. ... During those years, when he clashed with the palace and left Greece, he appeared somewhat differently from the older Karamanlis. ... Everyone agrees with this—even the Marxist left."[29] Several examples bear out this opinion. For instance, under domestic and international pressure, Karamanlis closed the communist exile camp of Agios Efstratios during his precoup tenure in office and relaxed most of the post–civil war, anticommunist measures. As he himself put it: "I found 4,498 Communists in prison and reduced them to 937. ... I found 898 Communists in exile and reduced them to six. ... This does not mean that in my time the state of Greece was idyllic, but it shows that there was a serious and honest effort to develop the country in a democratic framework."[30] Furthermore, the Lambrakis murder, usually argued to have been an attack on the left by the extreme right or by the parastate, and occurring some twenty days prior to Karamanlis' 1963 resignation, has been portrayed quite differently by some. As has been argued, the murder could well have been an attempt by right-wing officers in key positions of the military and police to undermine not the left, but rather Karamanlis' government, which, by this time, had openly threatened to restrict military and royal prerogatives.[31] Indeed, both this incident as well as the military's involvement in manipulating the 1961 elections appear to have alerted Karamanlis to the dangers of tolerating the parastate. Thus, when he entrusted the administrative investigation of the Lambrakis murder to a judge of the *Areios Pagos* (Supreme Court), he appeared to imply the identity of the culprits when he gave the express order that anyone recognized as responsible—whether from the administration or the police—should be discharged from his post immediately.[32] A further indication of Karamanlis' increasing unwillingness to tolerate the parastate came a few days prior to his resignation, when he called the leader of the General Army Staff, Lieutenant General Constantine Sakellariou, and requested that top army positions be reorganized. Apparently as a result of such efforts to restrict both military and royal privileges, Karamanlis was "visited" by four military officers "suggesting" in the name of the armed forces that he resign from government.[33] In light of such events, his abrupt departure from Greece may be more easily understood.

This argument—that the origins of Karamanlis' moderation preceded the post-junta period—is given further credence in a letter he wrote to the king in November 1967. In it he clearly reveals his awareness of the need for reform *prior* to the transition to democracy.

The most fundamental reason [for my refusal to return] was my belief that democracy could not function in Greece without a cleaning up and modernization of our public life, beginning with the constitution. ... The problem of removing the revolutionaries could therefore not be separated from that of removing the conditions which led to their "deviation." ... [A new government must be carefully chosen by the king] to assuage passions and create the psychological conditions for the reconstruction and modernization of political life; to draft a new constitution, which must be "strict but not undemocratic;" ... to restore discipline in the armed forces; and to settle the Cyprus problem. ... Lastly, the government should conduct a plebiscite [on the monarchy] and [hold national] elections.[34]

By the time the military extricated itself from power, then, Karamanlis as well as most other members of the parliamentary right appear to have acknowledged the need for significant political reform. As the civil war receded into history, the repressive post–civil war measures became unnecessary. Deputies of all political parties and military officers confirmed that by 1974, the fear of communism had disappeared in the minds of most Greeks, even among the most conservative members of the right. A deputy of the right confirms this: "We did not legalize [the left] back then because it had taken up arms against Greece. Now [in 1974] there was no fear; ... the fear [of communism] did not exist."[35]

In addition to the disappearance of the communist "threat," the passing of time also contributed to a blunting of the passions and hatreds brought about by the civil war. The importance of such attitudinal change is forcefully asserted by Víctor Pérez-Díaz in his analysis of Spain.[36] Approximately twenty-five years had passed from the time the civil war ended. As in Spain where two sets of ideology—that of national Catholicism on the right and social radicalism on the left—had to gradually fade away, in Greece too the passing of time helped dull the sharp division of society into "nationally minded" and "suspect" citizens. As one deputy of the right pointed out: "When did they want the right to legalize the Communist Party? When a civil war was taking place? Or when Bellogiannis[37] and others were coming from [behind the Iron Curtain] with wireless radios believing they could ignite another [conflict] in Greece? With the passing of time circumstances changed, and the sharp differences were dulled."[38] A former *Nea Demokratia* prime minister agrees:

[T]he guerrilla war had ended in August of 1949 and it was natural for the traumatic experiences to still be fresh during the period of 1950–1960. In the parties there were quite a few deputies which had fought against the communists and others who had many friends and relatives killed or wounded due to the communist rebellion. Thus, it was impossible for these facts to be forgotten quickly. In 1974, when *Nea Demokratia* was founded, the communist rebellion was an event of the past, as twenty-five years had passed since the end of the guerrilla war.[39]

In short, it is in the changed environment of the postcoup period, a period in which more than a quarter of a century had passed since the time of the civil war, that Karamanlis' moderate post-1974 decisions might best be interpreted. Simply put, circumstances had progressively changed in Greece, permitting him to bring about reforms that might not have been acceptable to the right in earlier years. As someone close to Karamanlis argued: "The passing of time healed wounds. ... [P]eople had matured [by 1974] to accept the legalization of the Communist Party.

He did not legalize it in the 1950s, because if he had, there would have been a revolt by the right!"[40] Another ND deputy adds:

[The reforms] could not have been carried out ... during [Karamanlis' precoup tenure in government]. They had to be carried out under different circumstances and when people would be mature enough to accept them and, in 1974, people were mature enough to accept these changes. ... Karamanlis was the same person [in 1974]. Karamanlis may have read more—this is correct. Karamanlis may have been influenced by different democratic models the years he was in self-exile—undoubtedly this took place. But his political axes and his political orientations were always the same. Simply put, he was only able to carry them out [in 1974] with a more politically mature electorate and under different circumstances.[41]

The Lessons of Dictatorship

In addition to the passing of time, another factor that facilitated the right's moderation was the dictatorship itself and the "lessons" it taught Greek political elites. The importance of "learning" is emphasized by Nancy Bermeo,[42] who contends that such learning occurs when people modify their political beliefs and tactics due to serious crises, frustrations, and dramatic environmental changes. These crises tend to push people, followers and leaders alike, to reevaluate ideas about tactics, parties, allies, enemies, and institutions. Moreover, elite awareness of the possibility for damaging conflict, usually brought on by memories of past conflict, often induces elites to take important measures to restrain such conflict.[43]

Indeed, the junta experience in Greece brought home to most political elites the critical importance of moderation and conciliation. As one centrist deputy put it at the time of the dictatorship, "The present dictatorship, if it does not last too long, may in the end prove to have been a good thing—negatively. It's amazing how much the Greek people have 'ripened' under it."[44] And,

The Colonels have become the common enemy against whom the Greek people united, regardless of their views on the social structure of post-Junta Greece. This *de facto* creation of conditions of political alliance among all the political camps is an event of great importance. Duly developed, it can ... greatly facilitate the smooth functioning of democratic institutions after the overthrow of the dictatorship. And to think that all this is due to the Junta![45]

Just as the old royalist versus republican cleavage was greatly attenuated when members of both camps perceived themselves threatened first by the Axis and then by communism during the occupation and resistance, so another common enemy—the colonels—united both the right and left against the dictatorship: "[T]he dictatorship helped unite the [different] political forces. ... What we could not obtain in peaceful and normal circumstances, the dictatorship offered us."[46] Another parliamentary deputy agreed: The junta "completed the spirit of reconciliation because the enemy was a common one—the collapse of democracy."[47] It is important to note that this perception—that the dictatorship contributed to moderation and elite consensual unity—was shared equally by members of all political camps. A member of the leftist resistance group Patriotic Front (PAM), Ioannis Leloudas, argued as early as July 1972:

[T]hese five years have taught us that we Greeks can cooperate, discuss, and decide about our future, getting over those old disputes, the anticommunism, all those things that brought us into open conflict. Right now we see that we are all united against a common enemy. And I think that the instant the junta falls, irrespective of our differences, I think we have learned that there is one, common national interest and on that issue we have nothing which divides us![48]

These lessons of dictatorship were reinforced by secret contacts between members of both right and left through organizations set up to fight the junta. Both camps appeared informally in demonstrations together and served time in the same prison cells, fighting for the same cause. Thus, when one deputy of *Nea Demokratia* was asked, "When did the civil war passions begin to be erased?" she answered: "The dictatorship was a catalyst for this because we found ourselves all together; we signed [declarations] together. ... [B]efore the dictatorship it would have been incomprehensible for a rightist to sign with Florakis[49] and nonetheless they signed. ... [I]t would have been incomprehensible for them to even consider it, and yet they did so because the common enemy was the dictatorship."[50] As one member of the National Unity Government of 1974 said, "The dictatorship was the grounds [for] ... communication, collaboration, agreement, [and] friendly relations [among the various political camps]."[51] Even an air force officer agreed: "The period of the dictatorship had a good effect—it gave the opportunity to some to revise their views, to be self-critical, to see the mistakes of the past. Unity was achieved—that is, it was not uncommon to see in a resistance organization both rightists and leftists. The walls came down. The leftist didn't see the rightist as a fascist, and the rightist didn't see the leftist as a Bulgarian ... or a bandit."[52]

In addition to uniting—albeit informally—the various political *parataxeis* (camps) against the dictatorship, the colonels also contributed to a process of self-critical reflection among politicians, leading most of them to realize that the practices of the past had contributed to the fall of democracy in 1967. As Bermeo argues, dictatorships can push people to reevaluate the nature of a particular regime, their enemies, as well as their own goals and behavior: "[T]he lessons of dictatorship can be profound ... and can produce important cognitive change."[53] Change of this sort is evident in a statement made during the dictatorship by Mikis Theodorakis, a prominent member of the left, on *The Free Voice of Greece* radio program:

The true responsibility [for the dictatorship] lies with all Greeks—with all of us, without any differentiation. ... We begin with the left: Its responsibility lies especially in the period of 1943–1949. In those years, the left carried out a series of fanatic political mistakes—mistakes which brought about the source of its dismemberment. As far as the right is concerned, from 1952–1963, it was the only ruler of government and it could not solve even *one* of the great national problems. Its only answer to the massive social deceptions was the ... communist sermons and the use of political oppression. In this way we reached the popular uprisings in 1963–1964 which brought at first the Center Union. But even the Center Union showed an inability to govern.[54]

Theodorakis' statement is echoed by Karamanlis when asked in a 1967 interview who was responsible for the abolition of democracy in Greece. He answered, "No one and everyone."[55]

Thus, the experiences of the dictatorship coupled with the passing of time strengthened Karamanlis' personal moderation by contributing to his own political learning. Respondents of this study claimed that Karamanlis changed during his eleven years of self-imposed exile in Paris, returning to Greece substantially more democratic than when he left in 1963. In the words of a former deputy of EDA, "Karamanlis return[ed] a different man. Not even we—the left—recogniz[ed] him anymore. He [was] no longer the same man he was then."[56]

This argument can be set forth quite succinctly. Karamanlis' years of self-imposed exile in Paris provided him the opportunity to study and reflect upon the political and historical life of the nation as well as the causes of the dictatorship. Living away from Greece for eleven years, Karamanlis was able to reflect upon Greek postwar history and to view it more objectively from afar. One scholar argues that "Karamanlis, having apparently profited from the chance for contemplation and reappraisal offered by eleven years of self-imposed exile, sought to modernize [Nea Demokratia] in the years after 1974."[57] Virginia Tsouderou, a deputy of the center, corroborated Karamanlis' transformation in September 1974:

Karamanlis ... left the serenity of Paris to return here at a very difficult moment to take over a ship that was sinking. Surely, his eleven years in Paris made him think of different things ... as they made us, too. ... He surely thought about and analyzed the fact that the laws we passed back then [from 1946–67], ... many of those frightful laws which led to the persecution of a portion of the Greek population, were used even against [the right] ... after 1967. I am sure that he has thought of all this and he knows that democracy must be equal for all citizens. Even if there exists one political prisoner, one injustice ... [this] is enough to lead to a political catastrophe.[58]

Contributing to Karamanlis' self-reflection and contemplation during his exile was the fact that he spent a great deal of time reading political, historical, and philosophical texts. As he argued in a 1977 interview, it is necessary for people to study history and to be taught by it so that they do not "make the same mistakes twice. ... [History] is the best lesson for the citizen because it teaches him what he should do and what he should avoid so that his country will progress."[59] Often, it is such historical comparisons that give rise to political learning: "The appeal of democracy increases as the historical comparison between concrete national experiences of democracy and dictatorship favor the former."[60] A statement made by Karamanlis during the dictatorship reveals that he, like other civilian elites, came to realize how poorly Greek democracy had functioned in the precoup years:

In the first place, I think one must note the feeling of acute, destructive national division which has paralyzed Greece since 1915. In spite of two World Wars, she remained rivetted. ... Hence internal disturbances, coups d'état and natural disasters—there was an embarrassing imbroglio for democracy. ... It must be realized that the old passions had very deep roots. They had survived, formed new shoots and stifled our last liberties. That is why in the end, I renounced politics. ... [Greeks] love democracy but they refuse to create or to accept the prerequisites of its functioning: Namely, a moderate political climate, civilized political habits and institutions adapted to their national realities. But the passions do not love moderation. And ours are such that they lead us dangerously astray into hot tempers and exaggeration.[61]

In addition to being fully aware of the problematic nature of precoup politics in Greece, Karamanlis also appears to have become fully aware of the need to bring about a radical transformation of Greek public life if democracy was to become consolidated and stable. He reveals this to a close friend during the dictatorship: "My experience persuaded me that there can be no democratic government in our country unless great changes take place in our national life."[62] Likewise, a centrist deputy maintained:

Clearly, there was a difference between the right of the 1950s and 1960s and that of the post-1974 period. The thinking which took place in the eleven years of Karamanlis' absence made the right change. ... Karamanlis, in his first period as leader of ERE, ... did not accept any influence ... from the democratic spirit which had taken root in the countries [of Western Europe.] ... Then he leaves and lives for ten years in France. And he engages in self-critique and sees the mistakes of fanaticism [and he returns transformed].[63]

Moreover, Karamanlis himself argues that while the core of his personality remained unchanged during his self-imposed exile, he adapted himself to changes in his environment, and his experiences contributed to this adaptation:

People do not change easily. It is circumstances that change and they necessitate us to adapt ourselves to new realities. The experience of the past simply helps this adaptation. ... That is exactly what I myself did after my return in 1974. Where, besides other things, I created new institutions, a climate relieved of the passions of the past and, finally, I legalized the KKE to normalize our political life and to adapt it to European models.[64]

This legalization of the Communist Party is the best example of a decision in which political learning contributed to moderation. By 1974 Karamanlis appears to have realized that state coercion could not and should not be a substitute for ideological opposition to communism.[65] In fact, at the first Congress of *Nea Demokratia* in 1979, Karamanlis argued that in the absence of genuine democracy, people are pushed to resort to extraparliamentary forms of political participation, endangering democratic stability and consolidation. When asked specifically about the legalization of the Communist Party, Karamanlis answered:

It was a necessary measure so that we would liken ourselves to the democratic countries of the West. If I had not done this, international assurance would not have been created that democracy had really been restored in Greece. Besides—*and this is the important point*—the Communist Party is more dangerous when due to its illegality it belongs to a larger party which it affects and in this way dangerously pollutes the political life of the country.[66]

Corroborating his statements, a close associate adds,

How could democracy have been consolidated in Greece ... without the legalization of a
party which represented ... at least twelve to fifteen percent of the Greek people. ... And,
furthermore, the danger would have been great because ... we must not forget that the illegal
has always had a certain special attraction. Thus, the Communist Party had to be present ...
as a democratic party in parliament. It would have been totally unrealistic if the first thing
Karamanlis did upon arriving here and deciding to restore democracy was decide not to
legalize the Communist Party.[67]

A second reason given by Karamanlis for this legalization was his intention to
"normalize" Greek political life and bring it into line with Western democracy.[68]
A deputy of *Nea Demokratia* sums up this argument nicely:

[I]t was the only way the country would be able to get out of the anomaly which was created
by the KKE's nonparticipation in the elections of 1946 and the underground activity which
it engaged in afterwards. Karamanlis believed and wanted Greece to acquire a new
democracy. ... And he [understood] ... that this schism between first and second class
citizens ... had been catastrophic for our country. ... Karamanlis deeply believed [in] and
wanted ... a new democracy—a new democratic parliamentary life, new habits, new
traditions, new people.[69]

A second major decision taken by Karamanlis was to hold a referendum on the
monarchy. Karamanlis' primary motivation behind his decision to hold the
referendum while publicly maintaining a neutral stance also appears to have been
born primarily out of a concern for democratic consolidation and stability. While
some deputies of *Nea Demokratia* as well as many of the opposition claimed that
this decision stemmed wholly from the fear that taking a position would split his
party, Karamanlis' unequaled authority and stature in 1974 indicate as well that had
he decided to take a position *against* the monarchy (as it appears he was personally
inclined to do),[70] the vast majority of *Nea Demokratia* deputies would have
probably, albeit grudgingly, remained in the party. This appears to be especially
true given Karamanlis' personal popularity at the time—a position solidified by
Nea Demokratia's resounding victory in the elections of November 1974. As one
deputy of the right exclaimed when he was asked whether Karamanlis' feared
splitting *Nea Demokratia*, "Don't be silly! Karamanlis fear the split of *Nea
Demokratia*? At that time he was all-powerful; at that time Karamanlis received
fifty-five percent of the vote. Let's not forget that."[71] Moreover, had Karamanlis
and *Nea Demokratia* been primarily motivated by electoral concerns in 1974, a
position against the vastly unpopular monarchy might have paid handsome
dividends in terms of electoral support. This is not to say, however, that the
possibility of splitting his party did not factor into Karamanlis' decision-making.
Instead, what was in the national interest—maintaining a neutral stance on the issue
in order to definitively resolve the conflict—also appears to have been in the best
interests of *Nea Demokratia*.

Karamanlis himself argued that his handling of the issue was designed to heal
what had been an open wound in Greek politics from 1915 to 1974. A vast number

of parliamentary deputies agreed. According to one *Nea Demokratia* deputy, for example: "[*Nea Demokratia*] did not take a position because it did not want to politicize the issue of the institution because if it had politicized it and the king had or had not returned, then he would not have been a king of all Greeks, he would have been a king of one party. ... [Karamanlis] allowed each citizen to express himself or herself freely."[72]

Yet a third issue area in which the national interest as well as the interests of *Nea Demokratia*—both internally and as a vote-seeking political party—appear to have been as one was the modernization of the right. While it is difficult to disentangle electoral motivations from those of genuine national interest, it suffices to say that the two need not be incompatible. Specifically, Karamanlis' decisions to found *Nea Demokratia* in 1974 and to modernize the right appear to have been partly based on his conviction that the party should be "freed from all the commitments and passions of the past" and thus be broader in political orientation.[73] Karamanlis openly expressed his desire to renovate the right by including within it more moderate elites than had traditionally belonged to the conservative camp—even before the founding of *Nea Demokratia*: "I believe that we must move as quickly as possible ... [t]o build a new party because ERE can no longer be renovated to form a wider *parataxi* and to include in it capable people who do not belong to ERE."[74]

Karamanlis' desire to broaden the right and to attract deputies as well as voters of other *parataxeis* reflects not only an attempt to build a broader-based modernized party of the right, but also the need to appeal to a changing electorate. In this vein Karamanlis' strategy for modernizing the right was reactive and reflected his recognition (or anxiety) that the creation of PASOK and the shift of the Greek political spectrum to the left meant that unless the right modernized it could easily become marginalized. Hence, Karamanlis' decision to modernize the right can also be interpreted as preemptive action in order to avoid future failure at the polls.[75] This example provides an interesting twist on the elite convergence theory insofar as the theory posits electoral motivations on the part of *opposition* parties occurring *after* failure at the polls. The example of Karamanlis differs in two ways: *Nea Demokratia's* moderation occurred *while* in government and *well before* any kind of electoral defeat.

Electoral and other motivations aside, the fundamental drive behind the founding of *Nea Demokratia* as with the decisions to legalize the communists and to hold a referendum on the monarchy appears to have been a conscious and deliberate attempt to reconcile Greeks. As one parliamentary deputy expressed: "[When] Karamanlis founded *Nea Demokratia*, he wanted to cut off from its body all the extreme [antidemocratic] right."[76] Karamanlis himself indicated as much in his speech inaugurating the party: "*Nea Demokratia* is the *politike parataxi* (political camp) which ignores the disputes and the schisms of the past—which brought so much suffering to our country—and it orients itself towards the broader and stronger forces of national unity ... and it promises that it will always and only serve the interests of the nation, which are found over and above the incorrect labels of right, center, and left."[77]

Generational Change

In analyzing the factors behind the right's moderation, we have thus far focused on changes at the individual level—that is, individual attitudinal change brought on by the passing of time and the "lessons" of the dictatorship. However, as previously alluded to, a parallel process resulting from generational turnover was also taking place at the societal level. Simply put, the distribution of attitudes within society was altered as those with direct civil war experience were no longer alive or were extremely aged by the time of the transition. In fact, according to Van Coufoudakis, an estimated one million seventeen- to twenty-year-olds who could not vote in the last free elections of 1964 were now of age and could vote in 1974. This influx of new voters constituted approximately 20 percent of those who voted in the 1974 national elections. These new voters, while having experienced the unrest of the 1960s and the colonels' dictatorship, had no memories of the Greek Civil War. In contrast, some 750,000 voters who were in their mid- to late-sixties in 1964 were either very old (and thus probably not voting) or deceased by the mid-1970s. Coufoudakis writes that "[t]hese were ... the people who grew up in the political culture of the civil war and the Cold War state. ... Thus, for the new voting generation issues such as those of anti-communism and the schism over the monarchy and the republic had lost their significance and had been replaced by the need for socioeconomic change, and for effective, stable, and credible democratic government."[78]

Public opinion surveys also bear out the claim that significant attitudinal change—as a result of generational change—did in fact take place in Greece. While two surveys conducted in Greater Athens in 1983 and 1985 are by no means conclusive proof for this hypothesis,[79] they may nonetheless be indicative of broad, general trends, indicating that the attitudes of young people differed significantly from those of older people. Their attitudes differed in two critical ways. First, younger people were much less anticommunist and much less committed to the Western Alliance than their older counterparts. While 56 percent of those under thirty-five agreed that Marxism was the best-ever interpretation of history, only 19 percent of those over forty-nine agreed. Similarly, when asked if they would ever vote for the hard-line Communist Party of Greece (KKE), 40 percent of young people, but only 24 percent of older people, reported that they would. Older people were also decidedly more committed to a pro-Western orientation for Greece—61 percent of those over forty-nine wanted Greece's closest ties to be with Western Europe compared to 23 percent of those under thirty-five. Fully 80 percent of young people claimed that Greece's relationship with the United States was detrimental to Greece compared with 38 percent for older people.

The second and most critical way in which Greek public opinion shows a significant generational difference is in attitudes toward the civil war and the role of communists in it. While 11 percent of young people blamed the communists mainly or exclusively for the civil war, 60 percent of those over forty-nine did. The percentages were reversed when the question was whether the government was mainly or exclusively to blame for the civil war—65 percent of young people, 26 percent of older people. Along similar lines, when asked if Greece would have been better or worse off had the communists won the civil war, young people by a count of 48 percent to 20 percent felt that Greece would have been better off. Older people, however, felt by a count of 65 percent to 19 percent that Greece would have been worse off. Clearly, attitudes toward communists and the civil war were highly differentiated by age.

Interviews conducted with parliamentary deputies and military officers similarly indicate that generational change contributed greatly to democratic consolidation. First, as would be expected, those who had personally experienced the civil war or post–civil war years or had family members who experienced the traumas of that period appeared far more bitter and less able to "let go" of their hatreds and fears than those who were removed from firsthand experiences with that period. In fact, officers who had fought in the war or leftist deputies who had experienced persecution and exile during the post–civil war period often broke into tears as they shared experiences. A retired officer, involved in local government during the civil war, cried while describing the following: "Let me tell you that which I have seen with my own eyes. In my village … I found the children and the wife of the gendarme of the village inside a bin burned to death. I … found all of the gendarmes … and a lieutenant … all of them killed. And in a wall we found little fingers of children, two- and three-year-olds, cut off by an axe."[80] Another officer who had fought under Napoleon Zervas against the Germans in the occupation and then against the communists in the civil war recounted[81]:

I was a young rebel in a battle against the Germans … a battle that we lost. Retreating, I came upon a unit of ELAS, of the communists, and I was taken prisoner. That made an impression on me; the fact that they put me up before a rebel court—a popular court, as they called it back then—with the accusation that I had [been paid off to go fight] with Zervas. … When I … heard this, an entire revolution poured out within me. … If I note that for this reason I was sentenced to death [by the communists] but escaped from the execution squad, you will understand how an entire psychology was created—as much in me as in an entire people.[82]

Finally, a former deputy of *Nea Demokratia* contended: "I am an ardent anti-Marxist because they, the communists, killed my father on 29 April 1943." This deputy's bitterness is very apparent when asked, "Do you believe that civil war passions have finally dulled?" "No! Not for me!" he exclaimed, "Not even now. It is impossible for the son of a killed father to forget his father."[83] Or, in the words of another deputy: "Would it be possible for you to welcome someone when they killed your father and they [suddenly] reappear?"[84]

In short, deputies of all political parties acknowledged that generational change contributed to democratic consolidation simply because men who had been involved in the civil war were no longer influential because of their old age. As a former PASOK deputy argued, "Today the people who are reaching seventy are the youngest who could have contributed to the national resistance. In 1944 they were nineteen- or twenty-years-old. … All the passions that were created were created by people who have been forgotten."[85] In addition, the death of intransigent leaders allowed other elites with different beliefs, priorities, and styles to come to the forefront of decision-making.[86] A center-right deputy put it quite well: "Back then I was young and I experienced [the dramatic events]; I am now eighty-three years old. How many people like myself are alive today? Most of them have died. ... I look around me at my friends; do you know how many of us are left? I see a friend once every six months. ... Thus, [the passions] are being dulled. The young did not live through those conflicts."[87] Put simply, as individuals came of age in times further and further removed from the experience of the civil war, attitudes changed accordingly. Attitudinal change, brought on in part by generational change, was a critically important factor in the right's moderation and thereby in the successful outcome of the Greek consolidation process. Thus, the right's moderation was a response to both elite moderation (triggered primarily by political learning, especially on the part of Constantine Karamanlis) as well as a response to larger societal attitudinal changes brought on by generational turnover and the passing of time.[88]

THE GREEK RIGHT'S MODERATION IN THEORETICAL AND COMPARATIVE PERSPECTIVE

The preceding analysis of the Greek right's role in the transition to and consolidation of Greek democracy has important implications for democratization theory, particularly when coupled with lessons from other democratization experiences. Theories of democratization have repeatedly argued that inclusive, nonpartisan leadership is most likely to assure a successful transition and consolidation process. The importance of such tolerant, inclusive leadership was highlighted in Spain where the successful transition to democracy was spearheaded by Adolfo Suárez and his efforts to reach broad, all-party settlements. In Portugal, however, the importance of "national" leadership was proved by its absence. There, the clearly leftist, radical nature of the transition leadership, composed of army captains in effective alliance with an orthodox Marxist-Leninist party (PCP), dramatically politicized the process. Propelling the country toward the left and engendering violent partisan reaction during the "long, hot summer of 1975," the radicalized leaders of the transition put the democratization process—at least temporarily—at risk. In the face of such radical left-wing reforms as extensive nationalizations and a formal constitutional commitment to socialism, conservative peasants and small property owners mobilized to prevent radical change. Had subsequent elite moderation not taken place, the dominance of the Portuguese transition by such a narrow set of partisan elites could easily have endangered democratization and consolidation efforts there.

As we have seen, however, Karamanlis' dominance of the transition process in Greece did not in fact jeopardize democratic consolidation and stability. The principal reason for this was that Karamanlis himself returned to Greece a moderate democratic leader, with a national, rather than narrowly partisan, vision. Karamanlis and his party of the right, *Nea Demokratia*, took moderate action that facilitated the transition and enhanced democratic stability and consolidation (yet not necessarily the quality of democracy), despite the fact that they enjoyed virtually complete dominance of political life throughout the mid- and late-1970s. In fact, this gradual, yet critical, transformation of Karamanlis and the Greek right had a close parallel in Spain where the conservative Alianza Popular (AP) underwent similar moderation during the Spanish transition. Despite their roots in the Franquist regime, its leaders adopted an unquestionably prosystem stance in the aftermath of the party's 1978 schism. In fact, party leader Manuel Fraga's wholehearted support of the new democratic constitution and his opposition to the failed February 1981 coup attempt was a conscious attempt to moderate AP's ideology and move it toward the center of the political spectrum.[89] Thus, once again, the value of intentionally proregime conciliatory behavior on the part of political leaders is revealed.

Clearly, the importance of the elite variable stands out in this analysis of *Nea Demokratia*, as it does in the other Southern European transitions. While impersonal factors such as the passing of time and generational change make things *possible*, people—and particularly political elites—make things *happen*. In Greece the prominent role played by a strong charismatic leader and his willingness—in fact, strong desire—to act as a national rather than as a purely party leader cannot be underestimated. Karamanlis, as an individual, and particularly one from the right, had a tremendous impact on the cause of democratization. A critically important figure, Karamanlis configured the entire transition trajectory and shaped the face of Greece's new democracy.

Critical to Karamanlis' success was that, as a respected former conservative prime minister, he was able to establish a certain continuity between the outgoing authoritarian regime and the incoming democratic one. Both military and civilian leaders perceived him to be the most capable and "appropriate," indeed the most credible, person to lead the transition to democratic rule. This significance of such credibility with outgoing authoritarians was highlighted in Spain by two key figures—King Juan Carlos and Adolfo Suárez. Like Karamanlis, Juan Carlos provided continuity during the transition to democracy by reassuring the Franquist elite that democratic change would be gradual and moderate. Later, his appointment of Adolfo Suárez—a politician with impeccable Franquist credentials—to head the first democratic government provided further reassurance to the right that the transition would not involve a radical lurch to the left, as had occurred in Portugal. Thus, in both Greece and Spain, some degree of continuity was maintained and military officers believed that an implicit assurance had been given that the transition would be "safe." With the military and the right reassured, and either loyal or at least quiescent, both Karamanlis and Suárez then acted decisively to democratize their two countries.

The importance of political elites notwithstanding, one cannot overlook the crucial role of structural-historical variables and the processes of long-term political learning, which clearly shape elite attitudes and actions. Placing a special emphasis on such factors in his analysis of the Spanish transition, Víctor Pérez-Díaz argues that the emergence of new democratic traditions, values, and institutions in civil society "preceded, and prepared the way for, the political transition of the 1970s"[90] in Spain. Thus, over time, Spanish collective memory was reconstructed and the civil war reinterpreted as an unavoidable tragedy. Collective memories of the traumatic collapse of the Second Republic, the ensuing civil war, and the Franquist dictatorship served to constrain political elites and helped avert damaging partisan clashes during the transition and consolidation processes. Spanish leaders have attested to the importance of historical memory. As the president of the Constitutional Committee, Emilio Attard Alonso, stated: "We are fully conscious that the dialectical undertakings of 1931 began in a quarrel and ended in a civil war."[91] Adolfo Suárez, in a 1984 interview, also revealed that his greatest concern following Franco's death was the possibility of yet another civil war.[92] But, by the end of the Franquist regime, most Spaniards had "explained away" the civil war as an unfortunate, but understandable, clash of opposing ideologies—a conflict to which they did not feel personally connected.[93] Thus, while Spanish elites did not feel obligated to "refight" the civil war with their political opponents by acting immoderately or punitively against them, they nonetheless recognized the dangers posed by extreme political conflict. In short, some ideological "house cleaning" and forgetting[94] was coupled with a desire to avoid severe political conflict—a combination that ultimately contributed to the success of the Spanish transition and consolidation processes.

Something similar also occurred in Italy where the memories of fascism and World War II greatly facilitated moderation in the postwar period. Having united in opposition to the German occupation and the rump of the Mussolini regime, Italian parties put aside deep historical and ideological divisions in order to fight their common enemy and free the country from fascism. Elites clearly moderated as a result of the lessons of dictatorship. As one Italian socialist wrote concerning his own contributions to the crises of prefascist Italy, "I must acknowledge ... that I would have been wiser had I been more moderate in my criticism of the ... system. ... Our criticism ... did not help to direct the evolution of Italian public life toward less imperfect forms of democracy but rather toward the victory of ... reactionary groups."[95]

As has been seen, parallel attitudinal change occurred in Greece. One public opinion survey published in 1990 reported that 41 percent of those interviewed blamed *both* the communists and government forces for their role in the Greek Civil War, and 32 percent of respondents did not even offer an opinion on the subject.[96] A number of factors—the passing of time, which allowed the civil war to recede into the annals of history; the harsh experience of dictatorship, which facilitated reconciliation between warring sides; and generational turnover, which greatly contributed to attitudinal change in 1974—facilitated and structured the right's moderation and taught many of them a lesson about the need for moderation and national reconciliation. In sum, then, the importance of more long-term, structural-historical variables should not be ignored in analyses of democratic transition and consolidation processes that focus primarily on elite action and interaction. To use a somewhat oversimplified analogy, if elites are the actors, or players, in the drama of democratization, scholars must not overlook the structural variables that create both the stage on which elites act as well as the environment—the set—that directly influences their behavior.

Finally, it is perhaps most important to note that while Spanish, Italian, and Greek elites acted with moderation during their countries' transitions to democracy, in many respects the ways in which they moderated were different. As this and previous chapters have been at pains to point out, while elite moderation was facilitated in Spain by an explicit and successful settlement between all significant political elites, in Greece the moderation of *Nea Demokratia* resulted from a process of convergence. As in France, where moderation began with the founding of the Fifth Republic in 1958 and was not consummated until the successful 1986 "cohabitation" of socialists and conservatives, or as in Italy, which experienced a protracted consolidation process beginning in the 1940s and lasting until the middle to late 1970s, the moderation of *Nea Demoktraia* proceeded slowly as the civil war period receded into the annals of history.

Specifically, convergence on the part of the right originated in the *precoup period* and came to completion only after the harsh experiences of dictatorship taught the right a lesson about the dangers of repressive laws and the exclusion of the left from public life. While the original convergence theory posits that such moderation is primarily triggered by *electoral* motivations, this study of the Greek right has revealed that a number of other factors also contributed to *Nea Demokratia's* and Karamanlis' personal moderation—the most important being a genuine desire to make Greek democracy consolidated, stable, and fully institutionalized. That is not to say that electoral motivations played no part in Karamanlis' 1974 decisions. Instead, electoral concerns were clearly secondary and were in a sense preemptive: Karamanlis, enjoying overwhelming popular support and electoral success, seems to have recognized that the average Greek voter had been moved to the left by the experience of dictatorship. Thus, the electoral need for the right to moderate its views in line with ordinary voters, as well as its need to build a modern party structure capable of long-term persistence, reinforced Karamanlis' personal desire to "modernize" and "liberalize" ND. In short, then, this chapter points to the fact that the process of elite convergence is often complex and multifaceted and the result of a number of motivations—electoral concerns, a genuine desire to consolidate democratic rule, and an aspiration to establish organizationally and ideologically modern, democratic political parties.

Thus, a constellation of interacting factors—personal elite variables, structural-historical constraints, and factors contributing to political learning and attitudinal change—contributed to the Greek right's moderation. I have argued that this moderation was fundamental to Greece's prospects for democratic consolidation and stability. However, the consolidation of democracy was not ensured solely on the basis of the right's moderation. The left, which had previously engaged in armed rebellion against the established bourgeois regime, would also have to moderate in order to undergo its own process of elite convergence and thereby facilitate democratic stability and consolidation. It is to that political family—the left—that we now turn.

NOTES

1. Michael Burton, Richard Gunther, and John Higley, "Introduction: Elite Transformation and Democratic Regimes," in John Higley and Richard Gunther, eds., *Elites and Democratic Consolidation in Latin America and Southern Europe* (Cambridge: Cambridge University Press, 1992), p. 24; Mattei Dogan and John Higley, eds., *Elites, Crises, and the Origins of Regimes* (Lanham, Maryland: Rowman & Littlefield Publishers, Inc., 1998); and John Higley and Michael Burton, "Elite Settlements and the Taming of Politics," *Government and Opposition* 33:1 (Winter 1998), pp. 98–115.

2. On the dangers of "descending into excessive voluntarism," see Terry Lynn Karl, "Dilemmas of Democratization in Latin America," *Comparative Politics* 23 (1990), p. 1.

3. "Regime Change and the Prospects for Democracy in Greece: 1974–1983," in Guillermo O'Donnell, Philippe C. Schmitter, and Laurence Whitehead, eds., *Transitions from Authoritarian Rule: Southern Europe* (Baltimore: Johns Hopkins University Press, 1986), p. 159.

4. See chapter 1. For additional discussion of the dangers of majoritarian, winner-take-all behavior, see Juan J. Linz and Arturo Valenzuela, *The Failure of Presidential Democracy* (Baltimore: Johns Hopkins, 1994). For a discussion of path-dependency, see also Juan J. Linz and Alfred Stepan, *Problems of Democratic Transition and Consolidation: Southern Europe, South America, and Post-Communist Europe* (Baltimore: The Johns Hopkins University, 1996); and "Toward Consolidated Democracies," *Journal of Democracy* 7:2 (April 1996), pp. 14–33.

5. As will be discussed below (see chapters 5 and 6), much of the opposition to Karamanlis in 1974 was more rhetorical than real.

6. Mikis Theodorakis, Interview given to *The Free Voice of Greece* radio broadcast (New York, NY, n.d.).

7. Interview conducted in Athens, Greece, on 21 March 1994 with a former deputy of PASOK.

8. Interview conducted in Athens, Greece, on 26 January 1994 with a former deputy of ERE who later joined ND.

9. P. J. Vatikiotis, *Greece: A Political Essay*, The Washington Papers, v. 2 (Beverly Hills: Sage Publications, 1973), p. 75.

10. Nikos D. Delepetros, *Apofasisa Na Mileso* (I Decided to Speak) (Athens: Estia, 1988), p. 307.

11. Interview conducted in Athens, Greece, on 31 January 1994 with a former deputy of ND.

12. Quoted in Potes Paraskevopoulos, *Ho Karamanlis sta Chronia 1974–1985* (Karamanlis in the Years 1974–1985) (Athens: Ho Typos, n.d.), p. 32.

13. Paraskevopoulos, *Ho Karamanlis*, p. 33.

14. Interview conducted in Athens, Greece, on 25 January 1994 with a former deputy of ERE who later joined ND.

15. Georgios I. Rallis, *Politikes Ekmystereuseis, 1950–1989* (Political Revelations, 1950–1989) (Athens: Proskenio, 1990), p. 143.

16. Interview conducted in Athens, Greece, on 1 November 1993 with a former deputy of EK.

17. Personal interview, quoted in Constantine Arvanitopoulos, "The Political Economy of Regime Change: A Case Study of Greece," Ph.D. Dissertation, American University, 1989.

18. "Political Leadership in Southern Europe: Research Problems," *West European Politics* 13:4 (October 1990), pp. 118–30.

19. Quoted in Tsatsos, *Ho Agnostos Karamanlis: Mia Prosopografia* (The Unknown Karamanlis: A Personal Account) (Athens: Ekdotike Athenon A.E., 1989), p. 91.

20. Woodhouse, *Karamanlis: The Restorer of Greek Democracy* (Oxford: Clarendon Press, 1982), p. 178.

21. Tsatsos, *Ho Agnostos Karamanlis*, p. 94.

22. Pavlos Tzermias, *Ho Karamanlis tou Antidiktatorikou Agona: Istorike Apotimese mias Duskoles Epoches (1967–1974)* (Karamanlis of the Antidictatorial Struggle: A Historical Appraisal of a Difficult Period [1967–1974]) (Athens: Ekdoseis Roes, 1984), p. 24.

23. Quoted in Richard Clogg, *Parties and Elections in Greece: The Search for Legitimacy* (London: C. Hurst and Co. Ltd., 1987), p. 155. For an up-to-date volume-length analysis of *Nea Demokratia*, see Takis S. Pappas, *Making Party Democracy in Greece* (New York: St. Martin's Press, Inc., 1999).

24. See P. Nikiforos Diamandouros, "Politics and Constitutionalism in Greece: the 1975 Constitution in Historical Perspective," in Houchang E. Chehabi and Alfred Stepan, eds., *Totalitarianism, Authoritarianism, and Democracy: Essays in Honor of Juan J. Linz* (forthcoming).

25. *The Daily Telegraph* (London), 22 June 1995.

26. *Ho Agnostos Karamanlis*, p. 120.

27. Panayiotes Kanellopoulos (Narrated to Nineta Kontrarou-Rassia), *He Zoe Mou: He aletheia gia tis krisimes stigmes tes Istorias tou Ethnous apo to 1915–1980* (My Life: The Truth about the Critical Moments in the History of the Nation from 1915–1980) (Athens, Dion Gialleles, 1985), p. 111.

28. David H. Close, "The Legacy," in Close, ed., *The Greek Civil War, 1943–1950: Studies of Polarization* (London: Routledge, 1993), pp. 217–18.

29. Interview conducted in Athens, Greece, on 11 December 1993 with a former deputy of EDA.

30. Quoted in C. M. Woodhouse, *Karamanlis: The Restorer of Greek Democracy* (Oxford: Clarendon Press, 1982), p. 167–68.

31. Basilios Evangelos Tsingos, "The Breakdown of Authoritarian Regimes: The Political Evolution of the Greek Military Dictatorship, 1967–1974," Honors Thesis, Harvard College, April 1990, p. 44.

32. Maurice Genevoix, *The Greece of Karamanlis* (London: Doric Publications Ltd., 1973), p. 160.

33. Giannis Ginis, *Ho Allos Karamanlis* (The Other Karamanlis) (Athens: I. Natsos, 1986), p. 93.

34. Woodhouse, *Karamanlis*, p. 186.

35. Interview conducted in Athens, Greece, on 8 February 1994.

36. Víctor M. Pérez-Díaz, *The Return of Civil Society: The Emergence of Democratic Spain* (Cambridge: Harvard University Press, 1993).

37. Bellogiannis was a communist leader who was eventually executed by firing squad.

38. Interview conducted in Athens, Greece, on 4 December 1993.

39. Written interview response of June 1994.

40. Interview conducted in Athens, Greece, on 21 June 1994 with a deputy of ND.

41. Interview conducted in Athens, Greece, on 21 June 1994 with a deputy of ND.

42. "Democracy and the Lessons of Dictatorship," *Comparative Politics* 24:3 (April 1992), pp. 273–91.

43. Arend Lijphart, "Consociational Democracy," *World Politics* 21 (1969), pp. 207–25.

44. George Mylonas, *Escape from Amorgos* (New York: Charles Scribner's Sons, 1974), p. 195.

45. Mylonas, *Escape from Amorgos,* p. 51.

46. Interview conducted in Athens, Greece, on 4 December 1993.

47. Interview conducted in Athens, Greece, on 18 April 1994 with a former deputy of the center who later joined ND.

48. Interview given to *The Free Voice of Greece* radio broadcast, July 1972.

49. Charilaos Florakis was a former party leader of the KKE.

50. Interview conducted in Athens, Greece, on 19 May 1994.

51. Interview conducted in Athens, Greece, on 25 May 1994.

52. Interview conducted in Athens, Greece, on 17 May 1994.

53. "Democracy and the Lessons of Dictatorship," p. 273.

54. Mikis Theodorakis, Interview, n.d.

55. Interview conducted with Eric Rouleau of *Le Monde* in November 1967. For a complete interview transcript in English, see Genevoix, *The Greece of Karamanlis*, Appendix I, pp. 191–97.

56. Interview conducted in Athens, Greece, on 11 December 1993.

57. P. Nikiforos Diamandouros, "Transition to, and Consolidation of, Democratic Rule in Greece, 1974–83: A Tentative Assessment," *West European Politics* 7:2 (April 1984), p. 67.

58. Interview conducted with Virginia Tsouderou by the *Free Voice of Greece* radio program, September 1974.

59. Takis Lambrias, *Ste Skia Enos Megalou: Meletontas 25 Chronia ton Karamanlis* (In the Shadow of a Great One: 25 Years of Studying Karamanlis) (Athens: Morfotike Estia, 1989), p. 140.

60. Bermeo, "Democracy and the Lessons of Dictatorship," p. 283.

61. Quoted in Genevoix, *The Greece of Karamanlis*, pp. 71, 186.

62. Quoted in Constantine Tsatsos, "Introduction," in Genevoix, *The Greece of Karamanlis*, p. 22.

63. Interview conducted in Athens, Greece, on 1 November 1993 with a former deputy of the center.

64. Quoted in Tzermias, *He Politike Skepse*, p. 155, 99.

65. For this argument, see Dimitrios K. Katsoudas, "The Conservative Movement and New Democracy: From Past to Present," in Kevin Featherstone and Dimitrios K. Katsoudas, eds., *Political Change in Greece: Before and After the Colonels* (New York: St. Martin's Press, 1987), p. 94.

66. Quoted in Tzermias, *He Politike Skepse*, p. 91. Emphasis added.

67. Interview conducted in Athens, Greece, on 4 April 1994 with a deputy of ND.

68. Proclamation of Karamanlis on the foundation of ND, quoted in Clogg, *Parties and Elections in Greece*, pp. 227–28.

69. Interview conducted in Athens, Greece, on 31 January 1994 with a former deputy of ND.

70. Evidence of this consists of Karamanlis' efforts to distance himself from the monarchy in the 1960s, his refusal to meet personally with King Constantine during the dictatorship, and his unwillingness to allow the king to return to Greece to campaign for the monarchy's return.

71. Interview conducted in Athens, Greece, on 21 June 1994 with deputy of *Nea Demokratia*.

72. Interview conducted in Athens, Greece, on 7 April 1994.

73. Quoted in Woodhouse, *Karamanlis*, p. 223.

74. Quoted in Rallis, *Politikes Ekmystereuseis*, p. 179.

75. P. Nikiforos Diamandouros, "Transition to, and Consolidation of, Democratic Politics in Greece, 1974–1983: A Tentative Assessment," in Geoffrey Pridham, ed., *The New Mediterranean Democracies: Regime Transition in Spain, Greece and Portugal* (London:

Frank Cass and Co., 1984). This opinion was also expressed in a private discussion with the author.

76. Interview conducted in Athens, Greece, on 31 January 1994 with a former deputy of ND.

77. Quoted in Paraskevopoulos, *Ho Karamanlis*, p. 74.

78. Van Coufoudakis, "The Democratic Transition to Socialism in Post-War Greece," *Modern Greek Studies Yearbook* 4 (1988), p. 17.

79. See Panayote Elias Dimitras, "Changes in Public Attitudes," in Featherstone and Katsoudas, eds., *Political Change in Greece*. See also, Jonathan Swarts, "Karamanlis and the Greek Transition to Democracy," unpublished manuscript.

80. Interview conducted in Athens, Greece, on 14 February 1994.

81. General Napoleon Zervas was leader of the National Republican Greek League (EDES). On EDES, see chapter 2.

82. Interview conducted in Athens, Greece, on 6 April 1994.

83. Interview conducted in Athens, Greece, on 10 December 1993.

84. Interview conducted in Athens, Greece, on 8 February 1994 with a former deputy of ERE who fought in EDES.

85. Interview conducted in Athens, Greece, on 24 March 1994.

86. Although not referring specifically to Greece, Nancy Bermeo makes this point in, "Democracy and the Lessons of Dictatorship," p. 279.

87. Interview conducted in Athens, Greece, on 26 January 1994 with a former deputy of the EK who later joined ND.

88. This point is argued by Pérez-Díaz, *The Return of Civil Society*, 6–26. Pérez-Díaz's view, however, is not fully in line with the argument being made here. Specifically, he argues that it was "the previous emergence of liberal democratic traditions in society" that shaped elite choices and preferences during the transition to democracy in Spain. Thus, elites are seen by Pérez-Díaz more as followers of public attitudes than as leaders of it. This study has found, rather, that the relationship between elites and the electorate tends to be more complicated, interactive, and bidirectional. Attitudinal change occurred in Greece at both the elite and mass levels of society and often had a reciprocal, interactive effect on the other.

89. Richard Gunther, Giacomo Sani, and Goldie Shabad. *Spain after Franco: The Making of a Competitive Party System* (Berkeley: University of California Press, 1986), p. 194. The organization of the AP is examined in Lourdes López Nieto, *Alianza Popular: Estructura y evolución electoral de un partido conservado (1976–1982)* (Madrid: Centro de Investigaciones Sociológicas, 1988).

90. Pérez-Díaz, *The Return of Civil Society*, p. 3.

91. *Informaciones*, 9 May 1978.

92. Quoted in Richard Gunther, "Spain: The Very Model of the Modern Elite Settlement," in Higley and Gunther, eds., *Elites and Democratic Consolidation*, p. 75.

93. Pérez-Díaz, *The Return of Civil Society*, p. 24.

94. Pérez-Díaz, *The Return of Civil Society*, pp. 3–5.

95. Gaetano Salvemini (Quoted in Bermeo, "Democracy and the Lessons of Dictatorship," p. 273).

96. See Panayote Elias Dimitras, "Greek Public Attitudes: Continuity and Change," *International Journal of Public Opinion Research* 2 (Summer 1990), pp. 92–115.

CHAPTER 5

Contagion from the Left: The Moderation of the Greek Communists

Given the Greek left's history of armed rebellion against the established order, its moderation, too, was a key element in the process of democratic consolidation. Had the left maintained its revolutionary tactics and rhetoric in the post-junta years, democratic consolidation and stability might have been seriously threatened. A significant antisystem position on the part of the left would have been perceived as a dire threat by both the remaining remnants of the extreme right and the armed forces—elements that only seven years earlier had intervened in democratic politics to "protect the nation" from the "communist threat." In this way the transition to democracy would have been jeopardized and Greece's nascent democratic political system destabilized. Moreover, given a political climate in which the attitudes of the electorate had been radicalized by the experience of military rule and in which anti-Americanism and antirightist suspicion were pervasive, a significant portion of that electorate might have been potentially mobilized into opposition to the new regime. Had such a left-led mobilization successfully raised critical questions of regime legitimacy, political instability and regime breakdown could have likely followed.

In the event, a mass mobilization did not occur. Rather, "the people of Greece were in effect non-participants in the transformation to civilian government."[1] This lack of popular participation (while perhaps negatively affecting the long-run quality of Greek democracy[2]) facilitated a nonviolent and successful transition to, and consolidation of, the regime. Far from challenging the fundamental legitimacy of the new regime, parties of the left promoted moderation and unity, and encouraged their followers to act prudently and responsibly. According to Michalis Spourdalakis: "References to a 'healthy climate', 'peace', 'maturity', 'national pride', etc. were common in the discourse of all the political parties. ... The accumulated problems and frustrations of the people came to be seen as secondary and were to be expressed in 'prudent and self-controlled' forms. ... The [communist parties] once again were a major, if not the major factor in this process."[3]

Given the left's moderate behavior in the transition to democracy, the question is: Why would a formerly revolutionary left go from attempting a violent overthrow of the established order in a bloody civil war to attitudinally and behaviorally accepting a bourgeois democratic regime? How had most leftists moderated and indeed become democratic by 1974? Despite their importance, the answers to these questions remain virtually unexplored in the literature on the Greek transition to democracy. The historical facts of the left's moderation do not produce sufficient answers—instead, a critical assessment of the left's motivation is necessary. Thus, by examining the motivations behind the ideological development of parties of the communist left in Greece, this chapter will show how, through a long history of interparty division, splits, and ideological conflict, the bulk of the Greek left arrived at system-supportive positions.

In this process of moderation, two distinct phases can be identified. First, I will demonstrate that just as the transformation of the right began in the precoup period and proceeded gradually and incrementally, the first phase of the left's convergence also preceded the dictatorship. Indeed, it originated in the immediate aftermath of the left's civil war defeat and took several decades to complete. However, in contrast to the right's moderation—which was decisively affected by the experiences of the junta years—the period of dictatorship does not seem to have had an appreciable moderating impact on the left. Rather, the experiences of the repressive post–civil war years had led many communists to adhere to democratic norms and procedures before the 1967 coup, so that a significant portion of the left had *already* moderated by the time the colonels came to power. Initially the motivation for moderation appears to have been strategic. Fearing reprisals from the Greek right for illegal activity and lacking support from a war-weary electorate, the left had to respond "realistically" to the limitations imposed upon it during the 1950s and 1960s. This "realism" implied the strategic adoption of democratic behavior.

Over time, however, this strategic behavioral adaptation was transformed into attitudinal support for democracy as many leftists, operating within the system, came to recognize that important policy outcomes could be achieved democratically. Thus, they came to value legal, democratic forms of political participation in principle, and not simply as a tactic. Contrary to the electoral logic of earlier convergence theories, then, the left's moderation—like that of the right's—was primarily triggered by more than simple electoral motivations. This chapter will illustrate that during their first phase of moderation, many leftists were not wholly motivated by electoral concerns. Instead, they were also motivated by a desire for democratization, national reconciliation, and democratic consolidation.

The second phase of the left's moderation—occuring after the collapse of dictatorship—was quite different. While one segment of the left moderated over the course of the postwar years, not even the experience of military dictatorship effected moderation from the orthodox Marxist-Leninist Communist Party of Greece (KKE). In fact, although the KKE was willing to tolerate Karamanlis during the 1974 transition, there is no evidence of ideological moderation until around 1985—a process that intensified in the late 1980s as the party engaged in electoral and government cooperation with the moderate Greek Left (EAR) and other political parties, including *Nea Demokratia*. In this phase moderation appears to have been triggered both by electoral motivations—as communists perceived an opportunity to attract PASOK voters in the wake of scandals implicating its leader, Andreas Papandreou—and by the demonstration effects of Gorbachev's *perestroika*. As I will argue, the desire to be incorporated into the logic of the parliamentary system initially impelled the KKE to adapt to the rules of that game and adopt a prosystem stance in the late 1980s. Behaving as a Downsian office-seeking and vote-maximizing party,[4] the KKE committed itself to moderate, democratic policies it believed would promote its electoral gains.

This moderation proved rather short-lived, however. Party hard-liners quickly reasserted their dominance in the party's central committee and in 1991 elected Aleka Papariga as its General Secretary. Curiously enough, however, this swerve back to a hard-line position also appears to have been electorally motivated. Given Greece's tri-modal distribution of public opinion,[5] and believing that the party had been punished by the electorate for its programmatic and ideological moderation in the 1988–90 period, KKE hard-liners—led by Papariga—reasserted the party's traditional antisystem positions. In short, while electoral motivations were an important factor in the party's 1988–90 moderation, they were equally important in the party's reradicalization. As a result, antisystem members are dominant forces within the party today. Despite these antisystem elements, however, and due to its relatively low level of popular support, the KKE has posed no threat to the long-term consolidation of Greek democracy.

THE MODERATION OF THE GREEK LEFT: A DRAMA IN TWO ACTS

Outlawed at the time of the civil war, the KKE was supplanted in 1951 by the United Democratic Left (EDA), which, as a legal party, became the official grouping of left-wing forces in Greece. Dominated by members of the KKE but encompassing within its ranks socialists and other leftists, EDA quickly became a highly divided, factionalized party. Moderate, revisionist, and even democratic tendencies began to emerge within the communist wing of the party, leading to clashes with the more radical orthodox and antisystem wing of the KKE exiled abroad. Conflict crystallized around diverging views of the role of the communist movement in democratic politics, its ideology, and tactics. On the one hand, moderate communist members of EDA repeatedly argued that they, unlike the KKE leadership abroad, respected democratic rules and were completely opposed to an overthrow of the established order. As a former General Secretary of the "revisionist" left argued,

We were totally opposed to all views of violent overthrow, violent abolition [of the bourgeois regime], dictatorship of the proletariat, etc. which the KKE . . . was supporting. ... Although the source of our spirit was Marxism . . . we believed in the renovation of Marxist ideas, the rejection of views which did not belong in our era. These were sources of ideological differences and clashes. Our theory was a Greek road to socialism with democracy and freedom . . . and this brought us to conflict with the KKE, which maintined . . . that a violent overthrow of the government might be necessary.[6]

As another leading member of the left put it, "Democracy was no longer the means to government as it was for the communists; it started to become the goal."[7]

At the Sixth All-Member Council of the central committee of the KKE in March 1956, the party tactically accepted legal forms of political participation and the "democratic way to socialism." As a result orthodox communists increasingly came to support the idea that the party must guard itself against revisionism and "right-wing opportunism." According to the "exteriors"[8] revisionism meant a denial of the leading role of the working class, a surrender of hegemony to the national bourgeoisie, an overestimation of the role of parliamentarism, an underestimation of illegal forms of struggle, and a rejection of democratic centralism. As one observer emphasized, the Ninth Congress of the Communist Party held that "[the revisionist group's] basic orientation led to the transformation of the Party into a small, bourgeois party in the social-democratic style, and a policy of submission to and collaboration with the liberal bourgeois class, and an anti-international, anti-Soviet direction."[9] According to a party hard-liner, "The leaders of this revisionist group [had] steadily been abandoning the principles of Marxism-Leninism and proletarian internationalism . . . and [had] centered their efforts on fighting our party."[10] As a result, KKE leaders—much to "interior"[11] members' chagrin—maintained that communists should remain prepared to support nonpeaceful avenues to power.

By the February 1964 election campaign, a clear schism had developed between exterior members who wanted to keep the fighting spirit of the civil war alive and interior members who advocated democratic participation. According to party moderates, "The insistence [of the exteriors] on justifying the 1946 decisions to enter into an armed struggle hindered popular reconciliation, objectively contributed to maintaining the anticommunist biases and the passions of the civil war, [and] produced opposition to the need for equal, broad democratic political cooperation."[12] According to EDA national progress could only be achieved through cooperation and unity among democratic forces in Greece. Toward this end, in 1956, the party had even gone so far as to form an electoral alliance with the center and a disaffected segment of the right in an effort to oppose ERE's discriminatory electoral law. For the majority of interior members, cooperation with the center meant backing the Center Union Party after its formation in 1961, as well as many of the center's progressive policies—such as increased cooperation with the Eastern bloc, a lessening of American influence in Greek affairs, and educational and military reforms. The moderate left's willingness to support the center was demonstrated again during the parliamentary elections of 1964, when EDA voluntarily and unconditionally withdrew candidates from constituencies in order to promote a Center Union victory. Later, when Center Union leader George Papandreou's disagreement with the monarchy during the parliamentary crisis of July 1965 led to his resignation as prime minister, Leonidas Kyrkos, a communist deputy of EDA, is purported to have exclaimed to EDA deputies: "We must give full support to the Centrists and the 'Old Man.'[13] . . . We must order all militants to go out on to the streets of Athens! We must find out all Papandreou's movements and we must never miss an opportunity to cheer and support him!"[14]

Given this undisguised revisionism, the conflict between the heretical moderates and the orthodox hard-liners became progressively worse. By the mid-1960s a majority of the KKE's politburo urged communist members of EDA to organize parallel, autonomous organizations at all levels of the party. Not surprisingly, the leadership of EDA vigorously opposed this action. As a result, the communist leadership decided in 1965 that EDA should cease to exist as a unified party organization and should become—as it had been prior to the dissolution of the KKE cells in 1958—a front behind which communists could develop their own clandestine organizations. Before these internecine quarrels could be resolved, however, the colonels came to power and brought democratic party politics to an end.

The imposition of the 1967 dictatorship precipitated yet another clash between the reformist and dogmatic wings of the communist party. This clash, reinforced by differences over the 1968 Soviet invasion of Czechoslovakia and the suppression of the "Prague Spring," led to a formal split when the communists of EDA criticized the leadership in exile as being dogmatic, bureaucratic, a "KKE Abroad," and with "having lost contact with Greek realities."[15] The invasion of Czechoslovakia became a turning point, impelling the KKE toward a less dogmatic version of Marxism. On 16 February 1968 The Twelfth All-Member Council approved a proposal by the KKE's Political Bureau to depose certain "interior" members, thus marking the official division of the central committee. In the view of hard-liners, when the revisionists failed to win a majority on the central committee and redirect the party, they decided to secede and form a new party—the KKE-Interior (KKE-I).[16]

For the duration of the dictatorship, EDA and the newly formed KKE-I continued to behave moderately, sharing many ideological and programmatic positions. Both groups engaged in negotiations with other democratic parties hoping to find a solution to the dictatorship. The KKE-I, for example, proposed the formation of a united front (National Democratic Antidictatorial Unity) of all Greek antidictatorial parties, resistance movements, and "patriotic" elements of the armed forces—irrespective of their political orientations—believing that such a movement could restore parliamentary democracy and thus allow the KKE-I to pursue its strategy of the "democratic road to socialism."[17]

Moreover, during the dictatorship, even orthodox members of the KKE were willing to collaborate with other antidictatorial political parties and movements to overthrow the dictatorship and to "restore the people's sovereign right to decide freely, by vote, on the political system of their country and the regime under which they are to live."[18] In fact, as discussed in chapter 3, when contacted by Scandinavian moderators, KKE general secretary Kostas Koliyannis is reported to have even agreed to support the "Karamanlis Solution." As long as a common enemy existed—the colonels—the KKE claimed it was willing to *temporarily* accept bourgeois democracy and cooperate with all antidictatorial parties on the designated objectives of bringing about the overthrow of the dictatorship, establishing political rights and freedoms for all Greeks, and convening a constitutional assembly.[19]

It is important to note, however, that the KKE's verbal commitments to democracy at this time appear to have been strategic. The experience of military dictatorship led only to a temporary willingness by the KKE to compromise and collaborate with other political forces. Although the party was willing to enter into alliances with other parties and resistance groups, the leadership continued to maintain that "[the working class] will [eventually] set up its own state, the state of proletarian dictatorship."[20]   In stark contrast to rightists and even Eurocommunists who argued that the years of the dictatorship had taught them the importance of democratic procedures and institutions, hard-line leader Koliyannis argued that the colonels' coup had taught him the importance of preserving a Marxist-Leninist party with strong underground organizations: "No matter how favorable the *international conditions may be for a peaceful revolutionary transition,* these do not . . . guarantee a peaceful development of the class struggle. ... What is needed is a close-knit *Marxist Leninist party* closely linked with the masses [and] capable of applying *all forms and means of struggle.*"[21]

In sum, the KKE refused to moderate its hard-line ideology throughout the dictatorship. Following the split of the the party in 1968, the hard-liners announced that the party's primary duty would be to build a strong Marxist-Leninist party with powerful clandestine party organs, to strengthen its ties of international proletarianism and solidarity, and to continue to subject itself to the Communist Party of the Soviet Union. It harshly denounced the "rightist, opportunistic, and anti-ideological opinions" of the KKE-I, which had become transformed into a "wing of social democrats."[22] Moreover, arguing that the noncommunist parties envisioned a post-junta "regime of bourgeois democracy of the pre-junta variety,"[23] the KKE announced that a "people's democracy" was its ultimate aim.

Following the downfall of the junta and Karamanlis' return to power, the moderate communists—much to the KKE's dismay—proposed that all parties collaborate with Karamanlis. According to one deputy of the left, "We saw that [Karamanlis] had changed. We saw differences. ... How could we not see the transformation and say that everything was the same?" According to the KKE-I and EDA, the 1974 transition was a *bona fide* victory for antidictatorial democratic forces and signaled a genuine change in political leadership. "The fall of the dictatorial regime and the formation of a civilian government by Constantine Karamanlis," argued KKE-I leader Leonidas Kyrkos, "are important events for the country and they constitute an important first step toward the restoration of democracy."[24] Elias Iliou, leader of EDA, argued that "[t]he formation of a civilian government . . . constitutes under any circumstances a very positive step. ... That is why we welcome the transition as a great positive step, as an opening toward democracy."[25] Manolis Glezos, another leading member of the communist left, maintained that "Karamanlis['] . . . taking the oath as prime minister was the official act which sealed the victory of the people against the dictatorship."[26]

In contrast, the KKE reacted angrily to the "new left" and its "national compromise" ideas. It denounced the KKE-I as being a "Karamanlis left," a "Karamanlist opposition," and its policies as "unity without principles."[27] In contrast to the Eurocommunists, the KKE argued that Karamanlis' assent to power did not constitute a dramatic democratic transition from the previous dictatorial regime: "The junta was thrust away from the direct governing of the country. However the substantive leadership . . . remains as before in the hands of the military junta."[28]

This hard-line stance was to continue throughout the 1970s. The KKE's Program, approved by its Ninth Congress in 1974 and amended by the Tenth Congress in 1978, emphasized that "the party should be prepared, and prepare the people" for both "peaceful" and "non-peaceful revolutionary" action. Furthermore, resisting calls from various party members, the leadership refused to substitute its call for a dictatorship of the proletariat with the more vague concept of "proletarian power." The party retained its traditional commitments to an internationalist policy, the principle of democratic centralism, and a rejection of ideological plurality.[29] In the view of then-party leader Charilaos Florakis, to accept ideological plurality would be to "turn the vanguard organization . . . into a [forum] for people propagating the views of the non-proletarian class and section of Greek society."[30]

Thus, the KKE entered the 1980s as an orthodox Marxist-Leninist Party, faithful to Moscow and abiding by the principles of proletarian revolution and dictatorship of the proletariat. Only during the 1985 election campaign, when Florakis indicated the possibility of postelection cooperation with PASOK on the basis of a joint program, was there any indication of possible programmatic moderation. That possibility proved to be short-lived, however. When Papandreou did not respond to the communists' proposition, the party leadership reverted to its traditional Marxist-Leninist, antisystem rhetoric.

Initially it even appeared that Mikhail Gorbachev's policy of *perestroika* in the Soviet Union would have no ideological or programmatic impact on the KKE despite the fact that it had been historically a most loyal adherent to the Moscow party line. The KKE leadership initially resisted Soviet reforms and during the Twelfth Congress in 1987 even indicated embarrassment over Gorbachev's domestic policies. The central committee's report reaffirmed that the KKE was still a revolutionary party, committed to the principle of proletarian dictatorship and prepared to operate clandestinely whenever necessary. The party's real attitude *vis-à-vis* programmatic and ideological moderation was probably best conveyed by Florakis' remark to a reporter, "The word 'renewal' gives me the creeps."[31]

Shortly thereafter, however, the KKE apparently succumbed to the force of international events despite vociferous objections from the party's more conservative faction. A 1988 statement by Florakis reveals a changing attitude:

Today we are following . . . what the party of Lenin is doing to restructure in a revolutionary spirit the life of Soviet society. It gives the Greek Communists special satisfaction that the CPSU (Communist Party of the Soviet Union) closely relates that process to the overcoming of dogmatism, outdated thought patterns and stagnation politics. ... The immense work of perestroika that the CPSU is carrying on today is very instructive for us. The [KKE] is trying to borrow from it what is useful to its own activity.[32]

Additional indications that the KKE was beginning to moderate its militant antisystem positions soon followed. In March 1988 a prominent communist argued that "while we do not say yes to the EC, at this moment it would not be correct for us simply to say no."[33] Later that year the KKE entered into an electoral coalition with the reconstituted KKE-I (renamed the Greek Left [EAR] in 1987) and other small progressive parties. A joint statement issued in December 1988 by the Coalition of Left and Progress (*Synaspismos*), as the coalition was called, signaled that the KKE had formally committed itself to the preservation of Greece's democratic, pluralistic system of government and had accepted the notion that democracy was the only road to socialism.[34] Kostas Kappos, a hard-line deputy expelled from the Party in 1988 for refusing to vote for the moderate program, argued that by emphasizing the "revolutionary" character of *perestroika*, the KKE had accepted the predominance of a market economy within socialism, denied the revolution and the leadership of the working class, and accepted parliamentarism: "Essentially, the congress abandoned the strategic desire of the socialist revolution and adopted [the principle] of transformation within the bounds of the system."[35] To the revisionists within the KKE, democracy had become "the means and goal of socialist transformation."[36]

The KKE's new-found moderate, democratic attitude was reinforced in June 1989 when *Synaspismos* entered into a coalition government with ND. This was followed in November 1989 by the formation of an "ecumenical," all-party coalition government in which both PASOK and ND participated in government with *Synaspismos*.[37] Finally, the resignation of Charilaos Florakis, the hard-line general secretary of the KKE, in July 1989, and his succession by Grigorios Farakos, a central committee member believed by many to be conciliatory toward the reformists, increased expectations that the KKE's moderate and prosystem stance might become permanent.

Explaining the First Act: Moderation of the "Interiors"

As argued above, moderation within the communist movement took place in distinct stages. During the 1950s and 1960s, communist members of EDA moderated their ideological and programmatic positions, eventually splitting from the KKE in 1968, forming their own party, and fully adopting a prosystem stance during the transition to democracy. How did interior members of the KKE come to believe that the party should follow a "realistic" and "flexible" policy in Greece, facilitating democratic change through peaceful means? What caused this transformation in attitudes? Interviews with deputies and party leaders of the left indicate that a number of factors—all of them connected with the political learning the left experienced in post–civil war Greece—triggered the first phase of moderation, causing some communists to abandon antisystem positions and to adopt moderate democratic attitudes in tactics and ideology.

The first division in KKE ranks developed almost immediately after the civil war. Mutual recriminations broke out between various factions of the left as disagreements arose over the communists' defeat. Over time many communists came to believe that the "dogmatic" and "sectarian" errors of the Stalinist KKE leader, Nikos Zachariades, and his supporters led the leadership of the party to incorrectly appraise the postwar situation, thereby making a number of very serious mistakes, including the decision not to participate in the elections of March 1946 and instead to take to the hills. The leadership, they argued, had underestimated peaceful forms of struggle and had turned to armed rebellion prematurely.[38] According to Dimitris Parsalidis, "[t]he Party leadership, led by Zachariades, disregarding the fact that the opportunities for a peaceful democratic solution still existed, that the masses were not convinced of the imperative need for armed struggle and that the situation was not altogether ripe for such action, adopted the tactic of armed struggle . . . and insisted on boycotting the 1946 general election."[39]

Disillusionment soon followed disagreement. Many leftists became deeply resentful of the KKE leadership. Mikis Theodorakis, in his *Journal of Resistance*, illustrates the disillusionment and resentment of communists as they learned about events that transpired during and after the civil war:

Now I learn that the moment that a party, a movement, a whole people, was offering its life to its leaders, those same leaders were intriguing among themselves and one half were devouring the other half. I also learn that they had even gone as far as to torture entire companies of partisans in order to elicit the confession that there were agents among them who were responsible for this or that defeat. I later learned that in a partisan hospital in a socialist country one of the leaders had beaten seriously-wounded men on their open wounds.[40]

Interior members also began to resent the influence of Moscow and the Comintern in the Greek Communist Party's internal affairs. Theodorakis, writing of the decision taken by the Twentieth Congress of the CPSU to depose Zachariades and his supporters, again illustrates this resentment: "[W]hen there was a new wind of change after the Twentieth Congress of the Soviet Communist Party, and Zakhariadis and his group had to go, it was still from our big brothers that the change came." For many interiors reactionary methods brought about what should have been a progressive change. Resentment soon turned to bitterness as many leftists began to feel that they had been betrayed both during the post–civil war period as well as during the junta years. Writing about the civil war, Theodorakis argues: "Oh, Greek people, you have been lied to too much. You have been beguiled with false hopes. Did they know, in the East and in the West, that it was impossible for you to bring your revolution to its term? So why did they push you? Who dared do it? With what aim? To serve what interests?"[41] About the dictatorship he adds: "The Greek Communist Party has been no help to us so far. ... After four months of clandestine struggle what have we received in the way of funds, material or any other form of assistance? Practically nothing. ... [T]he Greek Communist Party is only interested in us to the extent that we inspire confidence."[42]

In addition to disagreement and bitterness over the causes of the civil war defeat, a second source of conflict divided the Greek left even further. A split developed between the old leaders of the KKE—many of whom were outside of Greece in either forced or self-imposed exile in East European countries—and the leaders of EDA who were primarily communists living in Greece. The "old group" or the "exteriors" supported the existing policies, tactics, and program of the Eighth Congress, which, while emphasizing the possibility of a peaceful road to "democratic change," still reserved the right to resort to revolutionary methods if necessary. In contrast, the "new group," or the "interior" members of the Communist Party within EDA, desired tactical and programmatic changes that would, in their view, adopt KKE policies to contemporary issues and existing conditions in Greece.[43]

Several factors account for this split. When interviewed, revisionist deputies argued that EDA's leadership was composed of people—such as its chairman, Ioannis Passalides, and the leader of its parliamentary group, Elias Iliou—who had been elected in Greece and who, as parliamentarians, played a role in parliament and were facing "new experiences, new practices, and new problems." As one put it, "Even those who didn't condemn the civil war . . . didn't have the experiences of the civil war and they weren't creations of the civil war. They started from the new reality which had come about in Greece."[44] As a result, many communists increasingly came to see the old leaders and their insistence on revolutionary methods, as *passé* and out of touch with current political conditions.

Interviews also indicated that a number of "practical reasons" contributed to this division and isolation between the two groups of leaders. The geographic distance between communists in Greece and their leaders abroad limited the number of contacts between the two groups. Communication and dialogue were virtually nonexistent. Additionally, the communists of EDA argued that they "could not have relations with the [old leaders] because this was politically dangerous. It could lead to the dissolution of EDA."[45] Respondents argued that communists discovered having contacts with the clandestine organs of the KKE faced persecution and imprisonment in Greece. By 1956 many communists had reached the conclusion that these organs were causing harm to the left's efforts in Greece since they gave credence to the accusations of those who claimed that EDA was nothing more than a legal cover for the KKE. Thus, many supported the abolition of the clandestine party organs and a severing of ties with the leadership in the exterior.

With the passing of time, interior members also began to resent the fact that the exteriors insisted on directing party activity from abroad even though they lacked familiarity with the current political situation in Greece. According to the interior wing of the Communist Party,

[T]he directions that the leadership of the party in the exterior imposed reflected the excessive weight of events outside of Greece instead of trying to place themselves in harmony with the needs of the movement and with the desires of the Greek Communists. ... During the entire period, [the exterior] group formed a mistaken notion of political reality and of its dynamics. As a result, it determined and imposed an unrealistic political course on the movement. ... EDA [on the other hand]... revealed in its daily political action a different perception of problems, [and] it came into constant disagreement with the line of the KKE leadership in the exterior.[46]

Moreover, since directives were handed down from the exteriors to their comrades in EDA, EDA communists (who had little or no access to the KKE's leadership abroad) became increasingly embittered that they were the ones being persecuted in Greece for illegal activities, especially since those activities were becoming, in their view, increasingly ineffectual and unpopular.[47] As one interior KKE member expressed:

[T]hose who lived in Greece had an understanding of things here. They knew that they could not do the things that those from abroad—who did not know what was going on here—were telling them to do. It's one thing to live in an environment, to experience what's going on daily, and another thing to send orders from abroad. I'll give you an example. When Lambrakis was killed ... those from abroad said, "Now is the time to carry out a revolution." And those here said to them, "It is not possible for us to carry out a revolution at this time," because they saw the [right-wing] terrorism that existed. And they saw that if they attempted to do the tiniest thing, [the right] would wall them in and nothing could happen ... [and] the opportunity of the left would also be lost—lost yet again.[48]

Another respondent put it like this: "We ... believed that we had to maintain the underground organizations with huge efforts and huge sacrifices during the entire period after the civil war. ... Later we began to understand that this was not going well: All of us leftists would end up in jail. ... [In] 1956 it became clear that the clandestine organizations were harming the left."[49]

Over time, then, it became increasingly apparent to many interiors that revolution was unrealistic in the current Greek context. Many EDA deputies argued, for example, that the military under NATO could easily destroy the communist movement should it decide to revolt[50]: "[A]n armed struggle," argued one leftist, "would have to be carried out by the army. [We couldn't] arm a second army. All that [was] foolishness!"[51] In addition to realizing that they were militarily unprepared, many communists also understood that following the massive destruction of the civil war, the Greek masses were unorganized and even opposed to revolutionary struggle. As one official communist publication portrayed the situation: "[A] portion of the masses was duped by the anticommunist mania. Another [portion] distanced itself from the left either due to [rightist] terrorism or due to a strong mistrust of [the left's] competence to lead the democratic struggle and to give a realistic democratic perspective. In this situation ... the conservative political forces found themselves with an important mass base after 1949."[52] As Elias Iliou argued for the post–civil war period: "This is not the time for armed revolutions. Today, in Greece, no one wants trouble. We must persuade the people that we are the party of democratic tranquility and progress which will respect freedom and tolerate the existence of other democratic trends and that will study their problems and propose solutions aimed at ... the well-being of the people."[53]

In sum, interior members such as Iliou argued that the electorate preferred legal over illegal methods of political action in the post–civil war period. Since the state of the masses was unrevolutionary, the revolutionary tactics imposed by the dogmatic leadership of the KKE abroad produced counterproductive results, alienating people and turning them toward the right. In the course of interviews, many deputies referred to the KKE's clandestine party organs to illustrate the unpopularity of illegal methods of participation. They argued that the party's 1958 decision to abolish the organs and to urge all of its members to join EDA was prompted by the realization that the organs remained isolated and ineffectual even as EDA experienced tremendous electoral success. As a result, interior members argued that their insistence on the "democratic way" was rooted in the demands of the masses who desired democratization and gave their support to democratic parliamentary parties—not illegal organs.[54]

Organizational change was reinforced by the domestic experiences of Greek communists, as they participated in legal and peaceful forms of political struggle that led to increased moderation of their programmatic and ideological positions. Put simply, Greek leftists became acclimated to democratic parliamentary government. One leading leftist argued that

EDA's split was a reality immediately after the civil war—from that moment there were two centers, and this was especially true from the time EDA rooted itself in Greek circumstances and ... Greek reality. [Also] from that moment, there was a center [of power] abroad which thought in Stalinist terms ... and in terms of its own historical [experiences]—civil war, defeat, "Let's return [to Greece for another round]," and so on. And [then there was] the other center in Greece ... [which] had adapted itself to [domestic] political problems.[55]

As a result of such adaptation, many Greek communists argued that they came to value legal, democratic methods of political activity as the only appropriate basis of political participation. Interiors maintained that their involvement in such efforts as the gradual development of workers' movements, the founding of the Democratic Syndicalist Movement (DSK), the participation of EDA in municipal and national elections, and its electoral coalition in 1956 with centrists revealed to many of them that "the democratic way" could lead to important victories for the left.[56] As one leading revisionist put it, "Normal democratic life oblige[d] a large portion of the left to begin to think in parliamentary terms—that it must reenter the political game democratically. It must abandon the old revolutionary fantasies ... and think in the logic of parliamentarism."[57]

Yet another force driving the Greek left's adaptation to domestic circumstances during the 1950s and 1960s was the desire of the masses for national reconciliation and popular unity. As a result, EDA responded to this desire and adopted the masses' position. Thus, EDA deputy Mikis Theodorakis, an outspoken proponent of unity and reconciliation, argued in October 1962:

I am ready ... to extend my hand, to forget forever my past suffering and exiles, if we can all agree on a ... program which would secure the renaissance of our country. ... I can't define the content and the form of the unity of the people. As a man and as a Greek, however, who suffers for my country, I conceive this unity as being broad, very broad. Let all of us honest people unite, all of us who want the good of our country. ... Let us all be united.[58]

Thus, by the time the dictatorship was launched in 1967, the interiors had already recognized the importance of national reconciliation and had "pledged" their diffuse support for democracy.

The experiences of the dictatorial years simply reinforced the left's commitment to reconciliation as both rightists and leftists found themselves on the same side and, consequently, in the same prison cells with many of their erstwhile enemies. The effect this had on the left is reminiscent of the right's moderation under these same circumstances. A KKE-I publication illustrates quite well that the junta contributed to reconciliation:

[W]e must emphasize the great contribution ... of anonymous Greeks, who by endangering their lives ... gave hospitality to fighters of the resistance, leftists, centrists, and rightists. The members ... of the KKE-I, of "Rigas Feraios" and other resistance organizations of the left found ... protection not only in houses of the left, but also of centrists, and even rightists. This is ... a sign of the new great National Antidictatorial Unity, which was built and stabilized from our common struggle in the black years of the dictatorship.[59]

A statement by former conservative Prime Minister George Rallis during the transition gives further evidence of reconciliation:

The man who gave me the key to the Greek political situation was Elias Iliou. This leader of the left, a humanist respected by all, even by his most staunch opponents, has had an inhuman fate. At the time of the civil war, he was deported for five years ... and subjected to continuous torture during two of them. ... In 1967, the *coup d'état* took place, and the venerable leader ... was again deported ... and tortured. ... But nothing succeeded in making him submit. He has always spoken without fear. And now he is still speaking without hate.[60]

Iliou reciprocated: "Take Rallis' case: he was imprisoned by the military on the basis of laws he had himself issued against us. ... The traditional right fell victim to the arsenal it had built up to muzzle the left. This made it think. From now on, we are trying on both sides for mutual understanding."[61] In short, reconciliation begun in the years preceding the dictatorship was consolidated during the seven years of dictatorial rule. Following the harsh experiences of authoritarian rule in Greece and despite their earlier rejection of "bourgeois democracy," leftist leaders came to believe that maximalist strategies were no longer viable. Thus, their respective communist parties adopted moderate strategies and were loyal parties during the transition and consolidation processes. Both the KKE-I and EDA, for example, openly declared that democratic consolidation was their main objective.

Further cementing the willingness of Greek Eurocommunists to accept and even cooperate with Karamanlis during the transition was the fact that many of them genuinely believed that a serious threat of dictatorial relapse existed in the early period of the restored democracy. For example, Leonidas Kyrkos argued that only by supporting the Karamanlis government could the dictatorial threat be broken.[62] Even Theodorakis went so far as to argue that Greek communists had to propose to the Karamanlis government a "national compromise" comparable to the "historic compromise" of the Italian communists in order to prevent an authoritarian comeback.[63] In this way the Greek left bore out Adam Przeworski's argument that some leftists may choose to act within the emerging parliamentary structure rather than subvert it because they come to believe that even losing repeatedly under democracy is preferable to a future under an alternative, nondemocratic system: "After all, democracy ... offer[s] one fundamental value that for many groups may be sufficient to prefer it to all alternatives: security from arbitrary violence."[64]

Explaining the Second Act: The Moderation of the KKE

The moderation of the KKE was strikingly different from the more moderate Eurocommunist EDA and KKE-I. Specifically, its moderation was not achieved as easily or as quickly as that of the KKE-I and EDA. Instead, the KKE maintained its orthodox Marxist-Leninist positions throughout the transition to democracy and well into the 1980s, and supported the new regime only because it believed it to be a possible opening and means to socialism.

Nonetheless, the KKE did eventually moderate its position in the mid-1980s. In this section we will see how this came to pass. We will explore the reasons behind the KKE's willingness to moderate in 1985 by proposing collaboration with PASOK and why it was publicly willing to moderate its programmatic and ideological positions in 1988 when it joined *Synaspismos*.

Interviews with communist deputies indicate that several factors contributed to the KKE's moderation. The first, and most important, factor appears to have been electoral in nature. In the face of a number of public opinion polls in the late 1980s that clearly indicated that the Marxist-Leninists were losing ground in Greece, the KKE became increasingly willing to moderate. One such poll indicated that 56.1 percent of *Synaspismos* voters classified themselves as "Socialists," Marxist and non-Marxist, while only one in four classified themselves as Marxist-Leninist, and one in five claimed to be "Socialists but not Marxists."[65] In 1987 opinion polls also revealed that PASOK's electoral support was beginning to decline. In the wake of scandals over the alleged involvement of leading PASOK deputies (including Papandreou himself) in financial wrongdoing, phone tapping, as well as Papandreou's extramarital affair with an Olympic Airways flight attendant, it appears that the KKE saw an opportunity in 1988 to broaden its electoral appeal to dissatisfied PASOK voters.   The KKE thus relinquished its more radical ideological and programmatic features and cooperated with EAR and other moderate leftists, first, in the formation of the electoral alliance, *Synaspismos*, and, later, in the coalition governments of June and November 1989. Put simply, the KKE realized that on its own it could not attract disaffected voters of PASOK and thus went in search of a coalition partner, hoping to attract socialist defectors. As a former KKE deputy argued, the KKE moderated in 1988–89 "[b]ecause it want[ed] to participate in government."[66] A former EDA deputy also maintained that the left entered into the coalition because it "may have believed that by hitting PASOK, the EAM-ites would [leave PASOK and] return to [it]."[67] A PASOK deputy agreed: "[T]he left cooperated with the right for the first time in history ... out of a clear political interest. ... They thought Andreas would die and PASOK would be poisoned and they were trying to attract its electorate. They didn't do it for catharsis;[68] they simply believed ... that they could attract the old leftists back. ... [T]he communists believed that PASOK would be dissolved and they would replace it."[69] Similar to the moderation of the left in all four Southern European countries, the case of the Greek left reconfirms that, as the elite convergence theory holds, electoral motivations can indeed be an important factor behind ideological moderation.

In addition to electoral considerations, international diffusion effects also played an important role in accelerating the ideological, strategic, and organizational transformation of the KKE. Although the KKE was initially highly embarrassed by the changes in Eastern Europe, eventually its leadership warmed to the policy of *perestroika*. As an alternate KKE politburo member argued in 1989: "[W]e think it important to study [*perestroika*] and to learn the lesson of revolutionary transformation in the socialist world. Perestroika is very valuable to the theory and practice of the communist movement."[70] Another KKE deputy agreed:

With international developments and the overthrow of existing socialism, the Greek leftist movement was also affected. The movement was divided, since they wanted to move toward something new and away from the old models of socialism. ... [Thus] *Synaspismos* was formed. ...Renewal was necessary. Since the model of existing socialism was overthrown, we had to reformulate our ideas, maintaining intellectual socialism, certainly, but reexamining our ideology.[71]

Concerning the formation of the *Synaspismos* coalition, Leonidas Kyrkos, leader of EAR and founding member of the coalition, maintained that the process of moderation "beg[an] simultaneously with perestroika in the USSR. The Greek left forces would have been unable to achieve unity without perestroika, glasnost and new political thinking."[72] Thus, the KKE came to moderate its stance. When faced with dramatic ideological and political change at the communist core—the Soviet Union—it succumbed to the pressures for ideological change.

Under such international and domestic electoral pressures for moderation, the KKE entered the 1990s as a member of *Synaspismos* and an apparently prosystem party. And yet this moderation was not permanent, as the election of hard-line cadre Aleka Papariga as General Secretary on 27 February 1991 clearly indicated. Papariga, elected by the party's new central committee—in which conservatives outnumbered reformers sixty to fifty-one—announced on 15 June 1991 that she was withdrawing the KKE from *Synaspismos*. This announcement was followed by the dismissal of the central committee members who had resisted her decision to withdraw from the coalition.

The KKE's reversion to its previous hard-line position was confirmed by the party's expression of support for the attempted hard-line coup against Gorbachev in August 1991. In fact, Papariga, who only a few months previously had declared that "the ideas of perestroika ... contribute ... to the development of [a] modern theory of socialism ... [and make] socialism more attractive,"[73] now argued that the process of *perestroika*, "which has been presented as the political restructuring of socialism, is in fact a most savage ... restoration of capitalism." By the time of the party's Fourteenth All-Member Council (December 1991), the KKE leadership had reconfirmed its loyalty to Marxist-Leninist principles, proletarian internationalism, and democratic centralism.

Why did the KKE revert to a more radical position following its brief period of moderation? It is interesting to note that the same factors that facilitated its moderation in 1988–90—domestic electoral considerations and international factors—also contributed to its reradicalization in 1991. In terms of domestic electoral considerations, it is worth noting that while the KKE moderated in order to garner votes and enter government, sharing executive power with ND did not pay off electorally, as the electoral and governmental coalitions between left and right were not widely accepted by left-wing supporters. Many leftists, with vivid memories of the persecution, intimidation, and discrimination at the hands of the right in the post–civil war period, "seem to have suffered emotional revulsion at the prospect of co-government with the Right."[74] Thus, in the elections of November 1989, *Synaspismos'* share of the vote actually fell from 13.1 percent to 11 percent only to drop again in the elections of April 1990 to 10.6 percent. In just a little less than one year's time, the left lost one-fifth of its electoral support. In the face of this electoral loss, the orthodox leadership of the KKE appears to have decided that the coalition was no longer a political strategy worth pursuing. As a former deputy of ND put it, "[The KKE] believed it lost a percentage of its votes because it cooperated with ND."[75] For this reason "the soul-searching that went on in the party ... created a great rift within the KKE between those who wanted the renewal of the party and those who clung like limpets to traditional communist dogma."[76] It was those who clung like limpets to the old nostrums who predominated and as a result the *Synaspismos* coalition fell apart.

Moreover, events in the Soviet Union reinforced the electoral considerations of the hard-line leadership in Greece. As a deputy loyal to the *Synaspismos* coalition expressed, "As soon as he fell, as soon as they saw that Gorbachev was beginning to be doubted ... with coups and so on, they dissolved *Synaspismos*."[77] In short, then, just as the rise of Gorbachev contributed to moderation, his decline contributed to its rejection in the 1990s.

The orthodox Marxist-Leninist position was again officially restated during the party's Fifteenth Congress in May 1996. In a speech to the Congress, moderate politburo member Demetris Kostopoulos denounced the KKE's goal of withdrawal from the European Union, placed himself against the party slogan "Five parties—two politics," and criticized the party's opposition to cooperation with other parliamentary parties and its adherence to the term "dictatorship of the proletariat." As a result he and another moderate Eurodeputy, advocating similar positions, found themselves excluded from the list of central committee candidates. The hard-liners predominated yet again.

In the face of such events, one must question the KKE's true ideological and programmatic positions and its commitment to the democratic regime. Has the party adopted a prosystem position or is it as intransigent and antisystem as it has always been? Interestingly enough, despite formal party positions and actions to the contrary, many KKE deputies indicated in interviews that the KKE was beginning to abandon orthodox Marxist-Leninist principles. When asked whether the KKE was revolutionary, for example, one deputy answered: "What do we mean by revolutionary? .... Revolution means change; it does not mean artillery. ... This change consists of the old going out and the new coming in. Thus, the revolutionary character of a communist party does not stop when it has socialism as its goal. ... This party is revolutionary." He continued, however:

[T]he Communist Party is a loyal party to this regime, to this democracy. ... It accepts the constitution, it functions within the laws of the country, ... it competes to win the majority of the people in order to govern. Then [once in office] it will put into effect its own program. ... [T]his party ... has a program which has ... certain stages of development until it reaches socialism. ... It tells the people that [the KKE] is heading for socialism. However, at this moment I operate within the system.[78]

A hard-line Communist Party member also agreed: "There is an objective tendency for [party members] to continually restrict themselves to parliamentary methods. ... [A]s far as proletarian revolution and the like is concerned—the word "revolution" ... they don't even bring it up."[79] Despite such testimonials of moderation, it is important to note that the party remains highly divided. Other deputies and party cadres argue that, on the contrary, the party is, and should remain, revolutionary. A KKE member of the European Parliament, believed to be a moderate party member, stated the following: "In the past we would say that only with a mass revolution would Greece be able to pass to [higher stages of social development]. ... This reference is not a dream nor a vision, it is ... totally realistic. It might take a while. It might require sacrifices, but sooner or later it will happen. It will prevail."[80] Similarly, Kostas Kappos argued: "As for the frightful accusation that the communists desire a violent overthrow of the system: Yes, this is true. This is what they desire. ... Nowhere does the bourgeois class relinquish leadership of its own free will. It attempts to maintain it with violence."[81] Moreover, the party's Fifteenth Congress was clear indication of such division. While revisionists argued for an "opening" and for "cooperation" with other Greek political parties and movements, other politburo members argued that "cooperation and business deals ... with those political parties whose programs and politics move within the logic of the system cannot occur."[82]

Given such contradictory ideological and strategic positions, it is obvious that the Greek Communist Party is extremely divided internally. Indeed, its honorary president, Charilaos Florakis, pleaded at the party's Fifteenth Congress that delegates should remain united and steer a middle course between the hard-liners and the moderates. Concerning cooperation with other parties, he argued that party leaders "must not close the doors to tomorrow"[83] and should leave some room for political maneuvering in the future. Thus, despite the current dominance of hard-liners, the party remains in a state of flux and could undergo ideological and programmatic change in the future. As one former KKE deputy put it, "[A]fter the events in Eastern [Europe,] everything is being reexamined. ... [T]oday not even [the members] know [the party's positions.] ... [T]hey hesitate to clearly declare their position on different issues."[84] A former *Synaspismos* deputy agreed: "No one can say what the KKE believes. ... The KKE has always straddled between two beliefs—that of the dictatorship of the proletariat ... and the democratic functioning of the regime—but this is schizophrenic and no one can know exactly [where the KKE stands today]."[85] A former deputy of PASOK also maintained: "After the fall of the [Soviet Union], it [was] past its prime, losing its ideology, ... and it doesn't know where to go and what to do and what to believe in—whether it has or doesn't have an ideology."[86]

In sum, as has been shown in this analysis, the Greek left's moderation during the formative period of the transition facilitated democratic consolidation and stability. The left (especially the Eurocommunists) consciously refused to capitalize on the anti-NATO, anti-American, and antiestablishment positions of the radicalized Greek electorate. Refusing to contribute to the radicalization and mobilization of the masses, the communists stressed the importance of moderation and unity and urged their followers to act prudently and responsibly. Thus, the initial moderation of the communist left contributed greatly toward achieving democratic consolidation and stability.

By the early 1990s, however, a significant portion of the left had reconfirmed its loyalty to Marxist-Leninist principles, proletarian internationalism, democratic centralism, and the dictatorship of the proletariat. Despite such radical antisystem positions, however, the KKE does not pose a significant threat to democracy. Its efforts to appeal to a wider section of the electorate have been futile and the party appears more or less isolated on its traditional electoral base, which remains relatively small and is in seeming decline.[87]

Moreover, since the KKE's ideological and programmatic signals are ambiguous and since it is itself divided between hard-line and revisionist factions, it no longer represents a clear, unambiguous antisystem force. For example, one cannot be certain that the KKE's voters are clearly antisystem. A poll revealed that the vast majority of *Synaspismos* voters in 1989–90—74.2 percent—did not classify themselves as Marxist-Leninists.[88] Taken together with the fact that 70 percent of those *Synaspismos* voters also classified themselves as supporters of the KKE (rather than of the other alliance partners) at that time, it would appear that the vast majority of KKE voters do not consider themselves hard-line Marxists and thus are not as radical and antisystem as are their leaders.[89]

My own interview data also offer support to this argument. When KKE deputies were asked to describe a typical supporter of their party, many respondents indicated that the majority of KKE voters cast their ballot for the KKE based on a "sentimental" attachment to the party rather than on specific political considerations. Respondents indicated that historical family ties to the KKE, nostalgic memories of the occupation, resistance, civil war, and painful recollections of the oppressive post–civil war period connect KKE followers to their party. When asked to describe a typical KKE voter, for example, a former party deputy argued the following: "There are very few voters who will vote for the Communist Party today ... based on political considerations exclusively. ... The main reason ... has to do with nostalgia. That is, family origins, personal memories, sentimental attachments. ... It is not a rational choice ... [It is] an emotional [one]."[90] Thus, I contend that as long as KKE voters think of themselves as communists and vote communist based on emotional and sentimental grounds rather than on ideological adherence to Marxist-Leninist principles, it is very likely that they themselves are not a clear antisystem force. As a result, democratic consolidation and stability remains fundamentally unchallenged by Greek communists despite official programmatic and ideological positions to the contrary.

COMPARATIVE OBSERVATIONS AND
THEORETICAL IMPLICATIONS

This chapter has illustrated that the Greek left's convergence—like that of the right's—was incremental and gradual, having its origins in the precoup, post–civil war period. As with the right, the left's convergence ought to be seen as a departure from the animosities and hatred of the civil war and the postwar period. In sum, the hostilities and antagonisms that emerged during that critical period had to be dulled before convergence could occur. This chapter has also argued that convergence was brought about by several factors, including strategic concerns, party-organizational considerations, electoral motivations, and international influences. Moreover, as was the case with the Greek right, the left's moderation was effected by a process of political learning brought about by the harsh experiences of authoritarian rule, the repressiveness of the post–civil war period, as well as the practical lessons of democratic politics—particularly since 1958 when EDA gained formal opposition status.

As the elite convergence theory would predict, a principal motivation behind the moderation of the Greek left—as well as of the other Southern European communist parties—was electoral interests. In Greece the KKE's moderation in the mid- to late-1980s was triggered by a desire to appeal to dissatisfied PASOK voters and thus increase its own electoral strength. The Greek Communist Party was not alone in this regard. In Italy in the immediate postwar years, the PCI began to gradually relinquish its antisystem identity in the hope of broadening its electoral appeal and one day acceding to power. In Spain, too, the PCE— mirroring the KKE's cooperation with other moderate leftists to form the *Synaspismos* alliance—sensed that the Spanish electorate had come to reject the radical left-wing option and formed a coalition with the United Left (IU) in April 1986—all in the bid to increase its chances of electoral success. Even in Portugal, the formerly revolutionary PCP went in search of a coalition partner, and found the *Partido Renovador Democratico* (PRD)—again in an attempt to attract socialist defectors to its ranks. Thus, as all four cases demonstrate, electoral motivations are indeed an important factor behind ideological and programmatic moderation. However, as with the Greek right, electoral motivations are not the only force behind elite convergence.

A second factor contributing to convergence is long-term and strategic in nature. Forced to present itself as a moderate prosystem force during the repressive post–civil war period, EDA was compelled to display a democratic "face," participating in political contestation, electoral politics, and parliamentary debate despite the questionable democratic attitudes of many of its members. Over time, however, this strategic behavioral adaptation was transformed into genuine attitudinal support for bourgeois democracy as some leftists "learned" that important programmatic and public policy outcomes could be realized within the bourgeois regime. Put simply, the encounter of some leftists with democratic politics converted many of them to democracy.

Such transformations—based, in part, on the important process of political learning—were not unique to the Greek left. In fact, EDA's experience during the post–civil war period paralleled the more well-known actions of the PCE and the PCI. As in Greece, Spanish "exteriors"—communists living outside of Spain—were more likely to take hard-line, antisystem positions while those communists in Spain, under Franquist rule, often argued for more moderate, system-supportive positions—ones, they felt, reflected the need to adapt to current political realities.[91] The harsh experiences of the Spanish Civil War, decades of persecution under Franco, and the succeeding isolation of Spanish communists encouraged the PCE to moderate its ideology, adopting Eurocommunist positions. Thus, by the time of the Spanish transition, the PCE was already playing a dynamic and contributory role to the politics of consensus. It accepted the monarchy, participated in the constitutional engineering process, and took an active role in the *Pactos de la Moncloa*—thereby facilitating a successful transition and consolidation process.

For their part Italian communists also recognized the need for moderation following Italy's harsh experiences with fascism. Writing as the head of the Italian Communist Party in 1944, Palmiro Togliatti insisted that "[For the people who have] survived the harsh and heroic tests of clandestine work, of the Special Tribunal, of the prisons, of the islands of confinement, of exile, of the Spanish War … the need to be liberated from verbal extremism and the impotence of maximalism [is primary]."[92] Realizing that a revolutionary insurrection was not a viable option in Italy, the PCI, under Togliatti's leadership, reformed its party strategy, agreeing to participate in the Badoglio government in 1944, conceding to the inclusion of Mussolini's Concordat in the new constitution, and supporting a law granting pardon to some fascist leaders.[93]

In addition, all three Southern European communist parties saw the necessity for organizational transformation, eventually rejecting the classic Leninist organizational model. The need for such organizational restructuring is highlighted by the failure of organizational reform in the Portuguese Communist Party. As that case illustrates, while a tightly organized Marxist-Leninist party structure—a structure best suited for revolutionary and extraparliamentary forms of political action—suited it well during the initial "revolutionary" phase of the transition, with the shift from radical to more moderate democratic politics, the unchanged structure of the PCP actually proved to be a hindrance to successful democratic competition. In contrast, both EDA and the PCE abandoned their traditional cell-based organizational structure and reconfigured their party organizations so to better meet the demands of electoral politics. EDA's organizational transformation prior to the military coup has been described above. In Spain the PCE organizationally transformed itself from a party of functionally defined cells to a more open, territorially based local party during the country's transition. As in Greece, this transformation—as well as the PCE's ideological moderation into an openly Eurocommunist party—was explicitly effected so that the party would "fit better with the dynamics of competitive politics in the new democracy."[94] In short, the need for organizational transformation was a major factor contributing to both the PCE's and EDA's moderation.

A third factor contributing to convergence was the effects, both direct and indirect, of the international environment. Specifically, such events as the 1968 Soviet invasion of Czechoslovakia and the suppression of the "Prague Spring" and, more recently, the demonstration effects of Gorbachev's *perestroika* and *glasnost* were quite significant in prompting moderation on the part of all Southern European communist parties. In Italy the PCI—which had already undergone significant moderation prior to the collapse of "real socialism"—was propelled toward a more thorough ideological cleansing, renouncing its traditional identity and constructing an entirely new one.[95] The PCE similarly accelerated processes of moderation that were already well underway when faced with ideological and political change in Eastern Europe. In Greece and Portugal, on the other hand, the more orthodox and pro-Soviet KKE and PCP were actually compelled by Gorbachev's reforms to initiate the process of ideological change—even if it was halfhearted and ultimately short-lived. In short, traditional elite convergence theory correctly posits the importance of purely electoral interests in bringing about moderation; however, electoral motivations are not the whole story. As I have argued, factors such as strategic, long-range concerns, organizational problems and international influences all play their role in effecting moderation.

Perhaps the most significant theoretical finding of this study, however, has to do with the fact that many of these *same* factors that contributed to the Greek left's moderation in 1988–90 also impelled certain segments of that group to swerve back to their previous hard-line position in 1991. Believing that the party had been punished by the electorate for its moderation and willingness to collaborate with non-Marxist parties in forming *Synaspismos* and the "ecumenical" government of 1989, KKE hard-liners reasserted their dominance and reversed the party's tactics. Concluding that the *Synaspismos* coalition was no longer a strategy worth pursuing, they withdrew their support from that alliance. Based on this reversal, then, this chapter has argued that if electoral motivations can serve to moderate party programs and ideology, they can also have the reverse effect. Given the right stimuli, electoral motivations can easily serve a radicalizing as well as a moderating influence. The influence of international factors played a similar role, leading to both moderation and radicalization at different times. Just as Gorbachev's *perestroika* policies had initially "pushed" the KKE into moderating reforms, so, too, his demise had a radicalizing impact on the Greek Communist Party. No sooner did the KKE leadership see Gorbachev being challenged at home than it dissolved the *Synaspismos* alliance and reverted to its previous hard-line stance. In short, processes of democratic consolidation are neither unilinear nor unidirectional. Factors that contribute to party moderation and elite convergence can also contribute to radicalization. Democratization and consolidation can be arrested or even reversed.

Fortunately, the process of democratic consolidation was not reversed in Greece. Despite the formal dominance of hard-liners, the KKE poses no immediate threat to the long-term consolidation of Greek democracy. As argued above, the reason for this is two-fold: (1) the KKE continues to receive relatively low levels of popular support in national elections, and (2) its followers are not themselves as radical and ideologically committed as the party leadership. Two of the other three Southern European countries show similar moderation at the mass level. In Italy the PCI's electorate began to resemble the average Italian voter in the 1970s and 1980s as the representation of blue-collar workers diminished, while the representation of white-collar workers, teachers, and technicians increased. In Spain, too, thanks in large part to the formation of the IU, the PCE has managed to attract a relatively young, educated, urban middle-class electorate whose political attitudes are more moderate and closer to those of the average voter. In short, the KKE, like its sister parties in Italy and Spain, has a moderate base of support—one that, despite its leaders' intermittent bouts of ideological radicalism, is becoming increasingly moderate and system-supportive. Southern European communists—including Greek communists—have thus ceased to be a challenge to democratic consolidation and have in fact contributed to it.

Thus, if democratic consolidation and stability were to be severely challenged by a Greek political party during the transition to democracy, that challenge would have had to come from the Panhellenic Socialist Movement (PASOK). Unlike the traditional left, which systematically demobilized the masses during the transition, Andreas Papandreou's PASOK capitalized on the radicalized climate of the period by challenging the legitimacy of the transition, the leadership of Constantine Karamanlis and his national unity government, and the country's pro-Western orientation. Declaring that the fall of the dictatorship represented nothing more than "a change of the NATO guard in Athens," Papandreou appeared poised to seriously challenge the new democratic regime, its institutions, and rules of the game. To many observers, Papandreou's 1974 radical antiestablishment and antiright rhetoric represented the only significant antisystem voice of frustrated Greek citizens during the transition to democracy. This voice and its subsequent moderation is examined in the next chapter.

NOTES

1. Michalis Spourdalakis, *The Rise of the Greek Socialist Party* (London: Routledge, 1988), p. 60.

2. For this argument, see P. Nikiforos Diamandouros, "Beyond Consolidation: The Quality of Democracy in Contemporary Greece," Paper presented at Symposium '95, Modern Greek Studies Association, Cambridge, Massachusetts, November 1995.

3. Spourdalakis, *The Rise of the Greek Socialist Party*, p. 76.

4. Anthony Downs, *An Economic Theory of Democracy* (New York: Harper and Row, 1957).

5. See George Th. Mavrogordatos, *Rise of the Green Sun: The Greek Election of 1981* (London: Centre of Contemporary Greek Studies, King's College, 1983); "The Greek Party System: A Case of 'Limited but Polarised Pluralism'?" *West European Politics* 7:4 (October 1984), pp. 156–69; and Richard Gunther and José R. Montero, "The Anchors of Partisanship: A Comparative Analysis of Voting Behavior in Four Southern European Democracies," (unpublished manuscript).

6. Interview conducted in Athens, Greece, on 27 April 1994.

7. Interview conducted in Athens, Greece, with a leading *Synaspismos* deputy on 4 and 6 May 1994.

8. The "exteriors" were Greek communists who had been either forcefully exiled or who had fled Greece to the Eastern bloc in the civil war and post–civil war period and who maintained a staunchly Marxist-Leninist position.

9. Efstratios Demertzis, "Factionalism in the Greek Communist Party," Ph.D. Dissertation, New York University, 1979, p. 172.

10. Gregores Pharakos, "Banner of Struggle and Victory," *World Marxist Review* 12:11 (November 1978), p. 32.

11. In contrast to the "exteriors," the "interiors" were Greek members of the KKE who lived in Greece, were oftentimes members of EDA, and tended to espouse social-democratic, rather than Marxist-Leninist, tendencies.

12. "To Helleniko Kommounistiko Kinema apo to 1949 os to 1967" (The Greek Communist Movement from 1949 to 1967), *Kommounistike Theoria kai Politike: Periodiko tes K.E. tou K.K.E (es.)* (Communist Theory and Politics: Periodical of the Central Committee of the KKE-I) 9 (February–March 1976), p. 9.

13. "Old Man" was an affectionate term of reference to George Papandreou.

14. Quoted in Mikis Theodorakis, *Journal of Resistance* (New York: Coward, McCann & Geoghegan, Inc., 1973), p. 154.

15. Dimitri Kitsikis, "Populism, Eurocommunism and the KKE: The Communist Party of Greece," in Michael Waller and Meindert Fennema, eds., *Communist Parties in Western Europe: Decline or Adaptation?* (New York: Basil Blackwell Ltd., 1988), p. 100.

16. Pharakos, "Banner of Struggle and Victory," p. 32.

17. For this party line, see Babis Drakopoulos, "He Politike tes EADE stes Semerines Synthekes" (The Politics of EADE in Today's Conditions), 3 (March 1975), pp. 5–20; Leonidas Kyrkos, "EADE kai Demokratike Synergasia" (EADE and Democratic Cooperation) 8 (January 1976), pp. 3–9; Kostas Filinis, "Ho Demokratikos Dromos pros ton Sosialismo kai he EADE" (The Democratic Road Toward Socialism and EADE) 10 (April 1976), pp. 57–59, all in the Communist Party-Interior's publication, *Kommounistike Theoria kai Politike* (Communist Theory and Politics).

18. Vasilis Venetsanopoulos, "Triumph of Leninist National Policy," *World Marxist Review* 15:10 (October 1972), p. 114.

19. KKE, "Apofase tou 9ou Synedriou tou Kommounistikou Kommatos tes Helladas pano sten Ekthese Drases tes Kentrikes Epitropes" (Decision of the 9th Congress of the Communist Party of Greece on the Report of the Central Committee on its Activities), *Neos Kosmos* 3:4, p. 30.

20. Vasilis Venetsanopoulos, Vladimir Guliev, Sylwester Zawadzki, and Jaime Schmirgeld, "Notes on the History of the Idea of Proletarian Dictatorship," *World Marxist Review* 17:7 (July 1974), p. 72.

21. Kostas Koliyannis, "Leninism and the Experience of the Communist Party of Greece," *World Marxist Review*, 13:4 (April, 1970), p. 52. Emphasis in original.

22. KKE, "Apofase tou 9ou Synedriou," pp. 96–97.

23. KKE, "Apofase tou 9ou Synedriou," p. 74.

24. Leonidas Kyrkos, quoted in Potes Paraskeuopoulos, *Ho Karamanlis sta Chronia 1974–1985* (Karamanlis in the Years 1974–1985) (Athens, Ho Typos, n.d.), p. 33.

25. Elias Iliou, quoted in Paraskeuopoulos, *Ho Karamanlis*, p. 32.

26. Quoted in Paraskeuopoulos, *Ho Karamanlis*, p. 32

27. Michalis Papayannakis, "The Crisis in the Greek Left," in Howard R. Penniman, ed., *Greece at the Polls: The National Elections of 1974 and 1977* (Washington: American Enterprise Institute for Public Policy Research, 1981), p. 154.

28. From the archives of the Central Committee, KKE, 29 July 1974, quoted in Paraskeuopoulos, *Ho Karamanlis*, p. 33.

29. Pharakos, "Banner of Struggle and Victory," 31–35. See also Charilaos Florakis, "For Closer International Cooperation," *World Marxist Review* 22:3 (March 1979), pp. 72–75.

30. Charilaos Florakis, "Our Epoch and Lenin's Teaching on the New Type of Party," *World Marxist Review* 23:4 (April 1980), p. 12.

31. Quoted in Susannah Verney, "The Spring of the Greek Left: Two Party Congresses," *The Journal of Communist Studies* 3:4 (December 1987), p. 169.

32. Charilaos Florakis, "Turning Away From Dogmas, Forging a Closer Link With Reality," *World Marxist Review* 31:4 (April 1988), p. 8.

33. Grigorios Farakos, director of *Rizospastis*, quoted in Susannah Verney, "To Be or Not To Be Within the European Community: The Party Debate and Democratic Consolidation in Greece," in Geoffrey Pridham, ed., *Securing Democracy: Political Parties and Democratic Consolidation in Southern Europe* (London and New York: Routledge, 1990), p. 218.

34. *Rizospastis*, 8 December 1988.

35. Kostas Kappos, *He Epanastase pou Erchetai: Apantese sta Pseude tes Kyriarches Ideologias* (The Revolution which is Coming: An Answer to the Lies of the Dominant Ideology) (Athens: Gnoseis, 1991), pp. 67–68.

36. Kappos, *He Epanastase pou Erchetai*, p. 21.

37. See the Declaration of *Synaspismos* in *Rizospastis* and *Auge*, 8 December 1989.

38. Eighth Congress of the KKE (August 1961), reported in Dimitris Parsalidis, "The Communist Party of Greece in the Struggle for Democratic Change," *World Marxist Review* 5:1 (January, 1962), pp. 26–33; Kostas Koliyannis, "Leninism and the Experience of the Communist Party of Greece," pp. 48-53;and Zisis Zografos, "Some Lessons of the Civil War in Greece," *World Marxist Review* 7:11 (November 1964), pp. 43–50.

39. "The Communist Party of Greece in the Struggle for Democratic Change," p. 29.

40. Theodorakis, *Journal of Resistance*, p. 36.

41. Theodorakis, *Journal of Resistance*, p. 148.

42. Theodorakis, *Journal of Resistance*, pp. 67–68.

43. Demertzis, "Factionalism in the Greek Communist Party," p. 149.

44. Interview conducted in Athens, Greece, with a *Synaspismos* deputy on 4 and 6 May 1994.

45. Interview conducted in Athens, Greece, on 4 and 6 May 1994 with a former *Synaspismos* deputy.

46. "To Helleniko Kommounistiko Kinema," pp. 19, 20, 25.

47. "To Helleniko Kommounistiko Kinema," pp. 7–11.

48. Interview conducted in Athens, Greece, with a former *Synaspismos* deputy on 20 June 1994.

49. Interview conducted in Athens, Greece, on 4 June 1994 with a leading Eurocommunist deputy.

50. Letter sent by Panos Dimitriou to the Political Bureau of the Central Committee of the KKE on 1 March 1963, quoted in Panos Dimitriou, ed., *He Diaspasis tou KKE* (The Split of the KKE), 1 (Athens: n.p., n.d.), pp. 162–63.

51. Interview conducted in Athens, Greece, with a *Synaspismos* deputy on 4 and 6 May 1994.

52. "To Helleniko Kommounistiko Kinema," p. 7.

53. Quoted in Demertzis, "Factionalism in the Greek Communist Party," p. 199.

54. "To Helleniko Kommounistiko Kinema," pp. 9–10.

55. Interview in Athens, Greece, with a *Synaspismos* deputy on 4 and 6 May 1994.

56. "To Helleniko Kommounistiko Kinema," pp. 9–10.

57. Interview conducted in Athens, Greece, with a deputy of *Synaspismos* on 13 May 1994.

58. George Giannaris, *Mikis Theodorakis: Music and Social Change* (New York: Praeger Publishers, 1972), p. 195.

59. "Apo to 1967 os to 1974: Diktatoria, Antistase, Diamorfose tou KKE (esot.)" (From 1967 to 1974: Dictatorship, Resistance, Formation of the KKE [int.]), *Kommounistike Theoria kai Politike* (February–March 1976), p. 52.

60. *To Vema*, 4 March 1975.

61. *To Vema*, 4 March 1975.

62. Leonidas Kyrkos, "Poios—Poion? He Ethnike Antidiktatorike Enoteta; Axonas tes Politikes tou KKE-esot." (Who—whom? The National Antidictatorial Unity; the Axis of Politics of the KKE-int.), *Kommounistike Theoria kai Politike* 1 (March 1975), p. 6.

63. *Apogeumatine*, 6 September 1976.

64. Adam Przeworski, *Democracy and the Market: Political and Economic Reforms in Eastern Europe and Latin America* (Cambridge: Cambridge University Press, 1991), p. 31.

65. See *Anti*, 469 (28 June 1991), p. 24.

66. Kappos, *He Epanastase pou Erchetai*, p. 96.

67. Interview conducted in Athens, Greece, with a former EDA deputy on 30 November 1993.

68. Catharsis refers to the stated objective of this coalition government, namely, that it was formed to clean up public life following PASOK's alleged wrongdoing while in office.

69. Interview conducted in Athens, Greece, on 21 March 1994 with a deputy of PASOK.

70. Interview with Dimitris Caragoules in "The Strategy of Coalition: Greek Communists and Their Partners Say ..." *World Marxist Review* 32:10 (October 1989), p. 72.

71. Interview conducted in Athens, Greece, with deputy of KKE on 1 December 1993.

72. Interview with Leonidas Kyrkos in "The Strategy of Coalition," p. 71.

73. Quoted in *Pravda*, 25 June 1991.

74. Susannah Verney, "Between Coalition and One-Party Government: The Greek Elections of November 1989 and April 1990," *West European Politics* 13:4 (October 1990), p. 134.

75. Interview conducted in Athens, Greece, on 8 December 1993 with a former deputy of ND.

76. Anna Bosco and Carlos Gaspar, "Four Actors in Search of a Role: The South European Communist Parties," in P. Nikiforos Diamandouros and Richard Gunther, eds., *Politics in the New Southern Europe* (forthcoming).

77. Interview conducted in Athens, Greece, with a *Synaspismos* member on 20 June 1994.

78. Interview conducted in Athens, Greece, with a KKE deputy on 23 June 1994.

79. Interview conducted in Athens, Greece, with former KKE deputy on 31 May 1994.

80. Interview conducted in Athens, Greece, with a KKE Eurodeputy on 21 June 1994.

81. Kappos, *He Epanastase pou Erchetai*, p. 29.

82. See *Ta Nea*, 23 May 1996.

83. *Ta Nea*, 25 May 1996.

84. Interview conducted in Athens, Greece, with a former KKE deputy on 31 May 1994.

85. Interview conducted in Athens, Greece, with a *Synaspismos* deputy on 4 and 6 May 1994.

86. Interview conducted in Athens, Greece, with a former deputy of PASOK on 8 February 1994.

87. For example, from electoral support which averaged approximately 10 percent until the mid-1980s, the KKE dropped to only 4.5 percent in the 1993 general election, improved marginally to 5.6 percent in 1996, and garnered 5.5 percent of the vote in 2000.

88. The remaining proportion, 25.8 percent, did classify themselves as such.

89. See *Anti*, 469 (28 June 1991), p. 24.

90. Interview conducted in Athens, Greece, with a former KKE deputy on 6 June 1994.

91. Bosco and Gaspar, "Four Actors in Search of a Role."

92. Quoted in Nancy Bermeo, "Democracy and the Lessons of Dictatorship," *Comparative Politics* 24, 3 (April 1992), p. 277.

93. See Maurizio Cotta, "Unification and Democratic Consolidation in Italy: An Historical Overview," in John Higley and Richard Gunther, eds., *Elites and Democratic Consolidation in Latin America and Southern Europe* (Cambridge: Cambridge University Press, 1992); and Bermeo, "Democracy and the Lessons of Dictatorship," p. 278.

94. Leonardo Morlino, "Political Parties and Democratic Consolidation in Southern Europe," in Richard Gunther, P. Nikiforos Diamandouros and Hans-Jürgen Puhle, eds., *The Politics of Democratic Consolidation: Southern Europe in Comparative Perspective* (Baltimore: The Johns Hopkins University Press, 1995), p. 343.

95. See Bosco and Gaspar, "Four Actors in Search of a Role."

_____

CHAPTER 6

Taming the Green Guard: The Moderation of the Panhellenic Socialist Movement

In the formative period of Greece's transition to democracy, the emergence of the Panhellenic Socialist Movement (PASOK) did not appear to auger well for the new democracy. Fearing that the party might pose a serious deconsolidating threat to the regime, its institutions, and its rules of the game, many observers—both domestic and foreign—speculated on the uncertain prospects for regime instability and collapse. Some argued that PASOK's early condemnation of moderate social democratic policies, its demand for a new socialist constitution, and its promise of large-scale "socialization" and "an end to the exploitation of man by man,"[1] made it "realistic to assume that an attempt to realize the PASOK program would lead to intensified class struggles."[2] A former Dutch Ambassador to Athens feared, for example, that Andreas Papandreou would radically transform socioeconomic relations in Greece: "PASOK favours an almost total revolution of the political, economic and social structures. ... [It] aims at state socialism (really a kind of communism, at best of the Yugoslav type) and direct control by the people."[3] Others also speculated that significant change was in store: "Major uncertainty about the future of the system was generated by the prospect of a future electoral victory by a party pledged to rewrite the constitution and to destabilize Greece's global position by simultaneously claiming greater independence from the USA and blocking Greek entry to the EC."[4] Another observer hazarded the guess that Andreas Papandreou, the party's leader, was "determined to eventually lead Greece out of the Western camp in order to align [it] with the Third World, 'neutralist' bloc of nations."[5] Roy C. Macridis agreed: "[PASOK might take Greece] in the direction of socialism of a Third World kind, that is, a single party dictatorship."[6]

Within Greece as well, many political and military elites and some sections of the electorate seemed concerned by the prospect of a PASOK victory. For example, James Petras held that "important sections of the electorate continued to believe strongly that far-reaching socialist transformation would be forthcoming."[7]

On the right Constantine Karamanlis took to calling Papandreou and his PASOK "the left of the left," attempting to discredit the party by insinuating that it was more radical than the Greek communists. For their part the communists accused Papandreou of adventurism and irresponsibility, claiming that the preconditions for socialism were not yet ripe in Greece.[8]

The prospect of a Papandreou victory in 1981 was also perceived as a serious threat by military officers—so much so that the chiefs of the armed forces decided to resign when PASOK's victory was announced. This "creat[ed] uncertainty and [left] the way open for the military to intervene again in politics."[9] Even PASOK cadres feared that if the party won the 1981 elections, some "dark power" would prevent its accession to government. As a result, the left wing of the party believed that "if it insisted on enforcing its policies, it would be overthrown by a combination of military and allied opposition."[10] In short, there is little doubt that throughout the 1970s PASOK's rhetoric gave rise to serious concerns in many quarters about the possibility of its accession to power. Yet, despite PASOK's ideological and programmatic radicalism, the party did not hinder consolidation and the long-term stability of Greek democracy but, in fact, *contributed* to it. Over the short-term, the party quickly came to regard the regime, its constitution and rules of the game as legitimate and perfectly serviceable, abiding by those rules and playing within the confines of that system. Then, over the longer term, PASOK underwent dramatic change, significantly moderating its ideological and programmatic positions as well.

This chapter will attempt to explain PASOK's transformation. The logic of internal party building, for example, was a variable that contributed to this change. As the prospect for electoral success appeared over the horizon, Papandreou took an active part in ridding his party of radical militant activists and replacing them with parliamentarians capable of leading the party to electoral victory and eventually into government. As with *Nea Demokratia* and the communist parties, however, the motivations behind PASOK's convergence were not simply electoral, as the classic formulation of the convergence model would imply. Instead, like the other elites considered in this study, Papandreou engaged in a variety of games, only one of which was vote maximization. As this chapter will illustrate, a number of other factors also came into play. A second factor—one external to the party—also contributed to PASOK's convergence. The pressures of government as well Greece's membership in the European Union and its strategic location in the Eastern Aegean appear to have constrained PASOK, thereby facilitating its moderation.

This analysis of PASOK's convergence also emphasizes that a rhetorically antisystem stance does not always translate into explicit antisystem action and democratic instability. In the case of PASOK, the party's early radical rhetoric—due largely to the nature of Greek political culture, to electoral motivations, as well as to the early, more dogmatic composition of party activists—actually appears to have *contributed* to democratic consolidation and stability. As Nikiforos Diamandouros argues, it did so by attracting the support of dissatisfied and disaffected antiestablishment voters, allowing them to vent the pent-up frustrations of several decades of partisan discrimination.[11] PASOK's popular and charismatic leader, Andreas Papandreou, thus "empowered" these people, giving them a voice seemingly imbued with political strength, vigor, and authority. As PASOK toned down its radical positions and rhetoric, however, so did its electorate. By the mid-1980s PASOK and its supporters had become fully coopted into the new democratic regime—thereby securing and reinforcing the legitimacy of Greek democracy.

THE EMERGENCE OF THE "GREEN SUN"

In 1974 PASOK emerged in Greek politics with the motto "National Independence—Popular Sovereignty—Social Liberation." In many ways PASOK appeared as a radical, antisystem party, questioning the legitimacy of the post-1974 democratic regime, its rules of the game, and its international commitments. Drawing from neo-Marxist dependency theory,[12] Andreas Papandreou argued that: "Capitalism is in deep crisis not because it is blocked from development but because of the self-destruction caused by its dynamism. On a global scale, capitalism has to be held responsible for the more nefarious ills of mankind."[13] According to Papandreou Greece was an economically underdeveloped, politically subordinate, and dependent semiperipheral nation trapped in a metropole-satellite relationship. It had suffered exploitation and domination at the hands of the imperialist countries that had been its supposed "protectors" throughout the twentieth century. Moreover, a few economically privileged Greeks had undermined national interests by allying themselves with foreign compradore capital and exploiting the nonprivileged Greek majority.[14] Adopting the slogan, "Greece belongs to the Greeks," Papandreou called for a break with such "imperialism," arguing that this was the only way to achieve economic development and a healthy democratic regime:

Our national independence is inseparably bound to popular sovereignty. ... But it is simultaneously intertwined with the extrication of our economy from control by foreign monopolistic and domestic capital. ... And of course Greece must withdraw not only from its military alliance with NATO, but from its political alliance. And all bilateral agreements which have allowed the Pentagon to turn Greece into an outpost for its expansionist policies must be nullified. But behind NATO, behind the American bases are the multinational monopolies and their domestic agents.[15]

Given that "national liberation" was seen as a fundamental precondition for socialist transformation, PASOK opposed Greek membership in the European Economic Community. The EC was seen by Papandreou as a "club of the multinational monopolies," and Greece's accession to the Community served only to institutionalize the country's dependent status. As a result, PASOK denounced Greece's entry into the EC and called for complete withdrawal from it, arguing that it was a "counterpart to NATO," and an "impediment to an independent national economic policy."[16] PASOK also pledged the withdrawal of Greece from NATO and opposed the continued existence of U.S. bases in Greece with the very popular and effective slogan, "'Out' to the American bases of death!"

PASOK also pursued what it labelled the "third road" to socialism, rejecting both the "paternalistic, state socialism" of the Eastern bloc as well as West European social democracy, arguing that social democracy was simply "the human face of capitalism." Thus, the Socialist International was dismissed by PASOK as promoting the interests of contemporary monopoly capitalism. According to Papandreou the piecemeal reform efforts of West European social democrats had only prolonged the life of the bourgeois system rather than "radically chang[ing] it."[17] "Creeping socialism," he argued, never leads to change; instead, it allows "gradual unconnected and neutralised reforms [to be] absorbed by and integrated into the system."[18] Such gradual reforms, argued Papandreou, were not steps *toward* socialism, but measures of "staving it off."[19] In contrast, PASOK advocated that the "social relations of production must change fundamentally."[20] To this end, Papandreou openly declared to party cadres in 1977 that PASOK was a Marxist movement: "Are we Marxists, yes or no? We have no reason to leave these questions hanging. If by 'Marxist' we mean the historic method of analysis bequeathed to us by Marx, which speaks of class struggle, of the power structure, of evolutionary dialectics—if this is what we mean, then as a socialist movement we must say yes."[21]

Moreover, unlike European social democratic parties that accept the contractual origin of the state,[22] Andreas Papandreou and his PASOK party openly rejected both the contractual basis of authority inherent in the constitution and the concept of a neutral state, openly embracing the Leninist conception of the state as an instrument in the hands of a ruling class. Based on this view Papandreou argued that both national liberation and national sovereignty could only be achieved once the majority—"the underprivileged"—become part of the governing process.[23] According to PASOK *laokratia*—or direct popular government—together with decentralization would amount to direct self-government at the local, municipal, and regional levels, as well as at the firm, factory, and in the public sector. PASOK exemplified its position on this matter in the slogan, "PASOK in government, the people in power." To this end Papandreou argued that in moving toward socialism, Greece was following in Yugoslavia's footsteps.[24] As one scholar argued, "By its adoption of mass participation PASOK, in the manner of East European parties, ... affirmed the idea that it possesse[d] a 'natural' right to be the leading force in society."[25]

As far as specific economic and social policies were concerned, PASOK went so far as to advocate socioeconomic reforms that even the Greek communists were not ready to endorse.[26] Papandreou himself announced that, "Our programme ... goes further than that of the Communist Party."[27] Economically, the most important pledge, "socialization" of the means of production (distinct from nationalization) meant that representatives of central, regional, and local government would participate alongside employees in the management of the socialized industry. A number of industries—including banks, insurance companies, mass transport and the telecommunication companies, public utilities, the large mining companies, as well as those industries in the production of steel, cement, fertilizer, drugs, and national defense[28]—were to be socialized.

More importantly, PASOK went beyond radical public policy commitments and also took a markedly antisystem stance *vis-à-vis* the institutions and rules of the new regime. Initially, seeing the fall of the colonels' dictatorship as nothing more than "a change of the NATO guard in Athens," Andreas Papandreou declared that PASOK was not a political party operating within a democratic regime, but a national liberation movement struggling to free Greece from imperialist control. Important party cadres openly declared that PASOK's attitude *vis-à-vis* the newly founded regime was one of "structural opposition."[29]

It is within this logic of "structural opposition" to the regime, its rules, and its institutions that PASOK's openly hostile position during the entire constitutional engineering process should be viewed. Specifically, Papandreou not only renounced the 1975 constitution as "totalitarian," but he and his party walked out of parliament, taking with them the entire opposition. Even as late as 1979, Papandreou verbally challenged the legitimacy of that constitution, arguing that constitutions reflect class relations and economic interests and therefore must never be viewed as beyond the reach of socialist parties. Any attempt to change them, he argued, is legitimate: "In our country today there is a constitution which defines the institutions with capitalist socialist structures in mind. It is however, natural, that when PASOK comes to power [it will] push for a revision of constitutional provisions, so as to secure new foundations, which will facilitate the socialist transformation of society."[30]

Finally, PASOK also laid claim to the ideological heritage of the National Liberation Front (EAM)—the chief organization of resistance in World War II. Speaking only a few days prior to the 1981 elections, Papandreou promised that his generation would live up to the dream of the National Resistance without making the mistakes its leaders had made forty years earlier—failing to state, however, what those mistakes were.[31] Not only did Papandreou consider the EAM resistance, led by the Greek Communist Party, as "heroic," but that it was "also ... the 'sole instance' in modern Greek history that national sovereignty was achieved in its true form."[32] Dimitri Kitsikis argues that even the rising green sun of PASOK was reminiscent of the sun and the green of EPON, EAM's youth organization.[33] Moreover, the party's passionate speeches advocating "social justice" and "national independence," and its calls of "putting an end to the exploitation of man by man" revived strong memories of the resistance and made PASOK appear more radical in 1974 than any other political party. As a sign of respect and admiration for EAM, Papandreou, once elected to government, granted advisory positions in a number of key ministries to returning communist exiles, including the commander-in-chief of ELAS, Markos Vafiades.

THE CONVERGENCE OF PASOK

Despite such radical ideological and programmatic positions, however, once in power, PASOK did not threaten the established regime, its rules of the game, or its institutions, and democracy became stable and consolidated. A perceptible moderation of some of PASOK's most maximalist positions was evident as early as during the run-up to the 1977 elections. This moderation became even more pronounced during the extended 1981 election campaign. As Richard Clogg argues:

Not only was PASOK's ... previous insistence that it was a class-based Marxist party glossed over, but even the prospect of socialism was de-emphasized. Instead, in accordance with the strategy of "National Popular Unity" adopted by the Central Committee of PASOK in 1978, Papandreou went out of his way to offer re-assurance to the "average" Greek, with a house, a shop and a car, that he had nothing to fear from a PASOK victory.[34]

Eventually abandoning all references to specific socioeconomic classes, PASOK judiciously substituted these references with the vague and all-encompassing terminology of "privileged" versus "nonprivileged" Greeks. According to PASOK's formulation, "nonprivileged" Greeks were virtually all Greek citizens while the "privileged" constituted a very small group of families that supposedly were the financial and economic elite of the country. By pitting, in true populist style, the "nonprivileged" majority against the "privileged" minority, Papandreou was able to muster the support of a wide swathe of voters from across nearly the entire political spectrum.

After 1977 PASOK also abandoned its demand for a "socialist" constitution. In the run-up to the 1981 elections, Papandreou repeatedly emphasized "that PASOK, as a potential government party, [would] remain democratically accountable both to the people and to Parliament—that it [would] act not as a revolutionary movement but as a party that expect[ed] to move in and out of power."[35] The party's neutralist, Third World socialist stance was also abandoned and PASOK began to increase its contacts with West European socialist and social democratic parties. Over time, even the word "socialism" appeared less and less frequently until it was dropped from the party's discourse altogether. In its place emerged the rather ambiguous slogan, "*Allage*," or "Change." Moreover, by April 1981, in an effort to deemphasize its earlier calls for the socialization of the means of production, Papandreou declared that "the only thing endangered by the rise of PASOK [was] the right's monopoly of power."[36] Even the legitimacy of the 1975 constitution—which Papandreou had initially negated—was never called into question during the electoral campaign of 1981. Instead, one of the first statements made by Papandreou after PASOK's electoral victory was that "one of the principal lessons of the [electoral] contest was that Greece's *democratic institutions* had truly functioned."[37]

A similar moderation was perceptible in PASOK's foreign policy positions. As the 1981 elections approached, Papandreou asserted that PASOK had a constitutional duty to respect all of Greece's international commitments. On 10 November 1980, in a speech to the PASOK rank and file, Papandreou indicated that should Greece gain better terms for its participation in the EC and NATO, the party would agree to continued participation in both groups. Thus, although its electoral manifesto still pledged withdrawal from NATO and the removal of the

U.S. military bases, the party—playing on the Turkish threat—increasingly used the excuse that "PASOK would never allow the capability of the armed forces to be undermined,"[38] thereby admitting that "such installations [could not] be removed instantly."[39] Once in power the PASOK government participated in bilateral negotiations with the United States, eventually leading to the signing of a new five-year base agreement in the summer of 1983. At the time it declared that with the expiration of this agreement in 1988, U.S. bases would be completely removed from Greek soil. Soon, however, Papandreou indicated a willingness to extend the life of the bases past the 1988 deadline. To this end he began a new round of negotiations in the autumn of 1985, announcing to parliament that "if the price is right" he would allow the bases to remain.[40] He promised that once the new agreement was concluded it would be submitted to the electorate in a referendum for approval. No such referendum was ever called.

PASOK's promise to withdraw Greece from NATO was also broken. Initially, the party modified its original position for *immediate* withdrawal by arguing that it now viewed the issue in the context of the dissolution of *all* military blocs. Thus, withdrawal was seen only as a long-term, strategic objective. Over time, however, even this position was modified. PASOK soon argued that continued participation in NATO was critical given Turkey's membership in the alliance. According to Papandreou, "the two members of NATO [Greece and Turkey] [could] possibly collide in war and … the collision would be rendered inevitable if Greece were to withdraw from NATO."[41] Thus, withdrawal was never pursued seriously.

Not surprisingly, PASOK's promise to pull Greece out of the European Community was also abandoned. By late 1980 and early 1981, Papandreou began to hint that a shift was occurring in Western Europe—a shift that he claimed made the EC more politically independent from the United States. Soon, Papandreou tempered his demands for immediate and complete withdrawal to calling for "a special relationship *outside* the EC," to then demanding a "special relationship *inside* the EC," to eventually promising that a referendum would be held on the issue should PASOK be elected to government. Soon, even this was qualified. Papandreou argued that until a referendum could be held, the country would participate in the Community in order to mitigate the negative economic effects of Greece's membership. Several weeks after the 1981 elections, however, the call for a referendum was quietly dropped as Papandreou divulged to *Le Monde* that "Greece did not want to break its ties with Europe since it [was], 'above all,' European."[42] This statement paved the way for what was to follow.

Only months after PASOK's accession to power on 23 March 1982, the government submitted a memorandum to the European Commission describing the "peculiarities" and "structural malformations" of the Greek economy, enumerating the problems that membership would pose to Greece, and suggesting solutions to those problems, including increased Community financial support and permission for temporary derogations from EC rules. Thus, not only did PASOK *not* withdraw Greece from the EC, but it actually pushed Greece to become a more aggressive and actively involved member, pursuing as a primary objective the convergence of the developed North European economies with those of the less developed South

European ones and calling for a more effective regional policy to bring this about.[43] In a speech to the socialist group of the European Parliament on 8 September 1982, Papandreou explained:

PASOK had always held the view that full Greek membership in the Community would negatively affect the economic development of the country. This position has not changed. Today, however, we are members of the community and we are examining in good faith, with good intentions, within the Community, the possibilities for the establishment of a special arrangement—a special relationship—that would allay the negative consequences of the accession of a developing country into a Community of developed countries.[44]

In sum, as with the other foreign policy issue areas—membership in NATO and the maintenance of U.S. bases on Greek soil—PASOK moderated its position *vis-à-vis* the European Community as well. Thus, Greek membership in the Community was never endangered by the party.

EXPLAINING PASOK'S CONVERGENCE

In the course of interviews with political elites, a number of explanations for PASOK's transformation were offered. Some respondents argued that the logic of party-building moderated PASOK. They maintained that the way to government required purging the party of its most radical party cadres. As Papandreou realized this and began to purge the extremists from the party, PASOK became a moderate, pragmatic party. Other respondents argued that in the radicalized post-junta climate, PASOK's early rhetoric was simply a vote-getting tactic. Still others blamed a fundamentally antagonistic Greek political culture for PASOK's early radicalism. They argued that the combination of an acidic political culture and PASOK's electoral motivations were responsible for the seemingly semiloyal and even antisystem position adopted by PASOK in the formative period of the transition. They maintained that the party never intended to carry its radical policies to fruition. In this view both the party's initial radicalism and its subsequent moderation were electorally motivated and geared toward vote maximization.

Yet other respondents maintained that the early rhetoric was sincere and that PASOK was forced to moderate its ideology and program by international and domestic factors as well as by the constraints of being a party of government. In this section, I will argue that no one variable can fully account for PASOK's transformation. Instead, the most complete explanation for PASOK's convergence and moderation must incorporate all of these factors.

First there is Greek political culture and its impact on the nature of political competition in Greece. The style of political competition there is legendary for being extremely confrontational. One scholar asserts that "the struggle for power continues to be waged as an all-out war."[45] Debates in parliament take place within an extremely polarized bipolar atmosphere of competition in which rational political debate succumbs to simplistic, highly partisan attacks. In fact, by the 1980s a distinct parliamentary culture existed in which "a kind of silent consensus seemed increasingly to prevail between the two larger parties on the *nonconsensual* way in which the parliamentary game should be played."[46] Consider the constitutional engineering process of late 1974 and early 1975. Put simply, the debates on the constitution were extremely acrimonious and conflictual. Opposition parties, and especially Papandreou's PASOK, protested vehemently against the power accorded to the executive,[47] the inability of the opposition parties to have any real influence over the content of the constitution, as well as the so-called "superpowers" of the president. During this time interparty relations were extremely conflictual as highly charged debates between the government and opposition invoked populist rhetoric and impassioned exchanges.[48] George Mavros, the leader of the opposition, called the constitution "reactionary," while Andreas Papandreou declared that it was "totalitarian"[49] and "no better than the constitution of dictator Papadopoulos."[50] Eventually, tensions became so strained that when, on 21 May 1975, the government refused to revise an article in the draft constitution concerning the election of the president, the entire opposition stormed out of parliament and withdrew permanently from the remaining debates on the constitution. As a result, only *Nea Demokratia* deputies participated in the remaining sessions and they were the only deputies who voted to ratify the finished product in 1975.

To many observing the actions and rhetoric of the opposition during this crucial period of the transition, the constitutional engineering process appeared to have triggered a return to the old-style politics of the precoup period. Naturally, this raised many questions about the prospects for democratic consolidation. The opposition, in both its actions and rhetoric, indicated that it disapproved of the new regime's constitution, its rules of the game,[51] and its institutions.[52] As a result, many observers began to question the extent to which the new regime would be capable of withstanding such assaults to its very legitimacy. And, yet, democratic consolidation was apparently not hindered by the adversarial, highly partisan nature of those parliamentary discussions. Once ratified, both the spirit and letter of the constitution were fully observed by all parties—opposition and government alike. Even PASOK, whose leader had earlier claimed that if elected to power his party would "dissolve Parliament and call for the election of a constituent assembly to produce a constitution based on the people's sovereignty,"[53] fully respected the constitution during its tenure in government.

Contrary to expectations that this period of parliamentary life—a period in which, by many accounts, Karamanlis dominated decision-making, "rammed" the constitution through parliament, and was viewed by the opposition as "antidemocratic" and "authoritarian"—would be viewed negatively by opposition deputies, interviews with deputies of *all* parties indicate the opposite. Incredibly, nearly every deputy interviewed asserted that the early transition period—including the constitutional engineering process—was one of the "finest" periods of Greek democratic political life. As a former Center Union deputy who later joined PASOK argued:

Because I was a member of parliament in 1974 and experienced the period, I must say that that period of constitutional assemblies was one of the most ... brilliant periods of Greek parliamentary life. ... Despite the restrictions, rules of parliament, etc., many things were discussed. The opposition was able to carry out its criticism; it was able to pass certain things. ... The discussions were very congenial and interesting. ... I believe that the parliament of 1974 will be recorded as one of the best periods of parliamentary life in our country.[54]

More importantly, when deputies of PASOK were asked whether the opposition's antagonistic position and its abstention from the vote on the constitution were indicative of a lack of loyalty to the new constitution, they consistently and repeatedly argued that PASOK *was* loyal to the constitution promulgated in 1975, despite the party's seemingly antisystem stance. For example, when a deputy of PASOK was asked about the party's loyalty to the constitution, he answered, "We did not vote for [the constitution] but we supported it. ... [U]nder no circumstances did PASOK think of doubting the regime; it supported it back then."[55] Another PASOK deputy argued: "We accepted the constitution in 1975. We all recognized it. ... All of us accepted that constitution. That is why we call[ed] the constitution of 1975—with its 1985 revisions—the most democratic constitution our country has ever known."[56] Yet another deputy of the party adds that PASOK's abstention "did not manifest [a lack of loyalty]. It was probably a political act. ... It was as if someone was saying to Karamanlis and the others, 'Don't think that we are legalizing you. We are maintaining our reservations.'"[57]

If, as these interviews indicate, the opposition's fierce criticism and its abstention of the constitution did not constitute a lack of loyalty, it would appear that its emotional rhetoric as well as its apparently semiloyal stance suggest a feature of Greek political culture that has not been explicitly and systematically examined in the literature. Interviews conducted with deputies of all political parties indicate that the opposition's position on the constitution was at most a partisan political tactic. For example, when a deputy of ND is asked why the opposition behaved as it did, he answers: "The differences were clearly of a political character. ... They were clearly of the type, 'Since you say so and so, I will not accept it. If I accept it, then who will vote for me?' These were the considerations. Unfortunately, in Greece the first consideration in everything is the political cost."[58] Another ND deputy adds, "[W]e reached the point that whatever the government proposed, the opposition rejected!"[59]

Deputies of the center also agreed with this assessment. One leading centrist deputy argued: "When I am in opposition I cannot vote for that which the government is proposing—especially on such an important issue. ... Voting against the constitution did not mean voting against [its] substance. In substance just about everyone was in agreement."[60] Another centrist corroborated this argument: "When [the constitution] came to the floor to be voted on, I remember that we all voted against it. But this is always ... the stance of the opposition. 'Yes,' says the government. 'No,' says the opposition. Very rarely do they agree."[61] A member of EDA also indicated that the opposition's position on the constitution was driven by partisanship rather than substantive disagreement:

In Greece the opposition thinks it has the duty, regardless of whether it is *Nea Demokratia*, whether it is PASOK, whether it is the left—it thinks it has the duty that if the government says, "A," the opposition must say everything except for "A." It is a defect and a lack of maturity in political thought. ... PASOK's and the left's reason for not voting for the constitution [was that] ... oppositional tactics prevailed. ... Mavros [also walked out of parliament and abstained from the vote] for clearly oppositional reasons. ... To answer your question why the opposition did what it did in 1975, I must say that it [sprung] from the opposition's disposition not to agree.[62]

A PASOK deputy concurs: "All of that [radical rhetoric] ... [was] the practice of politics—especially of the left—to appear maximalist. This [was] more an issue of tactics than of political strategy."[63] In sum, the antagonistic nature of the parliamentary discussions in the early period of the transition was primarily a function of Greek political culture—a political culture that, despite its rancor, is highly prodemocratic. By the opposition's own account, such rhetoric and behavior did not signal a genuine lack of loyalty either to the 1975 constitution or to the newly established regime. The Greek case highlights the fact that partisan rancor and democracy can indeed coexist.

In addition to viewing PASOK's early rhetoric in the light of Greek political culture, deputies of all political parties have also maintained that the party's early discourse should be seen in the light of the radicalized post-junta climate. A relative swing to the left—noticeable in *all* parties—had occurred during the dictatorship. As already indicated in chapter 4, *Nea Demokratia* was no exception, as Constantine Karamanlis himself, following a near-consensus in Greek public opinion, decided to withdraw Greece from the military wing of NATO. However, it was Andreas Papandreou who, in 1974, appeared as the most articulate exponent of the radicalized climate, advocating Greek "independence," an end to American "interference" in Greek affairs, and the adoption of a foreign policy orientation that would supposedly no longer subject Greek national interests to foreign (NATO and U.S.) ones. Thus, much of PASOK's early rhetoric was perfectly in tune with popular perceptions, desires, and demands.

Specifically, most Greeks resented what they perceived as a long history of manipulation by external forces and powers. Greeks of all political and ideological persuasions were openly hostile to the United States, believing it to have been a willing supporter of the 1967 *coup d'état*, the colonels' attempted coup in Cyprus, and the partition of the island following the Turkish invasion. Greeks also questioned the worth of membership in the NATO alliance. In their view NATO had done nothing to assist Greeks in their efforts to overthrow the colonels' repressive military dictatorship. It had also allowed Turkey—another NATO member—to occupy the northern half of Cyprus. Thus, in the eyes of most Greeks, both the United States and NATO were seriously suspect. A number of surveys conducted during the transition indicated widespread criticism of both. Even as late as 1982, a Eurobarometer opinion poll showed that 87 percent of all Greeks still had little or no confidence in the United States.[64]

Within this climate of anti-American and anti-NATO feelings, Andreas Papandreou's outspoken accusations against the alliance, the United States, and other Western powers struck a nationalist chord in most Greeks. As a founding member of PASOK argued:

I don't know if Andreas believed or did not believe what he said [in 1974]. However, Andreas took what the people would have said to you if you entered a cafe [and repeated it]. What were the people saying? "Foreigners are controlling us. ... Who can possibly take on capital? It is powerful and, unfortunately, we cannot take it on" Andreas took these two things people were saying ... [and he developed] a sermon against foreigners. ... Thus, a leader came who said, "Follow me and I will take on capital."... And the people said, "Let's follow him; he will liberate us from foreigners and from the three hundred families that rule [Greece]"—because this is what we were telling them back then.[65]

A prominent PASOK deputy corroborates these views: "[By] using those slogans of democratization, of economic reform, ... of social advancement, justice, democracy, ... we were taking positions which corresponded with the spirit of the times. ... [W]e took on all of the slogans and problems of the Greek people."[66] A revisionist deputy of the Communist Party described the situation in the following way: "Truly, Papandreou [came] out onto the balcony to get rid of this and get rid of that and that. This is what the people desir[ed]. At that moment, the politician [was] expressing the unconscious and conscious desires of a people—as the people themselves were doing. ... Papandreou himself [was] deceiving the people, but the people themselves [were] prepared to be deceived."[67]

In sum, in the early stages of the transition to democracy, Papandreou articulated the sentiments and desires of the average Greek citizen. As Angelos Elephantis points out:

PASOK's main ideological themes were not invented by Andreas Papandreou. They [were] the offspring of contemporary Greek society, of its political adventures, and to a certain extent they reflect[ed] the actual demands of the popular strata. Papandreou [did] not exert his influence in a vacuum. There [was] something like a predisposition in the air, a feeling ready to be given shape. Andreas captur[ed] this element, and from the height of his campaign rostrum he return[ed] it to the crowd, almost unchanged in its essence but endowed with a political dimension.[68]

In short, PASOK's radical rhetoric while in opposition reflected a broad, albeit vague, public consensus: "Papandreou would never have been elected ... if the central, catalytic message of his political program ... did not strike a profound chord in the emotional core of most Greeks, all the way from the right to the left."[69] Thus, in the early period of the transition, PASOK's anti-American, anti-NATO, anti-EC rhetoric was, paradoxically enough, *consensual*.

Taking the electorate's post-1974 radicalism into consideration, deputies of all political parties contended that much of PASOK's early rhetoric was primarily motivated by a desire to attract electoral support. According to two ND deputies, "[Papandreou] said what the people wanted to hear so that they would vote for him. [PASOK's radicalism] was simply an electoral tactic to get the support of the left."[70] When asked why PASOK was so radical during the transition to democracy, a PASOK deputy argued: "[M]any times parties and leaders say things that cannot occur and things occur that cannot be said. In our life, we politicians always try to exploit moments."[71] Finally, a former PASOK deputy put it like this: "[Papandreou] act[ed] on what he believ[ed] and not on the words [he spoke]. Words [were] something else. ... Words [were] to enthuse."[72] In short, Papandreou never truly challenged the legitimacy of the regime, its institutions, and rules of the game but, instead, took radical positions in order to exploit mass feelings of discontent and translate them into enthusiasm and electoral support for PASOK.

Offering credence to such arguments were the clear inconsistencies between the party's rhetoric and behavior throughout the 1970s and 1980s, as Papandreou said "one thing to one group and another thing to another group."[73] In fact, it was not at all uncommon for Papandreou to engage in radical rhetoric on the one hand, but behave moderately and pragmatically on the other. A number of illustrative examples can be given concerning both foreign policy and domestic issues.

In January 1978 PASOK actually voted in favor of the second financial protocol under the Greek-EC Association Agreement, even while publicly opposing the EC and calling for Greece's withdrawal. A founding deputy of PASOK argued that even though Papandreou had decided by the late 1970s that Greece would not withdraw from the European Community, he continued to pledge withdrawal to the electorate: "We did not go out to bravely say that [withdrawal from the EC] was unrealizable. ... We did not have the manliness to say, 'We were mistaken,' or, 'We can't do it and that's that.' ... Many people were waiting for us to pull out of the EC. ... While it was not in Andreas' head for us to pull out, he would not go out and say however, 'We have made a mistake!' He would not say it. ... [H]e believed [it would cost him votes]."[74] All the while, PASOK continued to attack *Nea Demokratia* for its allegedly antidemocratic behavior, arguing that Karamanlis ought to have held a referendum on the issue,[75] and promising to call a referendum on Community membership should PASOK be elected to government. Given the fact that under the 1975 constitution only the president of the republic had the ability to call for a referendum, it would appear that Papandreou was cynically raising the hopes of many Greeks. By then Karamanlis was President and, as the architect of Greece's membership in the Community, it was highly unlikely that he would agree to hold this referendum. In fact, even raising the issue would have likely provoked a serious political crisis.

This notwithstanding, by the 1981 election campaign, PASOK still argued that it was committed to minimizing the negative effects of membership in the Community until a referendum could be called. By stating that the referendum would allow the electorate to choose between "full membership" or a "special agreement," PASOK's original promise for "withdrawal" was dropped. Following the elections it soon became clear that PASOK had no intention of reversing Greece's accession to the EC. In fact, only one week after emerging victorious from those elections, PASOK ministers made a statement to the first EC Council of Ministers in which they expressed Greece's long-term interests within the community framework.[76]

Similar tactical considerations also appear to have played an important part in PASOK's actions and rhetoric *vis-à-vis* the U.S. bases. On 1 July 1983, two weeks prior to signing a new agreement extending the life of the U.S. bases in Greece, Papandreou declared: "For us, the idea of having foreign bases on our soil is unacceptable."[77] Yet, negotiations followed in which the government energetically pursued concessions from the U.S. government, which would, among other things, increase military and economic assistance to Greece and provide guarantees against possible Turkish aggression in exchange for maintaining the bases.

Following the signing of an agreement, great controversy ensued over the specified termination date of the bases. According to the English version of that agreement, which stated that "this agreement is *terminable* after five years," no iron-clad guarantee was given that the bases in fact be gone after the 1988 termination date. In the Greek translation of this contract, however, the word "terminable" (implying the possibility of termination) was replaced by the term "*terminating*" (suggesting definite termination). Moreover, in an apparently deceptive move, Papandreou publicly presented the agreement as "a termination of Greek dependence." Speaking to PASOK's central committee, Papandreou argued that his government had signed a "historic agreement for the removal of the United States' bases from Greece."[78] As one prominent Center Union deputy indicated in an interview, there was a lot of doublespeak during that time: "At one point ... [Papandreou] agreed that the bases would remain. ... Nothing changed. However, the slogans which came out on the streets and in PASOK's newspapers were, 'The Bases Have Left! The Struggle Has Been Justified!'"[79]

Such inconsistencies also spilled over into economic issues. In February 1984 Papandreou attacked the international banking system as well as the monetarist policies of the Reagan administration, calling them the "social and economic counter-revolution of the ruling capitalist class." Assuring PASOK cadres that capitalism had outlived any positive contributions it may have been capable of offering, Papandreou maintained that it was "now looming as a destructive force within the framework of a forthcoming nuclear war." On the same day in New York, however, his Minister of National Economy was meeting with American business executives and bankers "to ascertain whether there was an interest in investments in Greece" and enthusiastically explaining to them that American investments were especially welcome.[80]

In sum, many deputies have argued that PASOK's radical rhetoric during the formative period of the transition was an electoral tactic designed to appeal to an electorate that had itself been radicalized by seven years of dictatorial rule. The party's rhetorical and behavioral inconsistencies throughout the 1970s and 1980s also appear to indicate that tactical considerations were at play. While engaging in radical rhetoric when speaking to party cadres and, in decreasingly frequency, to the electorate, PASOK was in fact pursuing a much more moderate and pragmatic course of action.

With the passing of time, the initial post-junta radicalism of the electorate began to cool. It became increasingly clear that socialism was not only not imminent but that it was also not desired by most Greeks. As a founding member of PASOK argued in an interview: "[T]he slogan, 'On the Eighteenth Socialism,'[81] really frightened voters. Socialism frightened people ... and people did not want socialism at all."[82]   Moreover, by 1981, the majority of Greeks (61.1% of respondents in one survey[83]) had come to believe that Greece ought to remain in NATO despite the alliance's inaction during the Turkish invasion of Cyprus. Even the EC began to be appreciated as the economic benefits of membership became clear. A Eurobarometer Survey, conducted at the time of the 1981 elections, indicated that there was now widespread support for the Community. Specifically, support for "efforts being made to unify Western Europe" had increased significantly, and Greeks' opinions of "their country's relations with the rest of Western Europe" were also very positive—more so than other EC member states. Similarly, Greeks' assessment of "'the understanding between the countries of the European Community' over the preceding twelve months" was the most positive among all member states. Greeks considered membership in the Community a good thing rather than a bad thing by a margin of two to one.[84]

Some deputies argued that largely as a result of these changed attitudes, Papandreou decided that the party should drop many of its extremist domestic and foreign policy pronouncements. Moreover, since much of PASOK's early radical rhetoric was almost certainly electoral in nature, deputies contended that it was conveniently dropped by Papandreou when it was no longer an electoral asset. As one study argues, as soon as PASOK achieved the status of formal opposition in 1977, its main goal became the attraction of former supporters of the decimated center, who were generally more conservative than most PASOK supporters.[85] In short, just as electoral considerations contributed to PASOK's initial radical positions, as time passed similar considerations appear to have led to the party's moderation. A former ND deputy argued, for example, that "[PASOK] softened [its position] so as not to scare a large portion of the center and therefore to reach government."[86]   Likewise, a PASOK deputy argued that "[Papandreou] slowly began to soften all [his radical positions] because the people did not want it—not even our own followers."[87] When another PASOK deputy was asked why the party moderated its positions and rhetoric, he, too, answered: "[The party moderated] in order to win government. It is very simple. With this, essentially, all of the centrist voters voted for it. And with this it got 48 percent of the vote. How else would it have gotten it? ... [I]t had to adopt more moderate positions, or it would have remained in opposition."[88]

Furthermore, as time passed and electoral considerations began to be accorded the utmost priority by the party leadership, the tendency toward moderation was reinforced by the need to build an electorally viable, professional party organization. The early composition of the party was militant. Members of Papandreou's Panhellenic Resistance Organization (PAK) composed the largest group in the party's central committee during 1974–75, its members played a predominant role in the party's creation, and their ideas and policies characterized the party's founding "Third of September Declaration." A founding member of the party described its early complexion as radical, largely composed of antidictatorship extremists: "[A]ll of those ideologically charged young people ... Trotskyites, Leninists, arch-Marxists, and certain other homeless leftists ... [who] had come from different countries ... with pictures of Marx and Lenin on their lapels, with hammers and sickles and other Marxist emblems"[89] originally had a major ideological influence on the party. As Michalis Spourdalakis argues, it was a small group of PAK activists, representing radicalized, politically progressive white-collar workers, who initiated discussions and formulated PASOK's radical program in 1974. Thus, the new party was left with the imprint of an original PAK program developed abroad during the years of dictatorial rule.[90] As a former PASOK deputy argued: "It appears that Andreas ... was influenced by certain leftist characters which he had brought with him [from abroad]. ... In the beginning, he too ... was very leftist."[91] A former centrist deputy also argued that "[Papandreou] escalated the anti-American campaign ... to satisfy his own small group that he started with—to satisfy the hard-liners."[92]

In addition to PAK activists, two other groups were also involved in PASOK's early discussions—radical student activists (many of whom had participated in the Polytechnic uprising and had contributed to the radical formulations in the party's original platform) and a group of former Center Union parliamentarians (who were well-versed in the art of electoral competition as well as the practice of patron-clientelism). As Nikiforos Diamandouros argues, however, in the early stages of the party's formation, the third group was less influential. Instead, the inner maximalist wing of the socialist movement attempted to build "a powerful, radical party capable of retaining its ideological cohesion and dynamism and serving as the central instrument for socialist transformation."[93] The parliamentarians quickly grew to object to the radicalism of the PAK and student activists. Despite their opposition, however, the "The Third of September Declaration" was distinctly similar to PAK's program, calling for national liberation and a socialist transformation of society. Thus, radical slogans such as "Down with Exploitation," "Get Foreign Capital Out," "Workers, Peasants and Students," "Forward to Build Socialism," "The Capitalist State Exploits You," and "Socialism on the 18th"[94] were characteristic of PASOK's early rhetoric.

As time passed and electoral victory appeared to be a real possibility, Papandreou appears to have realized that the way to electoral success was to cleanse the party of its extremist Trotskyist tendencies and to strengthen the more moderate parliamentary wing. Several waves of expulsions took place in which Papandreou himself ensured the ascendancy of the parliamentary wing of the party over the militants and consolidated his own personal power over the entire party apparatus. The first expulsions occurred during the spring of 1975. Later, when the 1977 elections made the prospect of future electoral success an immediate, rather than a distant concern, a second wave of expulsions took place. Realizing that the path to government ran through the center rather than the left of the political spectrum, Papandreou became concerned with developing the appropriate strategy to meet this new goal. As a former PASOK deputy articulated,

Something [radical] like this could not make progress; it could not be elected by the people and furthermore it could not become a party of government. ... For this reason, at some point PASOK eliminated all [extremists]. With a political decision he made himself, a slaughter took place. He erased them because he believed he could not enter government and the people would not follow him. ... Andreas' ambitions [were the reason]—he no longer wanted to remain on the periphery.[95]

As time passed the parliamentary wing of the party continued to consolidate its power. Commenting on this, one deputy of the radical tendency argued in an interview that, "the careerists who entered [the party during this time] swallowed us."[96] As the parliamentary wing of the party became disproportionately powerful within the movement, PASOK's radical program was downplayed until the word socialism disappeared altogether from the party's rhetoric. Radical jargon was replaced with vague notions of democracy and "rational" (non-rightwing) government.[97] As Diamandouros argues, what came to be a "'short march' [to power] strategy constituted a frontal challenge to the continuing ascendancy of the maximalist wing within the emerging party structures and opened the door wide for a fundamental shift of emphasis and orientation away from the radical goals associated with the old PAK group toward the more programmatic politics identified with the party's parliamentary wing and with its more moderate allies."[98] As members of the radical tendency articulated in interviews with Michalis Spourdalakis, "[A]s time passed, two things became clear: that Papandreou was not interested in any development of PASOK other than that which would lead to the expansion of its electoral influence; and that Papandreou was anything but committed to the idea of making PASOK a mass front of PAK."[99]

Finally, many deputies argued that it is simplistic to believe that all of PASOK's moderation was due to electoral strategy and party building tactics alone. A number of deputies pointed out in the course of interviews that while electoral considerations were paramount, PASOK—especially during the early transition period when the party was dominated by PAK activists—was not simply engaged in electoral deception. Many PASOK deputies both believed in and desired to bring about the radical transformation of society. As a former communist argued: "[While much of the rhetoric] was electoral, it was also [part of their] creed."[100] A former PASOK deputy agreed: "[U]ndoubtedly, [PASOK] exaggerated the slogans it used originally. ... However, a party never vocalizes a slogan just for the slogan. If it would have been able to achieve those goals, it would have done so. ... We did not say all that to fool [the electorate]. ... We simply [could] not do what we said."[101] And finally, "[PASOK] could not govern with the slogans of 'The Third of September'[102]—even though we would have wanted to keep them."[103]

Thus, just as Karamanlis was constrained by both domestic and foreign factors during the post–civil war period and was therefore unsuccessful in bringing about certain domestic reforms during that time, so, too, Papandreou was constrained once in office. As shown above, PASOK argued that withdrawal from NATO would have been dangerous given Turkey's membership in that alliance. Disengagement would have left Greece both isolated and vulnerable. Concerning the European Community, Susannah Verney has aptly pointed out that once a country's economy is integrated into the Community, the economic consequences of disengagement are "incalculable." The legal aspects alone of disengagement involve a "mountain" of complex problems. In short, accession itself erects serious obstacles to future disengagement.[104] Adamantia Pollis also argues that "[t]he

Greek socialists' striking reversal of EEC membership dramatizes the impact of domestic and international constraints on Greece's options." She contends that Greek withdrawal from the EC would have isolated Greece internationally by cutting it off from necessary export markets with Greek farmers suffering the loss of subsidies derived from the Community's Common Agricultural Policy.[105] Many PASOK deputies agreed that this was in fact the case:

Slowly ... PASOK recognized that many of [its early] positions were not realistic and thus it abandoned them. ... It would not have been easy [to pull Greece out of the EC]. It would have been very, very difficult because we had an economy in total dependence on the countries which were in the EC. ... With the passing of time [PASOK] slowly understood that these positions were wrong and that they were not realistic. [Our] moderation was an adaptation to a situation we could not change.[106]

The economic and security constraints of EC and NATO membership were not the only obstacles to the fulfillment of PASOK's radical program. Indeed, deputies argued that significant domestic constraints played an important role as well. Specifically, PASOK was forced to accept the seemingly universal truth that radical promises are easily made in opposition, but actual fulfillment of those goals is another matter entirely once a party has acceded to the responsibilities and realities of government. For example, one PASOK deputy argued that, "[G]overnment ... obliges one toward a more conservative view of things. One talks differently when one is on the course toward government [from] when one becomes government."[107] Another PASOK deputy maintained that, "[I]t is one thing to be the opposition and another to take over the government. ... It is compulsory when you enter government that you adapt. ... It is compulsory for you to adapt yourself to the new situations."[108] And finally, "Once you reach government you are restricted by being in government. You must balance a budget and not increase the pension of a farmer. ... You'd like to but you can't."[109]

SOME CONCLUDING REMARKS

As the preceding analysis has shown, PASOK appeared in 1974 as the most radical Greek political party. Demanding the large-scale "socialization" of the means of production, disparaging moderate social democratic policies and tactics, and ultimately questioning the legitimacy of the new regime, its institutions, and rules of the game, PASOK appeared poised on the verge of a radical transformation of Greece's new democracy should it be elected to government. By walking out of the vote on the new constitution, PASOK appeared to genuinely oppose the new democracy, placing itself in a position not unlike that of the Basque Nationalist Party (PNV) in Spain. It, too, walked out of parliament during the Spanish transition and had recommended to its supporters that they abstain from the 1978 constitutional referendum. The similarity was unsettling. PASOK's emergence as an apparently radical Marxist party thus led many reasonable observers to expect it to pose a serious obstacle to Greek democratic consolidation.

From the perspective of democratic consolidation and stability, however, such predictions were fortunately wrong. In a short period of time, it became obvious that PASOK respected the institutions of the new regime and would play the game of politics by the established norms of democratic behavior. In fact, this chapter has argued that PASOK was a fundamentally democratic political party as early as 1974 and that its rhetorically semiloyal positions were more a product of Greek political culture and electoral tactics than they were indicative of a truly semiloyal or antisystem position.

The most important point to arise out of this analysis of PASOK's moderation, however, is that contrary to the theoretical requirement that moderation of ideological and programmatic positions is necessary for democratic consolidation and stability to occur, the case of PASOK indicates that the party's radical position in the early years of Greece's transition actually *facilitated* democratic consolidation. It did so by attracting the support of dissatisfied and disaffected antiestablishment voters who might otherwise have withdrawn their support from the newly democratized regime. The potential for radical political parties such as PASOK to serve this regime-stabilizing purpose was also demonstrated in Spain, but by an extreme right-wing party. There, the conservative *Alianza Popular* progressively moderated, bringing its constituency of right-wing, Franquist sympathizers into full acceptance and participation in the new democratic game. In Greece PASOK did the same for those on the semiloyal left-wing, bringing them from decades of alienation and exclusion from Greek democracy to full participation in and respect for the new regime.

This was accomplished because the party's early radical rhetoric attracted the support of those sections of Greek society who belonged to what Nikiforos Diamandouros has termed the "underdog culture"—the underprivileged, the vanquished of the civil war, and those individuals suspected of being "non-nationally minded" during the post–civil war period.[110] As was argued in chapter 2, this was an electorate that was bitter, frustrated, and resentful at being excluded and marginalized from democratic politics. Its anti-Western, anticapitalist, and xenophobic worldview had only been reinforced by the experience of seven years of dictatorial rule. PASOK's emergence as a political party provided a viable political and ideological home for many of these people. As Richard Clogg argues, PASOK's early radical rhetoric "clearly had some attraction for members of the old left, who felt for the first time under the PASOK government that they were not being treated like second-class citizens."[111]

For these people PASOK's early antisystem positions, its subsequent accession to the role of formal opposition, and finally its election to government gave needed legitimacy to the new regime. As Theodore Couloumbis argues, "once in power, PASOK ... contribut[ed] to the 'enlargement' of the establishment, thus enhancing its legitimacy and long-term viability."[112] Even more importantly, by providing a loyal and democratic partisan alternative to the relatively large portion of society that had been disaffected and marginalized, PASOK left little space for the emergence of a truly semiloyal or antisystem political party. As discussed in chapter 5, the truly antisystem KKE has struggled to have any appreciable impact on the Greek political scene. Over time, as PASOK moderated its positions and rhetoric, it effected moderation in its supporters as well and thereby weakened the antisystem alternative. A reformist deputy of the Greek Communist Party put it well: "In essence, Papandreou prepared the people in stages to accept reality—that Greece belongs to the West. ... [T]he Greek people themselves [came] to understand [this]. ... [S]lowly, slowly, he himself [became] more realistic and he [made] the electorate more realistic too."[113] In fact, PASOK's abandonment of its early semiloyal or antisystem positions and its adoption of stances that were completely loyal to the democratic regime occurred very early in the transition process. Its forceful criticisms of the regime appear to have been the result of the rancorous nature of Greek political culture and of the fact that PASOK and the other opposition parties were all engaged in the game of partisan politics, Greek style. Such outbursts were not in reality genuinely semiloyal or antisystem stances on the part of the opposition. As deputies have since confessed, contrary to their rhetorical stances at that time, the opposition was in reality a loyal opposition to Greece's new democratic regime. No sooner was PASOK elected to government in 1981 than Papandreou triumphantly declared that his party's victory had confirmed that Greece's democratic institutions worked.

This analysis of PASOK points up a critically important point: the moderation of antisystem positions must be seen as distinct from the separate issue of the moderation of public policy positions. Programmatic and rhetorical radicalism—so long as it remains confined to issues of government policy and does not call into question the very institutions and rules of the new regime—can continue long after democracy has become consolidated and stable. In this way, programmatic radicalism and democracy can coexist.

This conclusion is born out by the Spanish socialists' ideological and programmatic positions during the transition to democracy in Spain. Despite the PSOE's prosystem stance during the Spanish transition, it was an ideologically Marxist, class-based political party that desired a radical break with the Franquist past. The party also supported Basque national self-determination and, like PASOK, took a decisively anti-NATO position, maintaining that the country's security interests would best be served if Spain were to remain disengaged from the politics of the main security alliances.[114] Moreover, while in opposition the PSOE gave the impression that, if elected to government, it would set out to transform economic policy by emphasizing the redistribution of wealth and the expansion of state intervention in the economy. In its 1976 party congress, the party declared that it was a "class party, and therefore of the masses, Marxist and democratic" and maintained that "the overcoming of the capitalist means of production through the seizure of economic and political power, and the socialization of the means of production, distribution and exchange by the working class" was its principal objective.[115] Clearly, during the early period of Spain's transition to democracy, the PSOE was an ideologically and programmatically "radical" political party. Despite this radicalism, however, the PSOE's commitment to the democratic regime was steadfast. In both Spain and Greece, then, the socialist parties were ideologically and programmaticly radical; however, their radicalism did not prevent democratic consolidation. In sum, the cases of PASOK and the PSOE illustrate that as long as political parties accept the regime, its norms, and rules of the game as legitimate, ideological, programmatic, and rhetorical moderation is not necessarily required before that regime can be considered consolidated.

Over time moderation of ideology and programmatic positions does, however, seem to follow from participation in democratic politics over the long-term. Like PASOK, the Italian and Spanish socialists are cases in point. In Italy the Italian Socialist Party (PSI) underwent both convergence and moderation. Loyalty to the existing democratic regime developed incrementally over the course of several decades from its initial trigger, the 1956 Soviet invasion of Hungary. Attempting to distinguish themselves from Italian communists, the PSI gradually moved from a position of semiloyalty to the regime to one of full loyalty through a process that often resulted in periodic splits between maximalists and revisionists concerning the direction "socialism" should take. Eventually, the pragmatic parliamentary wing of the party came to dominate and convergence ensued. Programmatic moderation followed. As general secretary Bettino Craxi realized that Italian society was being transformed by the emergence of a new middle class, he led the party to abandon the ideology of proletarian socialism, making an explicit electoral appeal to middle-class professionals while concurrently suppressing radical extremists.[116] As Alexander De Grand puts it, "One by one, the old symbols of the party were thrown overboard. The red carnation replaced the old rising sun and hammer and sickle ... [and] Marx gave way to the Harvard Business School's management theories."[117] The PSI clearly parallels PASOK: ideological and programmatic moderation definitely occurred, but prior to that, system support had already been established.

Similarly, in Spain it did not take long for the socialists to backpedal on many of their more radical stances. By the 1977 election campaign, the PSOE explicitly attempted to project itself as a moderate party, avoiding calls for extensive nationalization and other radical demands, focusing instead on noncontroversial issues such as "the need to elaborate a new Constitution, proposals to improve the quality of life of citizens, and the opportunity for integration of Spain in Europe."[118] Following its good showing in those elections, the party leadership then actively collaborated with conservative Adolfo Suárez, abandoning the party's most radical tenets. Party leader Felipe González led the way in forsaking the party's official Marxist ideology and setting about to reform the party's structure. After its accession to government in 1982, the PSOE experienced a further change of heart regarding NATO, eventually coming to campaign for the "yes" vote despite its earlier anti-NATO position.[119] Finally, its calls for the radical transformation of the Spanish economy as well as its support for Basque national autonomy were dropped. In this way the PSOE moderated its programmatic and ideological positions in the 1970s and 1980s in much the same ways as PASOK and the PSI.

Accounting for the convergence of the Southern European socialists follows a similar pattern to that of PASOK. The elite convergence argument—that parties moderate in order to attract votes and enter government—accounted for *some* of the moderation of Southern European socialists. In Greece, as this chapter has illustrated, Papandreou undertook a drastic transformation of party ideology and program, as well as a thoroughgoing purge of radical party activists, once it became clear that PASOK had a real chance of electoral success if it could attract moderate, centrist voters. Something similar was at work in Spain. Like Papandreou, Felipe González's embrace of a catch-all strategy, his adoption of moderate, centrist positions, and his acceptance of a capitalist market economy were prompted by his belief that the PSOE had a real chance of electoral success if it appealed to voters nearer the center of the political spectrum. In Italy, too, Bettino Craxi read the "political tea leaves" correctly during the 1970s and encouraged moderation. In appealing to Italy's new middle-class electorate, the PCI was "determined to detach and then represent the modern [and expanding] middle class electorate," perceiving that it was the future social base of political power in Italy.[120]

Thus, the logic of building a modern, mass-based electoral machine contributed to moderation. The Greek case illustrates that as time passed and electoral victory became the paramount concern for PASOK, Papandreou came to appreciate the need for organizational transformation, promoting the centrist and pragmatic parliamentary wing of the party over the more radical and ideological party activists. In Italy, too, from about 1978, Craxi began to strengthen executive authority within the PSI, while reducing the power of its grassroots. In Spain Felipe González's attempt to ideologically moderate the party had produced considerable intraparty upheaval by 1979, but it ultimately had the unforeseen consequence of enforcing greater internal party discipline and inhibiting factionalism within the PSOE. Transformed from a "radical, divided leftist party to a unified, centrist electoral organization dominated by strong leadership,"[121] the party became a cohesive election-fighting organization.[122] Put simply, electoral motivations were indeed an important moderating influence for Southern European socialist parties, but they were not the whole story.

In short, as has been seen in other chapters, the electoral motivations of the elite convergence model clearly explain some aspects of moderation. The "explained variance" is far from total, however. Other equally important factors play a role in convergence. It has been the task of this chapter to elaborate on those other factors and thus present a fuller picture of the elite convergence model.

As my analysis of PASOK's moderation has shown, the processes behind moderation are multifaceted and complex. Domestic and international factors, as well as the constraints imposed on parties once they leave opposition and enter government, also constrained socialists' behavior and facilitated moderation. In Greece PASOK realized that withdrawing Greece from NATO would pose a serious security threat given Turkish intimidation in the Eastern Aegean. When it came to NATO, it concurred with the PSOE leader who quipped that "getting a divorce is much more traumatic than not getting married."[123] In a similar vein PASOK discovered that withdrawal from the EC would present Greece with a serious financial burden—a burden all Southern European socialists realized was too costly to bear. Moreover, significant domestic constraints played an important role in socialist party moderation. As José María Maravall contends, the policy packages of these parties consisted of trade-offs between "economic and social policies, between wages and jobs, between taxes and the provision of social transfers and collective goods." Such contradictions between ambitions and possibilities, between ideology and reality, significantly constrained socialist actions.[124]

This chapter has thus shown how, despite its radical antisystem rhetoric during the early phases of Greece's transition to democracy, PASOK quickly became a loyal, system-supportive opposition party. Although PASOK maintained its ideological, programmatic, and rhetorically radical positions during the early period of Greece's transition, those positions did not hinder democratic consolidation and stability but instead contributed to it. Like all the other significant political parties in Greece, then, PASOK never posed a serious challenge to democratic consolidation and stability during the country's transition. If a direct threat to the regime was imminent in the post-1974 period, it would have to come from outside the field of "normal" democratic politics. In fact, it would have to have come from none other than the very group that had usurped power in 1967—the Greek military.

NOTES

1. James Petras, "The Contradictions of Greek Socialism," *New Left Review* 163 (May/June 1987), p. 8.

2. Heinz-Jürgen Axt, "On the Way to Self-Reliance? PASOK's Government Policy in Greece," *Journal of Modern Greek Studies* 2:2 (October 1984), p. 196.

3. Carl Barkman, *Ambassador in Athens, 1969–1975: The Evolution from Military Dictatorship to Democracy in Greece* (London: The Merlin Press, 1984), pp. 224, 226.

4. Susannah Verney, "To Be or Not to Be Within the European Community: The Party Debate and Democratic Consolidation in Greece," in Geoffrey Pridham, ed., *Securing Democracy: Political Parties and Democratic Consolidation in Southern Europe* (London: Routledge, 1990), p. 213.

5. See Jeffrey Schaffer, "Andreas Papandreou: [Political] Portrait of a Modern Socialist," p. 63, and Demetres Michalopoulos, "PASOK and the Eastern Bloc: A Growing Relationship," p. 352, in Nikolaos A. Stavrou, ed., *Greece Under Socialism: A NATO Ally Adrift,* (New Rochelle, NY: Aristide D. Caratzas, 1988).

6. *Greek Politics at a Crossroads: What Kind of Socialism?* (Stanford, CA: Hoover Institution Press, 1984), pp. 2–3.

7. "The Contradictions of Greek Socialism," p. 9.

8. Macridis, *Greek Politics at a Crossroads,* p. 26.

9. Memorandum concerning the events before and after the 1981 elections, written in February 1982 by Constantine Karamanlis, quoted in Michalopoulos, "PASOK and the Eastern Bloc," p. 352.

10. George J. Tsoumis, "The Defense Policies of PASOK," in Stavrou, ed., *Greece Under Socialism,* p. 99.

11. "Greek Political Culture in Transition: Historical Origins, Evolutions, Current Trends," in Richard Clogg, ed., *Greece in the 1980s* (New York: St. Martin's Press, 1983).

12. On the original formulation of dependency theory, see Andre Gunder Frank, *Capitalism and Underdevelopment in Latin America: Historical Studies of Chile and Brazil* (New York: Monthly Review Press, 1967), and *Latin America: Underdeveloped or Revolution* (New York: Monthly Review Press, 1969). See also Immanuel Wallerstein, *The*

Modern World-System: Capitalist Agriculture and the Origins of the European World-Economy in the 16th Century (New York: Academic Press, 1974).

13. Quoted in Matthew Nimetz, "Introduction," in Stavrou, ed., *Greece Under Socialism*, p. 2.

14. Andreas Papandreou, *Imperialismos kai Ekonomike Anaptexe* (Imperialism and Economic Development) (Athens: Nea Sinora, 1975), pp. 77–78.

15. PASOK, *Proclamation of Basic Principles and Goals of the Panhellenic Socialist Movement* (Athens, Greece: 3 September 1974).

16. George Drakos, "The Socialist Economic Policy in Greece: a Critique," in Zafiris Tzannatos, ed., *Socialism in Greece: The First Four Years* (Aldershot: Gower Publishing Company Limited, 1986), p. 41.

17. A. Kokkos and A. Mourike-Kostopoulou, eds., *Metavase sto Sosialismo* (Transition to Socialism) (Athens: Aletri Publishers, 1981), pp. 12–13.

18. Richard Clogg, *Parties and Elections in Greece* (London: C. Hurst & Company, 1987), p. 134.

19. Nimetz, "Introduction," p. 2.

20. Nimetz, "Introduction," p. 2.

21. Andreas G. Papandreou, *Gia mia Sosialistike Koinonia: Koinonekopoiese, Autodiacheirise, Apokentrose, Topike Autokioikise, Syndikalismos* (For a Socialist Society: Socialization, Self-management, Decentralization, Local Self Government, Syndicalism) (Athens: PASOK Press Office, 1977).

22. Brian R. Nelson, *Western Political Thought: From Socrates to the Age of Ideology* (Englewood Cliffs, NJ: Prentice Hall, 1982), pp. 159–90.

23. Nikolaos A. Stavrou, "Ideological Foundations of the Panhellenic Socialist Movement," in Stavrou, ed., *Greece Under Socialism*, p. 19.

24. Quoted in Michalopoulos, "PASOK and the Eastern Bloc," p. 354.

25. Stavrou, "Ideological Foundations," p. 36.

26. Roy C. Macridis, "Elections and Political Modernization," in Howard R. Penniman, ed., *Greece at the Polls: The National Elections of 1974 and 1977* (Washington: American Enterprise Institute for Public Policy Research, 1981), pp. 16–17.

27. *Le Nouvel Observateur*, 9 November 1974, p. 54.

28. Papandreou, *Gia mia Sosialistike Koinonia*, p. 29.

29. See, for example, Kostas Simitis, *He Domike Antipoliteuse* (Structural opposition) (Athens: Kastiniotis, 1979).

30. *Auge*, 4 November 1979.

31. Macridis, *Greek Politics at a Crossroads*, p. 32.

32. Stavrou, "Ideological Foundations," p. 25.

33. "Populism, Eurocommunism and the KKE: The Communist Party of Greece," in Michael Waller and Meindert Fennema, eds., *Communist Parties in Western Europe: Decline or Adaptation?* (New York: Basil Blackwell Ltd., 1988), p. 105.

34. *Parties and Elections in Greece*, p. 84.

35. Theodore A. Couloumbis, "Conclusion," in Penniman, ed., *Greece at the Polls*, p. 191.

36. *To Vema*, 26 April 1981.

37. Quoted in Clogg, *Parties and Elections in Greece*, p. 104. Emphasis added.

38. Quoted in Chrystos Lyrintzis, "Political Parties in Post-Junta Greece: A Case of 'Bureaucratic Clientelism'?" in Geoffrey Pridham, ed., *The New Mediterranean Democracies: Regime Transition in Spain, Greece and Portugal* (London: Frank Cass, 1984), p. 112.

39. PASOK, "Programmatic Declaration of the Government," 22 November 1981.

40. Quoted in Petras, "The Contradictions of Greek Socialism," p. 18.

41. Greek Parliament, *Minutes*, 23 January 1987, p. 2912.

42. Quoted in Charles W. McCaskill, "PASOK's Third World/Nonaligned Relations," in Stavrou, ed., *Greece Under Socialism*, p. 310.

43. Theodore A. Couloumbis, "PASOK's Foreign Policies, 1981–89: Continuity or Change?" in Richard Clogg, ed., *Greece, 1981–89: The Populist Decade* (New York: St. Martin's Press, 1993), p. 120.

44. Speech of Andreas Papandreou to the members of the Socialist Group of the European Parliament, Athens, Greece, 8 September 1982.

45. Susannah Verney, "Political Parties and the European Community in Regime Consolidation in Greece," Paper presented to the Political Studies Association, 1987, pp. 16–17.

46. Nicos C. Alivizatos, "The Presidency, Parliament and the Courts in the 1980s," in Clogg, ed., *Greece, 1981–89*, p. 70. Emphasis added.

47. The strong Greek president could, for example, dissolve parliament, call for a referendum, appoint as well as dismiss the prime minister, veto legislation that could only be overridden by a vote of three-fifths of the legislature, declare a state of emergency, and rule by executive order.

48. Kevin Featherstone, "Political Parties and Democratic Consolidation in Greece," in Pridham, ed., *Securing Democracy*, p. 189.

49. C. M. Woodhouse, *Karamanlis: The Restorer of Greek Democracy* (Oxford: Clarendon Press, 1982), pp. 230–31.

50. Quoted in Featherstone, "Political Parties and Democratic Consolidation," p. 183.

51. One obvious example is the opposition's criticism of the "reinforced" proportional representation electoral law, which, in allocating seats, favored large parties at the expense of smaller ones.

52. For example, the office of the president and the powers accorded to that office were strenuously challenged by the opposition. Eventually, the constitution was revised by PASOK and these "superpowers" were subtracted from the president and accorded to the prime minister.

53. Quoted in Featherstone, "Political Parties and Democratic Consolidation," p. 183.

54. Interview conducted in Athens, Greece, on 29 March 1994.

55. Interview in Athens, Greece, on 25 May 1994 with a prominent PASOK deputy.

56. Interview conducted in Athens, Greece, on 20 May 1994 with a former PASOK deputy.

57. Interview in Athens, Greece, on 24 March 1994 with a former deputy of PASOK.

58. Interview conducted in Athens, Greece, on 3 February 1994 with a former deputy of ND.

59. Interview conducted in Athens, Greece, on 4 April 1994 with former deputy of ND.

60. Interview in Athens, Greece, on 21 April 1994 with a leading Centrist deputy.

61. Interview in Athens, Greece, on 19 April 1994 with a former Centrist deputy.

62. Interview conducted in Athens, Greece, on 10 December 1993 with a former deputy of EDA.

63. Interview in Athens, Greece, on 25 May 1994 with a prominent PASOK deputy.

64. Eurobarometer, April 1982, quoted in Yorgos A. Kourvetaris, "The Southern Flank of NATO: Political Dimensions of the Greco-Turkish Conflict Since 1974," *East European Quarterly* 21:4 (Winter 1988), p. 442.

65. Interview conducted in Athens, Greece, on 8 February 1994.

66. Interview conducted in Athens, Greece, on 20 May 1994.

67. Interview conducted in Athens, Greece, on 13 May 1994.

68. "PASOK and the Elections of 1977," p. 117.

69. Peter Pappas, "The Eighteenth October of Andreas Papandreou: Some Thoughts on a Democratic Cult of Personality," in Theodore C. Kariotis, ed., *The Greek Socialist Experiment: Papandreou's Greece 1981–1989* (New York: Pella, 1992), p. 60.

70. Interviews conducted in Athens, Greece, on 29 March 1994 and 17 May 1994.

71. Interview conducted with a PASOK deputy on 9 June 1994.

72. Interview conducted in Athens, Greece, on 24 March 1994.

73. Interview conducted in Athens, Greece, with a former ND deputy on 29 March 1994.

74. Interview conducted in Athens, Greece, on 8 February 1994.

75. Susannah Verney, "From the 'Special Relationship' to Europeanism: PASOK and the European Community, 1981–89," in Clogg, ed., *Greece, 1981–89*, p. 134.

76. P. K. Ioakeimidis, *Ho Metaskhimatismos tes EOK: Apo ten 'Entole' sten Eniaia Europaeke Praxe* (The Transformation of the EEC: From the 'Mandate' to the Single European Act) (Athens, 1988), pp. 151–56.

77. Athens News Agency, 1 July 1983.

78. Macridis, *Greek Politics at a Crossroads*, p. 57.

79. Interview conducted in Athens, Greece, on 19 April 1994.

80. Athens News Agency, 9 February 1984, quoted in John O. Iatrides, "Papandreou's Foreign Policy," in Kariotis, ed., *The Greek Socialist Experiment*, p. 156.

81. The eighteenth referred to the day following the 1974 elections.

82. Interview conducted in Athens, Greece, on 8 February 1994.

83. See Kourvetaris, "The Southern Flank of NATO," p. 441.

84. Quoted in George Th. Mavrogordatos, *Rise of the Green Sun* (London: Centre of Contemporary Greek Studies, King's College, 1983), p. 58.

85. Angelos Elephantis, "PASOK and the Elections of 1977: The Rise of the Populist Movement," in Penniman, *Greece at the Polls*, p. 129.

86. Interview conducted in Athens, Greece, on 29 March 1994.

87. Interview conducted in Athens, Greece, on 21 March 1994.

88. Interview conducted in Athens, Greece, with a former PASOK deputy on 14 April 1994.

89. Panagiotes B. Katsaros, *He Eukairia pou Chatheke: Politikes Katagrafes kai Skepseis* (The Opportunity that was Lost: Political Writings and Thoughts) (Athens: Etairia Ellenikou Vivliou, 1990), p. 238.

90. *The Rise of the Greek Socialist Party* (London: Routledge, 1988), p. 62.

91. Interview conducted in Athens, Greece, on 21 March 1994.

92. Interview conducted in Athens, Greece, on 29 October 1993.

93. "PASOK and State-Society Relations in Post-Authoritarian Greece (1974–79), in Speros Vryonis Jr., ed., *Greece on the Road to Democracy: From the Junta to PASOK 1974–1988* (New Rochelle, New York: Orpheus Publishing Inc., 1991), p. 22.

94. Spourdalakis, *The Rise of the Greek Socialist Party*, p. 82.

95. Interview conducted in Athens, Greece, on 21 March 1994.

96. Interview conducted in Athens, Greece, on 9 June 1994.

97. Spourdalakis, *The Rise of the Greek Socialist Party*, p. 83.

98. "PASOK and State-Society Relations," p. 23.

99. Quoted in Spourdalakis, *The Rise of the Greek Socialist Party*, p. 147.

100. Interview conducted in Athens, Greece, on 13 May 1994.

101. Interview conducted in Athens, Greece, on 21 March 1994.

102. PASOK's founding proclamation, made on 3 September 1974, came to be known as "The Third of September."

103. Interview conducted in Athens, Greece, with a former PASOK deputy on 20 May 1994.

104. "To Be or Not to Be," pp. 207–8.

105. "Socialist Transformation in Greece," *Telos: A Quarterly Journal of Critical Thought* 61 (Fall 1984), p. 110.

106. Interview conducted in Athens, Greece, on 22 March 1994.

107. Interview conducted in Athens, Greece, on 29 March 1994.

108. Interview conducted in Athens, Greece, on 8 June 1994.

109. Interview conducted in Athens, Greece, on 29 March 1994 with a former PASOK deputy.

110. See, for example, Couloumbis, "PASOK's Foreign Policies, 1981–89; Diamandouros, "Greek Political Culture;" and Clogg, *Parties and Elections in Greece*.

111. *Parties and Elections in Greece*, p. 108.

112. "PASOK's Foreign Policies, 1981–89," p. 125.

113. Interview conducted in Athens, Greece, on 13 May 1994.

114. When PSOE entered government in 1982, participation in NATO was frozen and the government withdrew its delegates to the NATO working groups. See, for example, Víctor M. Pérez-Díaz, *The Return of Civil Society: The Emergence of Democratic Spain* (Cambridge, MA: Harvard University Press, 1993), p.45.

115. Quoted in Richard Gunther, Giacomo Sani, and Goldie Shabad, *Spain After Franco: The Making of a Competitive Party System* (Berkeley: University of California Press, 1988), p. 74.

116. See, for example, Spencer Di Scala, *Renewing Italian Socialism: Nenni to Craxi* (New York: Oxford University Press, 1988); and Alexander De Grand, *The Italian Left in the Twentieth Century: A History of the Socialist and Communist Parties* (Bloomington, IN: Indiana University Press, 1989), chapter 9.

117. De Grand, *The Italian Left in the Twentieth Century*, p. 158.

118. Quoted in Gunther, Sani, and Shabad, *Spain after Franco*, p. 75.

119. For the reasons behind this decision, see Felipe Agüero, *Soldiers, Civilians, and Democracy: Post-Franco Spain in Comparative Perspective* (Baltimore: The Johns Hopkins University Press, 1995), p. 203–4.

120. Diarmuid Maguire, "The Recent Birth of Modern Italy," in James Kurth and James Petras, eds., *Mediterranean Paradoxes: Politics and Social Structure in Southern Europe* (Providence, RI: Berg Publishers, Inc., 1993), p. 87.

121. Richard Gunther, "The Spanish Socialist Party: From Clandestine Position to Party of Government," in Stanley Payne, ed., *The Politics of Democratic Spain* (Chicago: Council on Foreign Relations, 1986), pp. 22–23.

122. Félix Tezanos, *Sociología del Socialismo Español* (Madrid: Tecnos, 1983).

123. Quoted in José María Maravall, "What Is Left? Social Democratic Policies in Southern Europe," Working Paper 36 (Madrid: Instituto Juan March, 1992).

124. Maravall, "What Is Left?"

Do Attitudes Matter? The Moderation of the Greek Military

As reviewed in chapter 1 of this study, the literature on democratic transition and consolidation processes provides several explanations concerning the varying capacities of militaries to place limits on democratization. Four explanations are particularly important to the case of Greece. First, it has been argued that the nature of the outgoing authoritarian regime can either facilitate or hinder the democratization path.[1] One of the critical factors in this regard is whether the outgoing authoritarian regime is militarized or civilianized.[2] In particular, militarized authoritarian regimes have a greater ability to influence the transition, maintain reserves of authority over policy decisions, and intervene when threatened by civilian reforms, thereby raising barriers to full democratization and hindering the establishment of a stable and consolidated democracy.

A second characteristic of outgoing authoritarian regimes that can influence the ability of militaries to place limits on democratization is whether the militarized regime was led by a hierarchical or nonhierarchical military structure.[3] Other things being equal, hierarchical military regimes—regimes in which the government is composed of or controlled by the highest-ranking military officers—are a greater hinderance to democracy than nonhierarchical military regimes—those led by lower-ranking officers such as colonels. Nonhierarchical military regimes risk being checked by the officers associated with the military hierarchy, especially if the regime faces severe economic difficulties it cannot solve, is threatened by invasion of a foreign power and cannot defend the nation, or finds that the capability of the armed forces is seriously impaired and the military divided. In such instances the military hierarchy is likely to launch a counter-coup of its own, overthrow the nonhierarchical regime, and call the civilians back to government.

Third, the specific transition path followed greatly influences the extent of the previous authoritarian regime's control over the transition process.[4] When authoritarian rulers are overthrown or when they collapse from power, their civilian opponents will be more likely to dominate the transition process virtually unencumbered by military officers. In addition, the way in which military issues are handled by civilians during the transition to democracy may either contribute to or detract from the military's willingness to remain in the barracks. If civilian elites move quickly to peripheralize the military, to discipline its officers for crimes committed under the dictatorship, or if they thrust structural, organizational, or educational reforms upon it, military officers are likely to intervene in an attempt to curtail such change. Often the best course of action may be to stagger reforms or other costly measures; in some cases it may even be better to forgo reforms completely rather than put the new democratic regime at risk.[5]

THE CASE OF GREEK MILITARY WITHDRAWAL

If one takes the case of Greece and "scores" its transition on each of these variables—the nature of the outgoing authoritarian regime, the nature of the elite directing the transition, the transition path followed, and the handling of military matters by civilian elites—it becomes clear that the transition trajectory followed in the Greek case was optimal for democratic consolidation. First, the military regime of 1967–74 was a nonhierarchical junta led initially by colonels. Thus, when the junta's botched coup attempt in Cyprus in July 1974 revealed the military's lack of preparedness to defend the country against a possible Turkish attack, the military hierarchy simply reasserted its authority and "invited" civilians back to government.

Specifically, the immediate catalyst for the military regime's collapse was its attempted overthrow of the Cypriot President, Archbishop Makarios, on 15 July 1974. In response to the regime's attempted coup, Turkey landed troops in northern Cyprus on 20 July. Faced with the possibility of war with Turkey, General Ioannides, the junta leader, gave orders for a general mobilization. The orders resulted in confusion and disarray. The chaos of the Greek mobilization effort and the obvious lack of military preparedness prompted officers outside the regime to take action.

On 22 July, 250 officers of the Third Army Corps stationed in Thessaloniki signed a declaration requesting the formation of a Council of National Salvation, consisting of both military and political leaders. The declaration requested that the Council elect Constantine Karamanlis as its president and "bestow (on) him the authority equivalent to a head of state and prime minister" and the power "to proceed with the conduct of free elections within six months."[6] On the following day the leaders of the air force and navy informed General Ioannides of the plan to transfer authority to civilians. Thus, just as a faction of the military had brought about the coup of 21 April 1967, so a faction contributed to its withdrawal in 1974.

Thanks in large part to the nonhierarchical nature of the military regime, seven years of dictatorial rule ended as quickly and bloodlessly as they had begun.[7]

Not only did the nature of Greece's outgoing authoritarian regime facilitate democratization, but so did the nature of its transition path—transition via collapse. In fact, the junta's collapse from power so discredited the military organization that the ability of officers to influence the transition process was virtually eliminated, leaving all decisions in the hands of civilian elites. Additionally, the gravity of the Cyprus crisis and the possibility of war with Turkey reinforced civilian elites' domination over the entire transition to democracy and, most importantly, refocused the attention of the military on its duties of external defense while reducing officers' time and inclination for domestic political interference.[8]

Finally, the way in which military matters were handled by civilians during and after the transition to democracy was crucial and makes Greece an example of how civilians can best finesse outgoing authoritarian regimes so as to facilitate depoliticization of the military. Both the conservative government of Constantine Karamanlis and the socialist government of Andreas Papandreou appear to have been cognizant of the possibility of a military backlash throughout the 1970s and early 1980s and were careful to treat the military with caution.

The Karamanlis cabinet, for example, took immediate steps to reassure the military that its corporate interests would not be harmed.[9] Fearful that a thoroughgoing purge would further weaken a demoralized military in the face of the Turkish threat or provoke a backlash from the hard-liners of the Ioannides regime, the Karamanlis government replaced only the upper echelons of the military leadership, increased military spending, and announced that "the careers of army officers shall be judged by their future behavior, not the past."[10] The *Nea Demokratia* government also increased the retirement allowances, medical care, and housing benefits of military personnel, and, when the leading protagonists of the 1967 coup were sentenced to death, Karamanlis immediately commuted their sentences to life imprisonment. Furthermore, when accused that the government had shied away from a thoroughgoing purge of the armed forces, Karamanlis' response indicates that he was aware of the dangers of doing so: "As for the demands for a more widesweeping purge ... half the Greek population would be in jail if I had not stood out against it."[11] Even socialist leader Andreas Papandreou, who had initially called for a thorough dejuntification of the armed forces, eventually argued that the dictatorship "was a product of a small minority of officers which had trapped the majority of the officers corps," and praised the military's "total devotion to their duties: the preservation of national independence and protection of the country's democratic institutions."[12] Clearly, dejuntification was kept to a minimum. Because the majority of officers never perceived that their personal self interests or their organization's corporate interests were threatened by democratization, it appears that officers were able to adapt more easily to civilian supremacy in Greece than they were in many Latin American countries where civilians quickly sought retribution for past crimes.

In sum, the case of Greece might appear to many students of democratic transition and consolidation processes as a "textbook example" of how an outgoing authoritarian regime dominated by a traditionally politicized military came to the eventual recognition that its proper role did not include intervention into the civil and political life of the nation and retreated to the barracks. The military hierarchy reasserted its authority over the junta and invited civilians back to power; the collapse of the authoritarian regime and the military's total preoccupation with the Cyprus crisis and the external threat posed by Turkey ensured civilians a free hand in shaping civil-military relations; and, last, both Karamanlis and Papandreou's cautious handling of military matters during the early years of Greece's new democracy reassured most officers that they had nothing to fear from a democratic government.

Despite this, there are clear indications that even in this seeming exemplary case of military withdrawal, full behavioral support for democracy was not achieved as early as most observers of Greek democracy might believe. Instead, as in Spain, where military factions opposed democratization until after the 1982 elections and where a 1981 failed coup attempt seriously threatened democratization, similar phenomena occurred within the Greek military. For example, a number of military-led coup attempts and conspiracies, as well as numerous attempts on Karamanlis' life, were reported during the 1970s and early 1980s. Two abortive coups have also been said to have taken place after Papandreou's accession to power, and there is little doubt that widespread unease and tension existed within the military due to the socialists' attempts to "democratize" the armed forces during the early 1980s.[13] A number of examples can be provided to substantiate this claim. While the veracity of each report cannot be entirely verified, the overall record leaves little doubt that significant groups within the armed forces were unwilling to fully and unconditionally submit to civilian rule.

As early as 29 July 1974, reports indicated that some military units were resisting government orders to remove the military junta's insignia from public buildings. Then, on 24 February 1975 a conspiracy by officers loyal to the former military regime to stage a new military coup was uncovered by the government. Announcing that the government would take steps to eliminate such "cancerous elements" from the armed forces, Karamanlis expressed that his own life had been in danger: "[O]f all persons, I am the most exposed to the wrath of the junta." Later, in autumn of that year, newspapers received a statement from the underground organization, the National League of Greek Officers, threatening to overthrow Prime Minister Karamanlis because of his government's treatment of the Greek officer corps. It was not long before this incident, according to some reports, that the navy and air force were called to stop unrest in an army and marine camp near Athens.[14]

Similar disturbances were to be repeated in ensuing years. In September 1976, following the arrest of a former lieutenant colonel for the illegal possession of arms, an investigation was ordered into allegations that weapons were in the hands of pro-junta sympathizers. In June 1977 an opposition deputy asserted in parliament that a 1975–76 conspiracy to assassinate the prime minister and overthrow the elected government involved as many as 300 officers. In August

1977 a Greek daily reported that yet another plot had been uncovered to force the government to free the leaders of the 1967 coup.[15] On 1 June 1979 ten members—including two army officers—of the Organization of National Restoration, an extreme right-wing organization supportive of the former military regime and aiming to destabilize Greek democracy, were imprisoned for a series of bombings in Athens over a two-year period.

Such manifestations of behavioral insubordination continued into the next decade. On 10 June 1981 *Nea Demokratia*'s Minister of Defense, Evangelos Averoff-Tossizza, announced that an antigovernment conspiracy by retired army officers planned for 1 June had been prevented by the rescheduling of military exercises.[16] Military insubordination, disturbances, and abortive coups were also alleged to have continued after the socialist government's ascension to power in October 1981. Based on an interview with Papandreou himself, James Petras reports that because of junta holdovers in top command positions, the socialists were "walking a tightrope between internal changes and securing military acquiescence."[17] In fact, it appears that only Karamanlis, by then the President of the Republic, was able to ensure the normal transfer of power to the new government. When PASOK won the 1981 elections, the chiefs of staff of the Greek armed forces refused to attend a meeting called by the new socialist government and instead resigned, "creating uncertainty and leaving the way open for the military to intervene again in politics."[18] Karamanlis reportedly visited the Greek Pentagon unexpectedly on 18 October 1981 and presided over a meeting with the heads of the military to ensure their submission to civilian control,[19] reassuring the chiefs "that PASOK's declarations before the elections were part of its tactics to gain power and that it would moderate its views once it achieved that goal."[20]

News reports also allege that two abortive coup attempts took place under the Papandreou government. The first attempt is said to have occurred on 31 May 1982. Concerning the second of the two alleged attempts, said to have taken place on 26 February 1983, news reports indicate that there was wide circulation of rumors of a coup attempt coinciding with military exercises in the Athens area scheduled for that month. Papandreou—largely believed to be reacting to the rumors—put the police and army on a "red alert" and mobilized supporters of his PASOK party as well as those of the Communist Party of Greece and the Communist Party of Greece-Interior. In subsequent days the government retired fifteen generals (stating, however, that the timing of the retirements was coincidental while denying all rumors of the coup attempt).[21]

Several observations are due here. First, the fact that both the conservative and socialist governments in Greece treated the military with caution and respect undoubtedly contributed to minimizing dissension and conspiracies within the armed forces, and care was consciously taken not to alienate or threaten the majority of officers by radical government action. While this contributed to keeping the majority of officers in the barracks and out of politics, reports of widespread unease and tension within the armed forces coupled with military disturbances, rumored coups, and assassination attempts[22] indicate that cautious handling of military matters by civilians is not by itself sufficient to achieve democratic consolidation. Assuming that reports of the abortive coup attempt of 26 February 1983 are accurate, one may conclude that sufficient behavioral acceptance of civilian supremacy was probably not achieved in Greece until some time in late 1983 when the behavioral manifestations of insubordination appear to have ceased.

More importantly, however, interviews indicate that undemocratic attitudes persisted in the officer corps long after democracy was restored in 1974, offering additional support to the notion that full elite convergence and, thus, democratic consolidation, was not achieved as quickly as most observers have argued. Did undemocratic attitudes persist in the military well into the 1980s? Empirically, this question must remain open until interviews can be conducted with active military officers. Theoretically, however, I contend that if the motive for behavioral acceptance of democracy rests on decisions made by the military to remain in the barracks so long as its interests are not being harmed by the government of the day, then behavioral manifestations of regime acceptance are not enough to consider a regime consolidated. Attitudinal support for democracy, which often follows from behavioral compliance, is clearly required for full democratic consolidation to occur. Furthermore, my interviews with retired officers point to the fact that the dynamics of permanent withdrawal are not explicitly addressed by the models described above. An understanding of these dynamics, I argue, is crucial for a fuller and deeper understanding of the military's willingness to remain depoliticized and to *permanently* submit itself to civilian supremacy.

Thus, by distinguishing two distinct elements of military withdrawal—the *initial extrication* of the military from politics and the *permanence* of that withdrawal—this chapter argues that factors conducive to the military's initial withdrawal, while facilitating a successful democratic transition, are not sufficient to keep traditionally politicized militaries out of politics. Extrication of the military regime in fact had little to do with an intrinsic concern or respect for democracy, democratic institutions, norms, and rules, or democratic pluralism, *per se*. As a result, long after the military had been confined to the barracks and had behaviorally submitted to civilian control, military officers indicated in interviews that the military reserved the prerogative to reintervene "if necessary." Thus, I argue that while behavioral support for democracy is adequate for partial democratic consolidation in the short term, attitudinal support is a necessary precondition for full democratic consolidation in the long run. In sum, the Greek military's extrication from power highlights the importance of achieving both behavioral and attitudinal support for a regime before that regime can be considered fully consolidated.

ANSWERING THE "WHY"

To fully understand the dynamics of military withdrawal in Greece, two critical questions need to be answered. First, why would a hierarchical military suddenly decide to reestablish the chain-of-command, forcing the putschists to retreat so quickly to the barracks? Second, given the Greek military's recurrent interventions into politics throughout the twentieth century—in 1909, 1922, 1926, 1933, 1935, 1936, and 1967—and the reasons given for its withdrawal in 1974, can anything be said about the permanence of military submission to civilian control?

Why did the militarized regime of 21 April 1967 retreat so quickly to the barracks, unlike its counterparts in Latin America? Simply put, the way in which the military was extricated from politics—by collapse following its failed coup attempt in Cyprus and its inability to carry out a general mobilization and defend Greece against war with Turkey—appears to have left the military with no preferable alternative but to submit to civilian control. As Linz, Stepan, and Gunther argue, "it is possible that, if the hierarchal leaders of the military come to believe that the costs of direct involvement in non-democratic rule are greater than the costs of extrication, they may conclude that the interests of the military-as-institution would best be served by abandoning governmental authority and allowing civilian elites to come to power."[23] This is largely what occurred in Greece. Officers perceived withdrawal to be in the best interests of the military organization.

In addition, my interviews point to two other reasons for military withdrawal: First, military officers perceived extrication to be in their personal self-interest as well as in the Greek "national interest." Second, the shame officers experienced due to the military regime's failures while in office prompted many of them to support extrication from government. In sum, interviews with former military officers indicate that the regime's failures taught them something about the destructive consequences of political involvement (both for the military organization and officers themselves, as well as for the Greek nation-state) and left other officers embarrassed and ashamed of the military's seven years in government.

It was, in fact, the case that the nonhierarchical military regime almost upon taking office had increasingly come to comprise a new threat to the armed forces. Specifically, the coup had overthrown the traditional military hierarchy and had moved authority from the senior leadership of the armed forces to lower-ranking officers. Moreover, it had brought about the emergence of a new power center—a surveillance and security system centered on the Greek Military Police (ESA)—that further threatened the Greek military hierarchy. The ascendance of this alternate power center under the colonels' regime increasingly alienated the armed forces from the regime. The fact that large numbers of officers in the armed forces had, at best, only halfhearted enthusiasm for the regime led the colonels to grant repressive state security functions to this quasi-independent military security organization rather than to the military itself. As a result, career officers either threatened or victimized by the new security system became increasingly disgruntled with the regime. Tension between the armed forces and the authoritarian regime thus led many officers to "consider how long such a situation could or should be allowed to continue."[24] As Basilios Tsingos argues, "when the threat posed to the Greek officer corps by continued authoritarian rule came to outweigh that posed by a return to civilian democratic rule, the armed forces marginalized the ruling military junta and ended the situation it had supported."[25]

Moreover, the officer corps of all three services felt that the outcome of the invasion of Cyprus totally discredited the military regime, exposed the military's inability to carry out its primary mission of protecting the nation against external attack, and led to Greece's diplomatic isolation internationally.[26] Interviews revealed that the great failures of the dictatorship became lessons for the armed forces as officers saw the destructive consequences of military intervention. As one officer expressed: "The armed forces in their totality [now] know of the tragic situations which come from the intervention of the army into politics—the catastrophes, or damages to the nation and of the damages to themselves."[27] Another officer commented on the negative effects military intervention had on the cohesiveness and professionalism of the military-as-institution:

In our country, constantly and repeatedly ... movements in the army took place ... . [T]he country was never peaceful ... because for a military movement to occur, it occurs from a portion of the army... . The others who are against [the movement] ... will lie and wait, will organize themselves, will set aside their military duties, and rather than occupy themselves with their military responsibilities they will occupy themselves with how they will overthrow their colleagues' coup which seized the leadership from them so that they will be able to get it back.[28]

Also prompting many officers to support military extrication from government was a deep sense of embarrassment and shame. A parliamentary deputy expressed the frustration of several friends who were Greek army officers in 1974: "[T]he squall of rain took all of the army with it. It was cheapened—the Greek army was cheapened in the eyes of the people. This [made] ... the officers ... embarrassed of wearing their uniforms in public."[29] Thus, the Cyprus situation and the excesses and failures associated with the dictatorship "tarnished the image of the armed forces, damaged its morale and 'castrated' the once proud Hellenic army."[30] This humiliation is perhaps most apparent in the words of one air force officer who felt dishonored by the harsh and brutal way the regime dealt with dissidents:

They [the officers] became disillusioned. They ... were embarrassed of being officers. They ... were embarrassed with everything that took place—the dirt, the shame, the crimes. When the tortures of ESA became known, they said among themselves, "God forbid! Did we support those people who burned the genitals of boys and girls? *They* are men?" Later, they recognized the harsh blow to the prestige of the armed forces—which was the shame of Cyprus, another military defeat. I too [was embarrassed] ... [when] some would say ... "Don't bother [him] too much, because he. ...s a colonel and you know how colonels strike." It was as if they were saying to [me], "Is it because you're incapable of being governed that you become colonels?" ... The shame was vivid. Everyone felt shame; I ... felt shame. [I asked myself,] "what percent of the responsibility was mine?" [And] I had the shame [of knowing] that from our own bad handling both the image of the country abroad and the economy had gone to pot.[31]

In sum, interviews with former military officers indicate that the military's reasons for submission to civilian control had little to do with an inculcation of democratic values. Instead, the military hierarchy realized that the capabilities of the military had been impaired by its seven years of political intervention. Faced with the possibility of war—embarrassed and ashamed—the Chiefs of the General Staff could do nothing but request the civilian elites' return. Thus, while most officers accepted withdrawal with some degree of satisfaction and even relief, their primary motivation for doing so was to protect their own personal and institutional self-interests as well as the national interests of Greece[32] while having very little, if anything, to do with attitudinal support or even an appreciation for democracy, the newly established democratic regime, its institutions, and rules.

This scenario of the Greek military's withdrawal from politics raises several important theoretical issues. While the nature of the military regime (nonhierarchical), the nature of the elite leading the transition (civilian), and the nature of the transition path (collapse) facilitated the transfer of power, the motivations of officers for doing so do not indicate a commitment to *permanent* withdrawal and depoliticization—a precondition for full democratic consolidation. Since the military's withdrawal in 1974 appears to have had little to do with the inculcation of democratic values, but rather was based on a kind of cost/benefit analysis of political intervention in which withdrawal was seen as the only way to preserve the professional interests of the armed forces as well as the national interests of the Greek state, are there circumstances under which officers might attempt another coup? That is, are there circumstances under which the military might decide to reintervene in politics based on the same perceptions of personal, corporate, or national interests that brought about its extrication from power in the first place?

Interviews conducted with retired military officers provide answers to these questions. Unlike civilian political elites who consistently argued that Greek democracy was fully consolidated and that they could not foresee another authoritarian regime taking power in the future, the overwhelming majority of both retired *pro-* and *anti-*junta officers interviewed indicated that, in their view, military intervention might again prove necessary to protect Greek national interests in the case of an emergency. The words of a pro-junta officer illustrate this point:

[O]ne lesson [the military learned] is that the army should not intervene in politics out of the blue. But … when there are great dangers for the country, and the politicians cannot [solve them], cannot unite, cannot come to an agreement to face those dangers, I believe that the army should not sit with its hands tied . … When the political leadership has proven to be powerless to face the situation … and the officers can offer better services than the politicians of the country … [they] must take a position. … [The] army will not intervene in politics unless such situations arise and such powerlessness appears on the part of the political leadership that someone will have to save this country. And no one else will remain but the officers.[33]

This attitude is reinforced by the answer of a former naval officer who was opposed to the junta, retired from the navy when the coup was launched, and was later arrested and imprisoned by the colonels for his involvement in the navy's 1973 counter-coup attempt against the military regime:

[A]s time passes, the army is becoming more and more democratic and does not think that it could ever be possible for an officer to rule the people. ... However, I cannot exclude that ... if politicians make tremendous mistakes, if extraordinary circumstances arise [an intervention may occur]. ... It will be difficult for another dictatorship to occur in Greece, but if you are asking me to exclude it, I cannot because I don't know what may arise. Perhaps such a situation will transpire the day after tomorrow.[34]

When a former army general who was also dismissed, imprisoned, and exiled by the dictatorship is asked to comment on the fact that the military appears to have permanently withdrawn from politics, he, too, argues,

Yes, certainly [it has]. Except if deviations occur which the human mind cannot conceive ... [and] if the deviations are influenced by events in the regions neighboring Greece. By this I mean the following: If we have some "anomalies" and the anomalies spread farther south from what is already happening in Yugoslavia, and if new anomalies arise from Turkish intervention ... and if it is confirmed that our old allies desire the destruction of our country, then the possibility of a deviation exists. Then, perhaps, even the people will accept the initiatives of the army to save the nation.[35]

Finally, another officer adds, "I am generally optimistic that a coup will not occur again on the part of officers. But on the other hand I believe totally that this is in the hands of politicians."[36]

Given the reasons for the military's initial withdrawal from politics in 1974 as well as the unwillingness of high-ranking retired officers to exclude future intervention, the permanence of the military's withdrawal becomes even more critical. Could significant groups, such as the military, which behaviorally submit to democracy without attitudinally supporting the regime pose an ongoing deconsolidating threat to it? Based on the comments of high-ranking military officers, one might argue that in the case of Greece such a potential existed long after Greek democracy appeared consolidated to most observers.

The responses of these officers are even more significant if one takes into account several earlier studies dealing with military intervention in Greece. While many of these studies dealt with former periods of authoritarian rule and some were even conducted during those authoritarian interludes, the continuity in officers' responses across time is striking. For example, one study of the Greek officer corps during the interwar period found that officers condemned intervention in principle, but felt that military intervention was justified during periods of national emergencies.[37] Comparable results were reported by a 1968 study that asked military officers, "What do you think was (were) the main issue(s) prior to the 1967 military intervention?"[38] All one hundred officers participating in the study gave one or more of the following answers as reasons for intervention: (1) a perceived fear of a communist take-over, (2) a breakdown in government efficiency and political order, and (3) a pervasive decay in public standards and morals. Furthermore, the study reports that while officers did not approve of military intervention in politics for its own sake, they did favor intervention given certain conditions: "Ideally the army should never intervene in politics but, when circumstances demand, the military cannot stand by when the nation is in mortal danger. ... [The military] would never have thought of intervening [in 1967] if the political leadership had been more stable and capable of creating a viable political system."[39] In fact, "the need to save the nation from disaster"[40] appears to be a recurring theme in virtually all military revolts occurring in Greece throughout the twentieth century.

In addition to citing factors such as national emergencies, "disturbances," and "anomalies" to justify interventionism, military officers participating in the 1967 *coup d'état* also stated that the Greek military was following historical precedent by instigating the coup.[41] In launching the dictatorship, officers perceived that they were protecting themselves and the state—which, according to officers, transcends in importance the government of the day—from "danger." Officers indicated that they perceived intervention to be in the "national interest," and since they saw themselves as the professional custodian of the national interest, it was their responsibility to intervene. One study argues: "The Greek professional officer ... make(s) a distinction between the state and the government in power. ... This concept is strongly reinforced by history, in that any civilian government or organization that threatens the status quo (the state) may motivate the Greek officer corps toward intervention."[42]

This discussion of the Greek military's withdrawal from politics provides several theoretical implications. First, since the original motivations for military withdrawal do not indicate a commitment to permanent withdrawal, and since nearly every officer interviewed raised the possibility of future intervention, I contend that factors facilitating the initial extrication of military regimes from power should be viewed as distinct from those factors conducive to *keeping* those regimes out of power. Since the motivations for extrication have to do with immediate gains (rather than with a genuine desire to return to democracy), the willingness of officers to reintervene in politics remains a tangible threat and a real possibility if civilians menace the vertical command structure of the armed forces, question the territorial integrity of the nation-state, challenge the country's international alliances, or attempt to prosecute officers for crimes committed under the dictatorship. Thus, it would appear that until officers are inculcated with democratic values and pluralist ideals, until they are coaxed to attitudinally support democracy or, at a minimum, until they come to reject the military's messianic self-image and to respect the democratic rules of the game, it is virtually impossible to draw solid conclusions about permanent military withdrawal. In order to assess the permanence of withdrawal, it is necessary to distinguish the factors—distinct from those surrounding the military's initial extrication—that will keep officers in the barracks and out of politics in the *long run*. In true convergence fashion, the Greek case highlights one such necessary factor—attitudinal change.

ATTITUDINAL CHANGE IN THE GREEK MILITARY

To this point it has been illustrated how although the Greek military had apparently behaviorally submitted to democracy by the early 1980s, some military officers reserved the prerogative to reintervene in politics "if necessary." If true, this indicates that the Greek military maintained its interventionist attitudes long after democracy was established in 1974 and the military had returned to the barracks. This notwithstanding, most observers classified Greek democracy as fully consolidated.

Felipe Agüero posits, in fact, that militaries can behave in a loyal fashion even while holding antidemocratic values. He contends that while in fully consolidated democracies the military accepts the supremacy of democratic institutions and procedures, in new democracies the military tends to hold on to its authoritarian ideology. He argues that changes in the military's ideology—while essential for democratic persistence in the long run—are not essential for the consolidation of newly democratized regimes: "Early demands for democratic indoctrination place the cart before the horse and may in fact trouble the military's practical acquiescence to democratization by unnecessarily sparking conflict with its prevailing ideological tenets and world views."[43]

In contrast, the findings of my study highlight the very importance of attitudinal change for democratic consolidation. The Greek case indicates that the specter of military intervention hangs over a newly democratized regime long after the military has been confined to the barracks and the regime appears to be consolidated. I contend that as long as military officers hold the interventionist and messianic views that were often expressed to me in interviews, they could substantially challenge any democratic regime. Thus, it is only after politicized militaries adopt more democratic attitudes and abandon their interventionist beliefs that a regime can be considered consolidated. Has such a change occurred in Greece? Has the military democratized? And if so, what factors contributed to its democratization?

On an empirical level, the question must remain open. On the one hand, the 1996 crisis in the Aegean over the islet of Imia raises fresh concerns regarding the nature and extent of civilian supremacy over the military. Specifically, questions were raised by the Chairman of the Joint Chiefs of Staff Admiral Christos Lymberis' seeming insubordination to his civilian superiors as he, first, leaked the minutes of a confidential war council he had had with Prime Minister Kostas Simitis on 30 January and, second, refused to resign from his post for doing so when requested by the government—actions resulting in his dismissal. In addition, it was widely reported in the days following the crisis that bitterness and unease were pervasive in Greek military circles as the military deeply resented being assigned the responsibility for what it perceived to be the government's poor handling of the crisis. Indicative of this resentment was the sharp tone of the announcement made by the Panhellenic Association of Retired Officers, challenging the actions of Prime Minister Simitis, Foreign Minister Theodoros Pangalos, and Minister of Defense Gerasimos Arsenis and declaring that "war is a very serious issue to be left in the hands of *irrelevant* and *impotent* politicians."[44] Then, in the weeks following the sacking of Lymberis, Prime Minister Simitis recanted his criticism of the military and stressed his trust in the readiness and battleworthiness of the Greek armed forces.

Despite this seemingly negative prognosis, if we recall the words of Dankwart Rustow in which he argues that behavioral support for a regime may eventually "spill over" into attitudinal support, we might not be so pessimistic concerning the prospects for Greek democracy. According to Rustow:

In explaining the origins of democracy we need not assume ... that beliefs unilaterally influence actions. Rather, we may recognize ... that there are reciprocal influences. Many of the current theories about democracy seem to imply that to promote democracy you must first foster democrats. ... Instead we should allow for the possibility that circumstances may force, trick, lure or cajole non-democrats into democratic behavior and that their beliefs may adapt ... by some process of rationalization or adaptation.[45]

If true, we would expect the Greek military to be little different from civilian political elites in Greece who moderated gradually through the process of elite convergence, adapting themselves ideologically and organizationally to the norms, rules, and institutions of the new democratic regime. Thus, as was the case with the civilian elites already analyzed in this study, we would expect such factors as political learning and generational change to contribute to the military's adaptation to democracy as well. This is, in fact, what occurred.

In order to fully understand the process by which attitudinal change may have followed behavioral change in the Greek officer corps, active, rather than former, military officers must be interviewed concerning their views on military professionalism and intervention. Research focusing on the attitudes of active officers and young recruits attending the military academies is greatly needed to provide us with indicators of attitudinal change and the motivations behind it. Until such a study has been completed, however, only tentative conclusions can be drawn.

However, based on my preliminary study of retired Greek officers, I argue that *if attitudinal support occurred* (as I presume it did), *it followed from behavioral backing* of the democratic regime, thereby completing the military's submission to civilian control. In Greece, a number of factors seem to have contributed to such attitudinal modification. One such factor, temporal distance from the dictatorship, may have provided sufficient time for generational change and may have contributed to attitudinal modification. Making this argument, one parliamentary deputy stated the following: "Today's officers are not the same people who emerged from the civil war. The previous officers were the officers of the occupation."[46] An officer adds: "The army is not of the mentality of that old period of the dictatorship. They are new people—especially educated about the political changes. They are influenced by the new postdictatorial democratic spirit."[47]

In addition to generational change, the "passing of time" has also contributed to a "learning" process that has changed the attitudes of many officers. For example, one great "lesson" for military officers came from the trials of the protagonists who were sentenced to life in prison and remained there until their deaths. This lesson, to use Rustow's term, helped to "force" officers into a more democratic mindset. As one PASOK deputy argued: "There were also the trials of the colonels and of the primary persons who administered the tortures; there were jail sentences—many of the convicted still remain in prison, others died in jail. ... Thus, anyone thinking about overthrowing the regime would know that if he failed, he would be sent to Korydalos [Prison] for life. ... They knew that they had to face the national justice system."[48] Another officer adds, "It is enough to note that the imprisoned protagonists of that period have not been amnestied yet. ... [I]f there were a foolhardy officer who would want to launch such a coup, he sees Papadopoulos still in prison and thinks twice about doing so."[49]

In addition to forcing and threatening military officers to adopt democratic attitudes by imprisoning the protagonists of the 1967 coup, potential coup makers may have also been "cajoled" by Karamanlis, President George Rallis, and Defense Minister Averoff throughout the conservatives' stay in power (1974–81). Averoff, in particular, believed that even those officers who had tacitly supported the military regime could be taught the virtues of democracy and civilian rule. In fact, one author's point of view that Averoff "desired more to submit the juntist officers to his own personal influence and protection and less to remove them from the armed forces" is not far from the truth.[50] As Averoff himself boasted: "I brainwashed them (military men) extensively on the merits of democracy. I think there is not a single officer ... (to whom) I did not speak personally at least three times."[51]

Even more importantly, the socialist government's efforts, beginning in 1983, to reform the curricula of military academies as well as the patterns of recruitment to these schools may have also contributed to changes in the mentalities of young officers and new recruits. Under these reforms admission to the military academies was integrated with the system of National University Examinations in which admission depends solely on performance rather than on investigations of the political persuasions of recruits and their families and friends. Furthermore, the reforms in the curricula of the academies were intended to impart a broader liberal background to cadets. Thus, unlike the young officers who, during the seven years of dictatorial rule, had graduated from the military academies, having received their military training under Ioannidis[52] and who subscribed to extremely radical and interventionist attitudes concerning the political role of the military, the post-junta cadets were educated with a more democratic mindset. According to one officer who was active in reforming the military academies in the post-1974 period, the efforts made to inculcate military officers with democratic attitudes seem to have been successful:

[We] began to change the curriculum in the academies and we had university professors teach ... twenty hours of sociology, twenty hours of constitutional law, [etc.]. ... Thus by teaching [courses on] constitutional law, the rights of citizens, human rights, etc., [the possibility of intervention] ... is becoming less and less likely. ... The boys who are now lieutenants have graduated under this system, and they understand more. ... They understand that each person is suited for his own job, and, furthermore, that the opportunity exists for those [officers] who want to run for [political] office. And there are officers in both parties—but not with weapons. They understand that it is one thing to command a military camp and another to command a ministry; and that is a totally different perception and mentality.[53]

Finally, there is even an indication that a trend has emerged within the Greek officer corps by which the military organization is moving away from "institutionalism" toward "occupationalism."[54] Charles Moskos states that members of an institution, such as the military, often perceive themselves as following a calling in life—captured by words such as *duty, honor*, and *country*—and therefore see themselves, and are regarded by others, as being apart from the broader society. Such groups also perceive their primary identification as being that of their institution; as a result, they are exclusionary and isolationist. This is the traditional "institutional military" model. The "occupational military" model, on the other hand, refers to the principles of the free market, viewing military service as comparable (in economic terms) to types of service provided by civilians. Thus, military service is simply one occupation among many within society. While the institutional model implies that there is only one legitimate interest—the interest of the institution to which one belongs—the occupational model implies that individual self-interests have priority over the institutional interests of the organization.[55] Military service is more of a job and less of a sacred calling.

It appears that the Greek military in the post-1974 period has undergone change in this dimension, moving from the institutional to the occupational model—both in terms of social organization as well as in civil-military relations. Traditionally, personnel in the Greek armed forces identified primarily with other military personnel, rather than with civilian social groups performing like occupational tasks. They made few friendships with civilians, social isolation was fairly complete, and senior officers even passed approval on the marriages of junior officers.[56] One study describes this precoup phenomenon: "What has emerged is a social isolation of the military families from other elements of Greek society, thereby creating a strong *esprit de corps* among the families and the officer corps. ... [T]his isolation by itself may be a leading factor in the lack of understanding on the part of the military community of the social, political, and economic events from 1965 to 1967."[57]

Today, this isolationism and exclusionary identification with other members of the armed forces is rapidly declining. A growing number of officers attend civilian universities in addition to the traditional military academies; draftees and officers are now allowed to wear civilian clothes when home on leave; wives of officers are increasingly likely to be professionals themselves, leading to nonmilitary friendships as officers interact with their wives' colleagues as well as with their own.[58] According to Dimitrios Smokovitis, such changes actually strengthen military effectiveness while subordinating the military to civilian rule.[59] Corroborating Smokovitis' claim, a retired military officer indicated in an interview that the integration of military personnel into civilian society is occurring and is enhancing the democratization of the armed forces:

[W]hat helped very much was the opening toward the people. ... [F]or the last fifteen years, since 1980, civilian [primary and secondary] schools have become more acceptant of military bases—to go, to see, to get on the weapons, to get in the airplanes, to see how the recruits are trained, and to speak to them. We have even suggested to the universities that we ought to conduct studies together. … Thus there [now] exists a mutual trust. Let me tell you the following: This country suffered because we had placed officers in a box which we had placed on a pedestal. But they themselves were unhappy. We [officers] were not paid well. We could hardly make ends meet. But we had to wear a tie, a uniform, this and that … Thus, [civilians were] … jealous of [us]. [And we officers were] jealous of [civilians].[60]

In short, the fact that officers were placed on a pedestal and greatly esteemed by civilian society contributed greatly to the military's messianic mindset and reinforced its self-perception as savior of the nation. The current trend toward occupationalism, however, is leading to a modification of such attitudes, rendering the military less likely to overthrow civilian supremacy in the future.

In sum, attitudinal support for democracy appears to have followed from behavioral support of the democratic regime in Greece and thus completed the military's submission to civilian control. However, this necessary condition for democratic consolidation—attitudinal change—has come slowly and has had little to do with the initial factors facilitating extrication. For attitudinal change to occur, time was required. The "passing of time" contributed to generational change, to a process of learning, to changes in the curricula and the recruitment patterns of the military academies, and to new patterns of civil-military relations.

THEORETICAL AND COMPARATIVE PERSPECTIVES ON THE GREEK MILITARY

The relative ease with which the Greek military regime was extricated from politics in July 1974 offers support to the various explanations found in the literature on democratic transition and consolidation processes concerning the varying capabilities of armed forces to place limits on democratization. First, concerning the nature of the outgoing authoritarian regime, the military hierarchy, acting as part of the state rather than of the regime, deposed the nonhierarchical military regime and invited civilian elites back to power. Second, the urgency of immediate extrication from power brought on by the Cyprus catastrophe and the military's inability to defend Greece from Turkey precluded the military from imposing any confining conditions on civilians and assured civilian elites of a free hand in directing the transition. Last, the cautious handling of military matters by both Karamanlis in the 1970s and Papandreou in the early 1980s reassured officers that they had nothing to fear under a democratic regime and contributed to a "hands-off" policy during the entire transition for the majority of military officers. In sum, if we were to judge the transition from military to civilian rule on these criteria alone, it would be difficult not to conclude that Greece's transition path was exemplary.

Despite the high "scores," the Greek case indicates that such factors do not say enough about the permanence of military withdrawal from politics. Since military extrication may have nothing to do with a conversion to democratic values, and since diffuse support for democracy as well as explicit support for democratic rules, norms, and institutions may not exist at the time of withdrawal, the prospects for democratic consolidation are initially uncertain in countries where the military has been extricated from power. In fact, evidence offered by the Greek case indicates that in many such countries officers might be willing to reintervene in politics although the military has been successfully withdrawn from power and has behaviorally submitted to civilian rule. Thus, officers who behaviorally submit to their civilian superiors without attitudinally supporting the democratic regime, its institutions, and rules might pose a significant deconsolidating threat until they come to respect the democratic rules of the game. *Behavioral submission to democracy is simply not enough for democratic consolidation to take place.* It is only after the military has been *attitudinally democratized*—once it comes to fully accept its submission to civilian elites—that a fuller and deeper consolidation of democracy can occur. The Greek case shows that such changes in military attitudes can, in fact, occur, but they, like those of civilians, usually require a long period of time.

The case of the Spanish transition to democracy offers further credence to this argument. Even there—where the outgoing dictatorship was civilian—civilian elites were clearly cognizant of the importance of appeasing rather than alienating military circles during the transition in the hope of gradually inculcating them with a respect for the new democratic regime, its rules of the game, and its institutions. As in Greece, Spanish elites were conscious of the possibility of a military backlash in the early stages of the transition and were therefore careful to treat the military with caution and respect. Following the failed military coup attempt in February 1981, for example, King Juan Carlos, rather than admonishing officers, echoed some of their very own criticisms, castigating "political acts ... [and] press campaigns which foster[ed] conditions that create[d] uneasiness, annoyance and concern in the Armed Forces."[61] Even during the trials that followed the coup attempt, care was taken not to irritate the military—very few officers had charges brought against them and even a majority of those participating in the assault were left unprosecuted. Then, a year later, during the *Pascua Militar*[62] of January 1982, the king thanked the armed forces for their discipline, emphasizing that they had come to expect more consideration, dignity, and respect and sympathizing with those surprised by "the indispensable freedom of expression ... , the changes in the ways of public treatment of military affairs, and the imposition of silence on those who perform this profession."[63] Moreover, following the army's warnings that a state of undiscipline would be unleashed should members of the *Unión Militar Democrática* (UMD)[64] receive amnesty and thereby be permitted to reenter the army, the Spanish Cortes, acknowledging the warning, declined amnesty to the organization. Even the Spanish socialists pointed out the outdated state of the armed forces, blaming Franquism for its backwardness, and, like the Greek socialists, pledged modernization, higher levels of military spending, and even the development of a local military industry should they be elected to government.

Despite such cautious handling of military matters, behavioral manifestations of a lack of military submission to civilian superiors also endured in Spain throughout the 1970s and into the early 1980s. In fact, Agüero maintains that as the costs of military acquiescence increased with the dramatic upswing in terrorist activities and the explosion of micronationalist demands, the hard-liners within the military reverted from disgruntled consent to active opposition to democratization, particularly after the founding elections of 1982. Certain military factions actively opposed democratization until after the founding elections of 1982. Examples are numerous. The military was openly angered when the minister of the interior, Manuel Fraga, publicly stated in 1976 that the legalization of the Communist Party was imminent. And, when the communists were finally legalized, not only did an official communique indicate "general repulsion in army units," but a number of army generals had to intervene to stop mobilization orders issued by junior officers.[65] Although more minor, another military effort to arrest democratization, *Operación Galaxia*, was an attempt in 1978 by a small group of mid-level officers to prevent the constitutional referendum from taking place. When Vice President Gutiérrez Mellado traveled around Spain to explain government policy and the draft constitution to officers, he was met with instances of a lack of discipline. In January 1980 conspiratorial meetings held in divisional headquarters were discovered. Then, in the most dramatic example of military unrest, on 23 February 1981, a heavily armed unit of the Civil Guard held the Cortes at gunpoint while large army units in and around the capital mobilized in their support. As Felipe Agüero maintains, "the episode ... highlighted the vulnerability of the new democracy, which could not be considered consolidated as long as the 'military problem' remained unsolved."[66] Agüero argues that even after the failed coup attempt, "[l]arge sectors of the army continued to harbor an overt repudiation of democratic institutions, and overt contestation and undiscipline continued to challenge civilian authority."[67] For example, plans were later discovered to assassinate the king and members of government by disgruntled military officers who disliked the way the monarchy had dealt with the 1981 failed coup attempt.[68] Even as late as 1987, there remained small groups in the military capable of engaging in seditious activity. As the then–Secretary of State for Defense warned: "The problem is over as a whole, but there remain smoldering minorities that should not be overlooked. We have to be cautious as serpents and never forget this possibility."[69]

In Spain as in Greece, however, a slow but steady learning process contributed to the military's attitudinal change. Like Karamanlis, Rallis, and Averoff "cajoling" the potential coup makers in Greece, King Juan Carlos was instrumental in reminding the Spanish army that it "ought to know how to interpret the Constitution with prudence and accuracy and to understand that the security of the Fatherland is not aided with thoughtless actions which place the Armed Forces and the State in critical situations, for which there can be no dignified way out."[70] Nonetheless, this important lesson was not learned overnight. In fact, it was not until after the failed coup attempt and the inauguration of the Calvo Sotelo administration (which devoted itself to terminating the hard-liners' threat to democracy) that officers slowly but gradually came to realize that democracy was there to stay and that the military ought to accommodate itself within it.[71] Specifically, the realization that military officers ought to submit themselves to their civilian superiors was brought about by the recognition that the most significant hard-liners had failed in their efforts and were now facing long prison terms. This, as well as the inappropriate behavior of the prosecuted senior officers during televised trials, demoralized the army and especially lower-ranking officers who were disillusioned with behavior that, in their eyes, lacked military honor. Thus, like the Greek case, attitudinal change in the Spanish military also appears to have followed from behavioral backing of the democratic regime. While conclusive evidence is unavailable, the discrediting of antisystem options is widely believed to have influenced military officers to such a degree that "no significant sector of the Spanish military today holds out any hope for an antidemocratic alternative to the present regime."[72]

In short, in both Greece and Spain, civilian elites embraced the new democratic regime; however, certain military officers did not and were initially unwilling to submit themselves to democratic rule. Thus, I submit that in both countries there was only a partial consolidation of the democratic regime, with most significant parties in full compliance with democracy, but with factions of the military maintaining their semiloyal and antisystem positions. In the early stages of both transitions, then, the Spanish and Greek militaries were the greatest threat to democracy since they remained outside the overall elite consensus.

In sum, this chapter has again highlighted that attitudinal changes are long-term phenomena, requiring years for new democratic outlooks to take shape and for old antidemocratic attitudes to be modified. In the immediate aftermath of extrication, democratic civilian elites can best keep the armed forces out of politics by reassuring the military that its corporate interests will not be harmed, maintaining (even increasing) current levels of military expenditure, praising the military's devotion to its duties, and gently reminding officers of the harm politicization can do to the capabilities and professionalism of the armed forces. Put simply, forcing, tricking, luring, and cajoling nondemocratic military officers to remain depoliticized in the early phases of the transition is imperative in order to buy the time required to bring about attitudinal support for democratic norms and institutions—a requisite for democratic consolidation. In short, military elites are little different from their civilian counterparts. They, too, must converge around democratic norms and principles before the regime can be considered consolidated. In the Greek case it just happened that military elites were the last players to be "tamed" and to accept democracy as "the only game in town."

NOTES

1. See Juan J. Linz and Alfred Stepan, *Problems of Democratic Transition and Consolidation: Southern Europe, South America, and Post-Communist Europe* (Baltimore: The Johns Hopkins University Press, 1996); and "Toward Consolidated Democracies," *Journal of Democracy* 7: 2 (April 1996), pp. 14–33.

2. Felipe Agüero, "Democratic Consolidation and the Military in Southern Europe and South America," in Richard Gunther, P. Nikiforos Diamandouros, and Hans-Jürgen Puhle, eds., *The Politics of Democratic Consolidation: Southern Europe in Comparative Perspective* (Baltimore: The Johns Hopkins University Press, 1995); and Agüero, *Soldiers, Civilians, and Democracy: Post-Franco Spain in Comparative Perspective* (Baltimore: The Johns Hopkins University Press, 1995).

3. Juan J. Linz, Alfred Stepan, and Richard Gunther, "Democratic Transition and Consolidation in Southern Europe, with Reflections on Latin America and Eastern Europe," in Gunther et al., eds, *The Politics of Democratic Consolidation.*

4. Agüero, "Democratic Consolidation and the Military."

5. See David Pion-Berlin, "Between Confrontation and Accommodation: Military and Government Policy in Democratic Argentina," *Journal of Latin American Studies* 23 (October 1991), p. 549.

6. Quoted in Constantine P. Danopoulos, *Warriors and Politicians in Modern Greece* (Chapel Hill, NC: Documentary Publications, 1985), p. 126.

7. On military extrication from politics, see Constantine P. Danopoulos, "From Military to Civilian Rule in Contemporary Greece," *Armed Forces and Society* 10:2 (Winter 1984), pp. 229–50, "From Balconies to Tanks: Post-Junta Civil-Military Relations in Greece," *Journal of Political and Military Sociology* 13:1 (Spring 1985), pp. 83–98, *Warriors and Politicians*, "Beating a Hasty Retreat: The Greek Military Withdraws from Power," in Danopoulos, ed., *The Decline of Military Regimes: The Civilian Influence* (Boulder: Westview, 1988), "Democratizing the Military: Lessons from Mediterranean Europe," *West European Politics* 14:4 (October 1991), pp. 25–41, "Farewell to Man on Horseback: Intervention and Civilian Supremacy in Modern Greece," in Danopoulos, ed., *From Military to Civilian Rule* (London: Routledge, 1992); Danopoulos and Larry N. Gerston, "Democratic Currents in Authoritarian Seas: The Military in Greece and the Philippines," *Armed Forces and Society* 16:4 (Summer 1990), pp. 529–45; Danopoulos and Kant Patel, "Military Professionals as Political Governors: A Case Study of Contemporary Greece," *West European Politics* 3:2 (May 1980), pp. 188–201; and Thanos Veremis, "The Military," in Kevin Featherstone and Dimitrios K. Katsoudas, eds., *Political Change in Greece Before and After the Colonels* (New York: St. Martin's Press, 1987).

8. For this argument see Theodore A. Couloumbis, "Defining Greek Foreign Policy Objectives," in Howard R. Penniman, ed., *Greece at the Polls: The National Elections of 1974 and 1977* (Washington: American Enterprise Institute for Public Policy Research, 1981), p. 166; and Theodore A. Couloumbis and Prodromos M. Yannis, "The Stability Quotient of Greece's Post-1974 Democratic Institutions," *Journal of Modern Greek Studies* 1:2 (October 1983), p. 372.

9. This was unlike Argentina where drastic steps were taken to purge the military of officers involved in repression, to imprison the protagonists, and to cut military spending, thereby pushing military officers to repeatedly intervene so as to "defend" themselves against civilians.

10. Quoted in Danopoulos, *Warriors and Politicians*, p. 133.

11. *Keesing's Contemporary Archives*, 23 (1977), p. 28686.

12. Quoted in Danopoulos, *Warriors and Politicians*, p. 140.

13. "Democratization" should not be confused with "dejuntification." The later involves an effort to purge and prosecute officers associated with the previous military regime. In contrast, democratization is a longer-term process involving educational reform and an opening of the officer corps to recruits of all parties and political persuasions. Obviously, democratization of the armed forces is a much less personal threat to military officers than is dejuntification.

14. *Facts on File*, 34 (1974), pp. 129, 166, 626; *Facts on File*, 35 (1975), pp. 129, 809; and *Keesing's*, 21 (1975), p. 27090.

15. *Keesing's*, 23 (1977), p. 28689; and *To Vema*, 31 August 1977.

16. *Keesing's*, 26 (1980), p. 30267.

17. "Greek Socialism: Walking the Tightrope," *Journal of the Hellenic Diaspora* 9:1 (Spring 1982), p. 15.

18. Memorandum concerning the events before and after the 1981 elections, written in February 1982 by Karamanlis, quoted in Demetres Michalopoulos, "PASOK and the Eastern Bloc: A Growing Relationship," in Nikolaos A. Stavrou, ed., *Greece under Socialism: A NATO Ally Adrift* (New Rochelle, NY: Aristide D. Caratzas, 1988), p. 352.

19. Nicos Alivizatos, "The Presidency, Parliament and the Courts in the 1980s," in Richard Clogg, ed., *Greece, 1981–89: The Populist Decade* (New York: St. Martin's Press, 1993), p. 67.

20. Memorandum concerning the events, quoted in Michalopoulos, "PASOK and the Eastern Bloc," p. 352.

21. Danopoulos, *Warriors and Politicians*, pp. 147–48; *Daily Reports: Western Europe*, 7 (1 March 1983–22 March 1983) (Washington: Foreign Broadcast Information Service); *Keesing's*, 29 (1983), p. 32587; and Nikolai Todorov, *The Ambassador as Historian: An Eyewitness Account of Bulgarian-Greek Relations in the 1980s* (New Rochelle, NY: Aristide D. Caratzas, Publisher, 1999), pp. 165–66.

22. For details on this, see Danopoulos, *Warriors and Politicians*, pp. 134–35.

23. "Democratic Transition and Consolidation," p. 85.

24. Basilios Evangelos Tsingos, "The Breakdown of Authoritarian Regimes: The Political Evolution of the Greek Military Dictatorship, 1967–74," Honors Thesis, Harvard College, April 1990.

25. Tsingos, "The Breakdown of Authoritarian Regimes."

26. Danopoulos, "Beating a Hasty Retreat," pp. 238–39.

27. Interview conducted with military officer in Athens, Greece, on 6 April 1994.

28. Interview conducted with military officer in Athens, Greece, on 17 March 1994.

29. Interview conducted with PASOK deputy in Athens, Greece, on 8 February 1994.

30. Danopoulos, *Warriors and Politicians*, pp. 136–37.

31. Interview conducted with military officer in Athens, Greece, on 17 May 1994.

32. See also Danopoulos, "Beating a Hasty Retreat;" and James Brown, "The Military in Politics: A Case Study of Greece," Ph.D. Dissertation, State University of New York at Buffalo, 1971, p. 225.

33. Interview conducted with military officer in Athens, Greece, on 17 March 1994.

34. Interview conducted with military officer in Athens, Greece, on 9 April 1994.

35. Interview conducted with military officer in Athens, Greece, on 6 April 1994. The lack of specificity of the terms "deviation" and "anomaly" indicate, I believe, the ambiguity of the officer's perception of threats requiring military rectification.

36. Interview conducted with military officer in Athens, Greece, on 17 May 1994.

37. Thanos Veremis, "Some Observations on the Greek Military in the Inter-War Period, 1918–25," *Armed Forces and Society* 4:3 (Spring 1978), p. 530.

38. George A. Kourvetaris, "Professional Self-Images and Political Perspectives in the Greek Military," *American Sociological Review* 36:6 (December 1971), pp. 1043–57.

39. Kourvetaris, "Professional Self-Images and Political Perspectives," p. 1055.

40. S. Victor Papacosma, "The Military in Greek Politics: A Historical Survey," in John T.A. Koumoulides, ed., *Greece in Transition: Essays in the History of Modern Greece 1821–1974* (London: Zeno Booksellers and Publishers, 1977), p. 184.

41. For this argument see Brown, "The Military in Politics," p. 118.

42. Brown, "The Military in Politics," p. 183–84.

43. Agüero, "Democratic Consolidation and the Military," p. 125.

44. *Ta Nea*, 2 February 1996, emphasis added. For information on this crisis see *Ta Nea*, 31 January 1996–9 February 1996.

45. Dankwart Rustow, "Transitions to Democracy: Toward a Dynamic Model," *Comparative Politics* 2:3 (April 1970), p. 344.

46. Interview conducted with *Nea Demokratia* deputy in Athens, Greece, on 10 December 1993.

47. Interview conducted with military officer in Athens, Greece, on 6 April 1994.

48. Interview conducted with PASOK deputy in Athens, Greece, on 7 February 1994.

49. Interview conducted with military officer in Athens, Greece, on 6 April 1994. Papadopoulos, the leader of the 1967 coup, died in prison in June 1999.

50. Potes Paraskeuopoulos, *Ho Karamanlis sta Chronia 1974–1985* (Karamanlis in the Years 1974–1985) (Athens: Ho Typos, n.d.), p. 159.

51. Danopoulos, *Warriors and Politicians*, p. 138.

52. Besides being the head of ESA, Ioannidis was also Commandant of the Greek Military Academy. Thus, he was in charge of the recruitment and training of all new army officers.

53. Interview conducted with military officer in Athens, Greece, on 17 May 1994.

54. See Charles C. Moskos and Frank R. Wood, eds., *The Military: More Than Just a Job?* (Washington: Pergamon-Brassey's International Defense Publishers, Inc., 1988).

55. Charles C. Moskos, "Institutional and Occupational Trends in Armed Forces," in Moskos and Wood, eds., *The Military*, pp. 16–17.

56. Dimitrios Smokovitis, " Greece," in Moskos and Wood, eds., *The Military*, p. 251.

57. Brown, "The Military in Politics," p. 183.

58. Smokovitis, "Greece," p. 252.

59. Smokovitis, "Greece," p. 253. For a discussion of how today's officers have been incorporated into civil society to an unprecedented degree, by twentieth-century standards, see Thanos Veremis, *The Military in Greek Politics: From Independence to Democracy* (Montreal: Black Rose Books, 1997).

60. Interview conducted with military officer in Athens, Greece, on 17 May 1994.

61. Quoted in Aguëro, *Soldiers, Civilians, and Democracy*, p. 171.

62. The *Pascua Militar* is a Christmas celebration in which the top brass meet with the king and exchange salutes.

63. Quoted in Agüero, *Soldiers, Civilians, and Democracy*, p, 171.

64. A clandestine organization that had been sentenced and expelled from the army in 1975.

65. Agüero, *Soldiers, Civilians, and Democracy*, p. 84.

66. Agüero, *Soldiers, Civilians, and Democracy*, p. 135.

67. Agüero, *Soldiers, Civilians, and Democracy*, p. 168.

68. Agüero, *Soldiers, Civilians, and Democracy*, p. 211.

69. Quoted in Agüero, *Soldiers, Civilians, and Democracy*, p. 211.

70. Quoted in Agüero, *Soldiers, Civilians and Democracy*, p. 171.

71. Agüero, *Soldiers, Civilians, and Democracy*, p. 174.

72. Richard Gunther, Hans-Jürgen Puhle, and P. Nikiforos Diamandouros, "Introduction," in Gunther et al., eds., *The Politics of Democratic Consolidation*, p. 22.

Achieving the Golden Mean: The Complex Dynamics of Elite Consensual Unity

Throughout this study I have argued that the moderation of elite attitudes and behavior was fundamental to the achievement of a stable and consolidated democratic regime in Greece. Unlike the literature on consolidation that associates the concept of democratic consolidation with the enhancement of the quality of democracy or with its deepening, in this study I have treated consolidation as distinct from issues regarding the quality or deepening of democracy. In taking this position I have adopted the stance of Juan Linz, Alfred Stepan, and Andreas Schedler,[1] among others, who maintain that, within the category of consolidated democracies, one may find both high- and low-quality democracies, both democracies that have been deepened as well as others that have not. Thus, I argue that, for a number of reasons, Greece is without doubt a consolidated, yet low-quality, democracy. As Linz and Stepan point out in their study of democratic consolidation:

When we circulated earlier drafts of this book, ... colleagues frequently expressed reservations about our calling Greek democracy consolidated. They correctly pointed out that former Prime Minister Andreas Papandreou and other leaders of his government were under indictment for corruption, that Greece's budget deficit was the highest in the EEC and that no government of any stripe could bring it under control, that the style of political discourse seemed dangerously acrimonious, and that two general elections in a row (June 1989 and November 1989) had produced hung parliaments.[2]

Indeed, a great number of problems can be enumerated to illustrate the low-quality of Greek democracy. Take, for example, the way in which successive post-transition governments have sought to bolster their electoral support by adding thousands of employees to the public payroll during election years. This patronage-based recruitment to the public sector has increased steeply since democratization, with the public sector now employing an astounding 30 to 40 percent of the population—about double the OECD average.[3] As I have noted elsewhere,[4] this colossal growth of the public sector has been an enormous drain on state revenues and has been responsible for the highest budgetary deficit in the EU.[5] It has led to overstaffing and underemployment, while the professionalism and overall quality of public service has suffered badly.

A second area in which the quality of Greek democracy—indeed the quality of Southern European democracy as a whole—has remained relatively poor is in the area of social welfare provision. Despite an overall increase in aggregate-level expenditures and other important welfare reforms legislated by Southern European governments, the Portuguese, Spanish, Italian, and Greek social welfare states do not compare well with the generous, universalistic models of welfare provision present in much of the Western industrialized world. Rather than being characterized by the principles of universalism, the Greek welfare state remains fragmented, corporatist, and particularistic. Greeks (and the other citizens of Southern Europe) enjoy widely varying levels of entitlements in pension, unemployment, and other benefits depending on their position in the labor market, their gender, age, and place of residence. Moreover, traditional patron-clientelist practices, with roots in agricultural society, have been transplanted into the urban centers and have been incorporated into the modern social welfare state, further limiting its political accountability and universalism. In sum, while post-transition politics and ideology have greatly expanded the scope of the Greek welfare state, an employment-driven corporatist model of welfare continues to produce a highly uneven pattern of social insurance coverage.[6]

Specifically, clientelist practices within the social welfare state (and elsewhere) are pervasive, as successive governments use public resources to manage consensus. Typically, this has taken the form of a direct exchange of some kind of favor—unemployment benefits, disability and old-age pensions, employment in the public sector, or income assistance—in return for electoral support. The origins of such practices lie in the period preceding democratization, when in the absence of truly participatory, representative workers associations, clientelism became a method by which Greece's repressive post–civil war regime received legitimacy as well as complacency and support from key societal sectors.[7] Such clientelistic trade-offs remain intact in Greece and represent an obvious departure from the standards of high-quality democracy.

Despite these and other shortcomings, however, Greek democracy is today stable and consolidated. No major threat to the regime, its institutions, or rules exists. Across the political spectrum Greek political and military elites consciously adopted more moderate and consensual political attitudes regarding the legitimacy of existing institutions and rules of the game and they conformed to the norms of democratic behavior. In so doing they secured the consolidation and long-run stability of democracy. Without this critical element of convergence, Greece would likely have returned to the divisive politics of the pre-junta period, thereby threatening the new democratic regime and potentially precluding successful democratic consolidation.

This focus on the role that elites and their attitudes play in cases of successful democratization is not new. Recognizing the critical importance of elite consensual unity, a variety of scholars have attempted to explain how it can be achieved. This study has considered two such models of elite moderation—the elite settlement and elite convergence models.

As I have argued, neither model can fully account for the successful consolidation of Greek democracy. The problem lies in their complexity. Being overly aggregated concepts, neither the logic of the elite settlement model—interelite negotiations leading to consensual unity and a formal agreement—nor that of the elite convergence model—elite moderation resulting from electoral pressures and motivations—adequately captures the complexity of the Greek experience. Since both models focus exclusively on a single factor—the presence or absence of a settlement, on the one hand, and the moderating pressure of electoral competition, on the other—they fail to incorporate what was in the Greek case an often bewildering variety of elite motivations and dynamic processes. A superficial look at the Greek case suggests a lack of conformity with the dynamics inherent in these two models. However, a closer examination of the Greek consolidation process reveals that the causal mechanisms underpinning convergence can be identified in Greece, but that they did not function in quite the ways the model suggests. The prime theoretical contribution of this study, then, has been to disaggregate the complex phenomena of elite convergence into its component parts, thereby refining our theoretical understanding of the various ways in which elite consensual unity can be achieved.

MODEL I: ELITE SETTLEMENT

First, there is the elite settlement model. As discussed in previous chapters and as best illustrated by the Spanish transition to democracy, elite settlements involve face-to-face negotiations behind closed doors between all significant political elites. Such negotiations are successful when an explicit agreement regarding the specific rules, norms, and procedures of the new democratic regime is achieved. This study has repeatedly made clear that *no elite settlement or pact* was successfully negotiated in Greece. In fact, at no time during the junta years or the transition period did all politically significant elites even meet together in the same room to discuss their political goals. Instead, informal negotiations and contacts progressed by fits and starts prior to the transition, but never came to any kind of fruition.

The literature on elite settlements has identified a variety of structural conditions antithetical to successful settlements. Chief among these are an excessive level of elite fragmentation and a lack of institutionalization of secondary organizations.[8] The Greek case points to a novel third structural characteristic that may preclude elite settlements. In Greece a critical factor in the failure of these negotiations—and indeed a significant influence on the transition and consolidation processes themselves—was the impact of political culture. In a political culture such as Greece's, personal distrust and deep partisan animosity are part and parcel of political life. Politics is viewed as a fundamentally win-lose, zero-sum competitive game—a game in which decisively defeating one's opponent is the ultimate goal. Thus, compromise and conciliation are viewed, at best, as the evidence of a lack of political will and, at worst, as the outcomes of "dirty" deals between unprincipled political players. Clearly, such attitudes toward consensual politics undercut the capacity of political elites to be pragmatic and to make concessions. It should thus come as little surprise that the political rule of the day is "principled," divisive position-taking, with little time for moderation, pragmatism, or conciliation.

The nonconsensual nature of Greek political culture was clearly a major impediment to the successful achievement of an elite settlement during the junta years. It is incredible that even in the face of a common enemy that was nearly unanimously despised by all civilian elites, Greek elites were unable to compromise and effect a united antidictatorial front. Though the imperative of unity among all antidictatorial forces was universally acknowledged, calls for unity did nothing to bring elites together. Deeply resistant to the very idea of partisan compromise, Greek political leaders were simply unwilling to hammer out a common front. Thus, despite the significant number of informal contacts that took place during the military dictatorship between leaders of all political parties and resistance groups, partisan and personal animosities, mutual feelings of distrust, and a general unwillingness to compromise doomed these attempts at concerted anti-junta action. Simply put, an elite settlement was never concluded in Greece because Greek elites were unwilling to reach agreement and bring informal negotiations to a successful conclusion.

Greek antipathy to partisan cooperation and consensus carried over into the democratization process as well. Unlike Adolfo Suárez in Spain who spearheaded broad all-party settlements, Karamanlis, during the Greek transition to democracy, consciously and deliberately excluded as many people as possible from political power, believing that negotiations and compromise would only lead to unnecessary delay, even stalemate and immobilism. As a result, no successful negotiations took place during the constitutional engineering process between the *Nea Demokratia* government and the opposition, as they did in Spain between Suárez's UCD and the opposition. Instead, the Greek government presented parliament with its own draft of the constitutional text and was only willing to accept opposition revisions to articles of secondary importance. Not surprisingly, parliamentary debates followed the usual pattern—highly polarized and confrontational political attacks.

Paradoxically enough, this tendency toward partisan conflict did not seem to impede or jeopardize the process of democratic consolidation in Greece as extreme partisanship endangered the transition in Portugal for a time. Instead, Greek elites and the general public seemed to understand well that parliamentary "warfare" was simply the appropriate expression of legitimate partisan differences. The opposition's rhetoric—and especially that of PASOK—was interpreted by many Greeks as merely verbal and electorally motivated. For instance, surveys indicate that a sizeable proportion of PASOK's electorate did not take its socialist platform seriously in 1981[9] and that half of its prospective voters viewed it as a "socialist non-Marxist party" despite Papandreou's pronouncements that PASOK was in fact Marxist.[10] Moreover, elite interviews revealed that deputies of all parties perceived the early transition period as one of the *finest* periods of Greek democratic life—this despite opposition rhetoric that, at the time, bemoaned the alleged undemocratic tyranny of the new government. Interestingly, opposition deputies argued that neither their antagonistic positions nor their abstention from the vote on the constitution were indicative of a lack of loyalty either to the new constitution or to the new democratic regime. They were, at most, partisan political tactics. As the Greek case illustrates, partisan rancor is not necessarily antithetical to democracy and democratic consolidation.

The Greek case thus highlights an important point. In societies in which an unwillingness to negotiate or compromise is an integral part of political culture, the lack of formal negotiation and partisan compromise does not necessarily imply a lack of consensus regarding the specific procedures and institutions of the new democratic regime. The Greek case also points up that while elite convergence on the specific rules and institutions of the new regime is clearly a precondition for democratic consolidation and stability, ideological, programmatic, and rhetorical moderation is not necessarily required. Instead, rhetorically antagonistic relations between elites ought to be seen as potentially a part of "normal" partisan politics and not an automatic threat to democratic stability. Indeed, to take the point one step further, in societies in which negotiation and compromise are viewed as "selling out" or as a weakness of political will (and especially where the electorate is itself highly polarized), extended elite negotiations behind closed doors as well as ideological, partisan, and rhetorical moderation can actually be perceived as nonrepresentative and fundamentally *antidemocratic* in nature, thereby casting doubt on the legitimacy of the new democracy and jeopardizing the process of democratic consolidation.

In fact, the case of PASOK shows that radical rhetoric and ideological stances need not threaten democratic consolidation and stability, but may in fact *facilitate* it. As I argued in chapter 6, much of PASOK's radical rhetoric in the early period of Greece's transition was motivated by electoral concerns and thus was not indicative of a fully antisystem or semiloyal position. Papandreou's impassioned criticism of the Karamanlis government, Greece's constitution, and the new democracy, as well as his calls for socialism and withdrawal from the European Community and NATO, were clearly aimed at mobilizing the support of an electorate radicalized by seven years of dictatorial rule. In this case, as with the KKE in 1991, electoral motivations were instrumental in *radicalizing* rather than moderating PASOK in the early period of its existence as a political party.

However—and this is the crucial point—contrary to much of the literature that posits that ideological and programmatic moderation is necessary for democratic consolidation and stability, the case of PASOK provides us a clear example of the opposite—that Papandreou's initial radicalism actually *facilitated* democratic consolidation. It did so by voicing the grievances and frustrations of dissatisfied antiestablishment voters who might otherwise have withdrawn their support from the newly democratized regime. While most analysts argue that such radicalism has the potential of mobilizing sectors of the population into active opposition to the new regime, in Greece the reverse occurred—PASOK's radicalism actually facilitated democratic consolidation and stability by providing a viable political and ideological home for many disaffected voters. Later, as PASOK moderated its radical positions and rhetoric, so did its electorate. In this way, by the mid-1980s, PASOK supporters had become fully coopted into the new democratic regime.

This analysis of PASOK's radicalism highlights an extremely important point: the moderation of radical programmatic public policy positions must be seen as distinct from the moderation of semiloyal or antisystem positions. While the moderation of truly semiloyal or antisystem positions is fundamental to democratic consolidation and stability, the moderation of radical *public policy* positions is not necessarily required. This theoretical point may also be illustrated by reference to the Spanish Socialist Party that did not begin programmatic moderation until about 1977—long after it had committed itself to Spanish democracy—as well as to the Italian Socialist Party, whose programmatic moderation actually occurred decades after its acceptance of the regime, its rules of the game, and its institutions. As the cases of PASOK, PSOE, and the PSI confirm, democratic consolidation can indeed occur in the absence of programmatic moderation.

Largely as a result of Greek political culture, then, elite contacts during the dictatorship did not result in a formal agreement concerning the transition trajectory or the shape of Greece's new democracy. This study has shown, however, that the many informal contacts between elites that occurred during the dictatorship did not simply go to waste. Instead, these seemingly fruitless and unproductive attempts at forging interelite cooperation and compromise actually succeeded in producing mutual civility and a diffuse sense of unity among many elites, helping them to slowly build relationships of respect and friendship—something that proved to be of significant and lasting value in the early days of the new democracy. Contacts during the junta years enabled elites to realize their opposite numbers were not as menacing as they had imagined and they learned that, at a minimum, they all shared a mutual interest in democratizing Greek public life. A diffuse general consensus opposing the junta and desiring a return to democracy thus emerged between all significant political elites despite the absence of explicit and successful face-to-face negotiations. The achievement of a sudden and explicit elite settlement concerning the specific rules and institutions of the new democratic regime is not, then, the only option. Instead, informal contacts—even if apparently unsuccessful—can, over the long run, greatly facilitate attitudinal transformation and elite consensual unity. Informal negotiations between Greek elites did exactly that: they contributed directly and decisively to the process described by the second democratic consolidation model—that of elite convergence. Thus, elite settlements and elite convergence should not necessarily be viewed as distinct processes. In fact, as the case of Greece illustrates, an element from the elite settlement model—informal elite interaction—may actually be directly relevant to the process of elite convergence.

MODEL II: ELITE CONVERGENCE

This study has helped disaggregate the phenomenon of elite convergence into several dynamic processes. Specifically, my analysis has illustrated that while the posited electoral logic of the original convergence model was clearly at play in Greece, the Greek case also demonstrates that convergence can be motivated by a wider variety of interests during transitions to democracy. This study stresses the importance of an additional motivation behind convergence. While Greek elites were clearly influenced by the necessity to build long-lasting, electorally successful party organizations, they (like many of their Southern European counterparts) were also motivated by a genuine desire for democratization, democratic consolidation, and national reconciliation. Put simply, the process of elite convergence is dynamic and multifaceted.

First, as theory predicts, electoral considerations were critically important to the moderation of Greek elites. Unlike the original argument that convergence is mainly a reactive response of *opposition* parties against their failure at the polls, however, the case of *Nea Demokratia*'s moderation illustrates that the logic of elite convergence can effect the moderation of *governing* parties as well. When Karamanlis moderated the right's ideological and programmatic positions in the early days of the transition, *Nea Demokratia*, unlike the French and Italian opposition parties that underwent convergence, was not an opposition party that had suffered defeat at the hands of voters. Rather, Karamanlis dominated the entire transition process, excluding virtually all other political forces from that process and essentially shaping the face of Greece's new democracy single-handedly. Karamanlis' *Nea Demokratia* was also electorally successful, emerging from both the 1974 and 1977 elections with clear parliamentary majorities. Thus, unlike French and Italian opposition parties, *Nea Demokratia* was not an opposition party needing to change its electoral tactics in order to win elections and enter government. Yet, this study has shown that some of the motives underpinning increased moderation on the part of *Nea Demokratia* were indeed electoral. Acting preemptively, Karamanlis decided to moderate the right, apparently calculating that the electorate would refuse to support an unreconstituted and undemocratic right in future elections. In sum, as theory holds, electoral motivations clearly played their part in the convergence of Greek elites—but with both opposition and *government* parties alike.

However, the case of the Greek Communist Party clearly indicates that there is no guarantee that electoral motivations will not effect the reverse—leading elites to adopt radical, semiloyal, or even antisystem positions. The KKE clearly exhibited such behavior after its temporary cohabitation with *Nea Demokratia* and PASOK in the coalition governments of 1989–90. The same factors that facilitated the party's moderation in 1988–90—domestic electoral considerations—also contributed to its reradicalization in 1991. Realizing that its coalition with the right was not widely accepted by left-wing voters, party hard-liners reconfirmed the party's commitment to traditional antisystem positions. Thus, the case of the KKE clearly shows that electoral motivations can be equally important in causing *radicalization* as they can be in bringing about *moderation*. This is an important caveat regarding electoral motivations. Such motivations do not act in a unilinear fashion—had the KKE been an electorally significant antisystem party, it could have promoted the reradicalization of political positions regarding the regime and its rules of the game and raised the specter of democratic deconsolidation.

A second important factor—closely related to electoral motivations—that is also critical to the convergence of political elites is the "logic of party-building." In Greece this "logic"—the desire to build a professional party organization capable of mobilizing support and winning elections—manifested itself across the political spectrum. However, in no party was the drive to build such an electorally viable, professional party organization more pronounced than in PASOK. This was unquestionably one of the primary motivations behind PASOK's convergence. As the prospects for electoral success improved following the 1974 elections, Papandreou actively began ridding his party of radical militant activists and replacing them with moderate, centrist political figures capable of leading the party to electoral victory and into government.

A similar party-building logic also informed and motivated the transformations of both the far left during the precoup era in Greece as well as the right in 1974. Like the Spanish Communist Party, which, during the Spanish transition to democracy, abandoned its traditional cell-based organizational structure and reconfigured itself into a more open, territorially based local party so as to better meet the electoral demands of politics, the Greek left also undertook a similar project of transformation. Many Greek "revisionists" came to gradually realize during the post–civil war era that illegal activities were becoming increasingly ineffectual and decidedly unpopular with the electorate. As they came to value legal and peaceful forms of struggle, they set out reforming the KKE's organizational structure, abolishing its clandestine party organs and attempting to restructure it around the model of the United Democratic Left (EDA)—an increasingly modern and democratic mass party. On the right as well, Karamanlis' efforts to modernize the right in 1974 and to be broader in political orientation were an explicit attempt at party building. His decision to modernize the party was based on the belief that only a well-institutionalized right-of-center mass party would be truly capable of playing a central and constructive role in the new political system of post-1974 Greece. Thus, he created *Nea Demokratia* in such an image.

Electoral and party-building motivations aside, the Greek case highlights that another important motivation—perhaps the most important motivation—behind convergence was the genuine desire of political elites to see public life become democratic and stable. Karamanlis' decisions in 1974 to hold a referendum on the monarchy, to legalize the KKE, and to modernize the right-wing of the political spectrum were clear indications of elite convergence motivated by a conscious and deliberate effort to forge national reconciliation, do away with the destabilizing schisms of post–civil war politics, and to ensure long-run democratic stability. The value of such deliberately supportive proregime behavior on the part of rightist parties was also revealed in Spain where the conservative *Alianza Popular* consciously moderated its previously pro-Franquist ideology and brought its right-wing constituency into full acceptance of the democratic regime. The Southern European right was not alone in this regard, however. The precoup convergence of Greek communists was also brought about by a genuine concern to democratize Greek public life. While strategic concerns appeared most important initially, over time such behavioral adaptation to democratic procedures and norms was transformed into a genuine attitudinal commitment to liberal democracy, its institutions, and procedures. In this way, Greek communists were little different from Spanish and Italian communists who also recognized the need for moderation following the Spanish Civil War and decades of persecution under Franco, on the one hand, and Italy's harsh experiences with fascism, on the other. In sum, Southern European communists came to value democratization, national reconciliation, and democratic consolidation as ends in and of themselves and not simply as tactical means to other goals. This study thus demonstrates that a sincere desire to democratize one's nation and to consolidate that democracy should be seen as a potentially decisive factor motivating elite convergence.

Closely related to this desire to see public life democratized and stable is the critical cumulative process of political learning that took place with the passing of time and whose effects in Greece were similar to those in Spain and Italy. In Spain the collective memories of the Second Republic's traumatic collapse, the Spanish Civil War's brutality, and the Franquist dictatorship's repressiveness served to constrain and moderate Spanish elites during that country's transition to democracy. In Italy vivid recollections of fascism and the devastation of World War II drove Italian elites to behave in a moderate and conciliatory way during the postwar period in order to ensure Italian democratization. And in Greece the process of political learning that took place during the post–civil war period, coupled with the learning of the dictatorial experience, helped dissipate the visceral anticommunist hatred characteristic of post–civil war Greece. By the time of the Greek transition, over a quarter of a century had passed since the end of the Greek Civil War and in that time many rightists had come to realize that the repressive post–civil war measures were no longer necessary or acceptable. Indeed, many had even concluded that these exclusionary measures were partly to blame for the collapse of democracy in 1967. Thus, many rightists—and certainly Karamanlis himself—emerged from the period of dictatorship fully aware of their previous mistakes and ready to transform Greek public life, making it genuinely democratic. On the left of the political spectrum, too, the passing of time and the process of political learning to which it contributed led many Greek and Spanish communists to increasingly view their dogmatic leaders abroad as *passé* and out of touch with current domestic realities. Many Greek and Spanish leftists thus increasingly resented the undemocratic practices imposed on them by their exiled leadership and came to regard democratic parliamentary activity as the only viable mode of political participation, coming to adopt system-supportive positions and eventually an explicitly Eurocommunist stance.

A similar process of extended and gradual learning also contributed significantly to the military's convergence in both Spain and Greece. This study has illustrated how civilian elites such as Constantine Karamanlis and others in

Greece, as well as King Juan Carlos in Spain, were instrumental in "cajoling" and gently reminding military officers that their proper role did not include intervention into politics. Such verbal reinforcements as well as subsequent changes made to the curricula of military academies appear to have "democratized" the attitudes of soldiers, reinforcing the importance of the military's submission to civilian rule. Recognition of this imperative did not occur overnight, however. Since the initial decision to hand power back to civilians (Greece) or to accept democratization already underway (Spain) was one of default rather than of choice or conviction, military officers were slow to change, only moved by the gradual realization that no alternative to democratic rule remained. In both countries the military repeatedly questioned democratization efforts, attempting to halt or reverse it from time to time and did not fully accept its own subordination until attitudinal change occurred, despite earlier manifestations of behavioral submission.

A critical point to emerge from this study of the Greek military is that a crucial distinction between behavioral and attitudinal support for democracy must be recognized—a distinction of critical significance when dealing with those who have a legal monopoly on violence. Specifically, I have shown that factors conducive to the military's initial withdrawal from power, while facilitating democratic transition, are not sufficient to keep traditionally politicized militaries out of politics. The Greek case illustrates that the reasons behind the military hierarchy's decision to remove the junta from power in July 1974 had to do with the specific interests of the armed forces and the military's perception of Greece's national interests. Extrication of the military regime had nothing to do with an intrinsic interest or a respect for democracy and civilian supremacy *per se*. As a result, long after the military had been returned to the barracks and had behaviorally submitted to civilians, military officers indicated that they still reserved the prerogative to intervene in politics again "if necessary." Unlike their civilian counterparts, who argued that Greek democracy was fully consolidated and that it faced no threat of another authoritarian interlude, the overwhelming majority of officers interviewed would not exclude the possibility of another military intervention. Instead, most retired officers indicated that, in their view, military intervention might again prove necessary should the need arise to protect Greek national interests from a national "emergency," a "disturbance," or an "anomaly." Thus, while behavioral support for democracy may be sufficient in the short run, full attitudinal support for the regime, its institutions, and rules of the game is necessary for long-term consolidation and democratic stability. As long as military officers reserve the right to intervene in politics, the democratic regime cannot be said to be free from the threat of military overthrow. Behavioral support for democracy may do in the short run, but lasting consolidation and stability depend upon full attitudinal support.

As critical as it may be, however, full attitudinal support for the democratic regime is not achieved either quickly or easily. While this study concludes that attitudinal support on the part of the Greek officer corps was eventually achieved, this necessary condition for democratic consolidation came slowly and had little to do with the military's initial motivations for extrication. Instead, attitudinal change was affected by a number of other factors—"the passing of time," generational turn-over in the officer corps, changes in the curricula and the recruitment patterns of the military academies, and new patterns of civil-military relations. In fact, *attitudinal change* was largely the result of the military's *behavioral* backing of the democratic regime. This analysis thus shows that factors that facilitate the military's initial extrication from power should be viewed as distinct from those factors conducive to keeping them out of power. For attitudes to be changed, time is required. Civilian elites must remain patient and moderate, buying the time required to bring about both the discrediting of antisystem options as well as attitudinal support for democracy among military officers, thereby ensuring full democratic consolidation.

This study has thus been at pains to illustrate that during transitions to democracy elites converge for a variety of reasons—including, but not limited to, a desire to compete successfully in elections, a need to create lasting, electorally successful party organizations, and a commitment to the restoration and stability of democracy. As the Greek case shows, there is no single path to convergence. Instead, a number of dynamic processes and motivations impel political elites—both in government and opposition as well as in the military—to move toward consensual, cooperative positions in support of the existing institutions and rules of the game. However, while conformity with norms of democratic behavior and an acceptance of the specific rules and institutions of the regime is absolutely fundamental for democratic consolidation and stability, the Greek case highlights that ideological, programmatic and rhetorical moderation is not necessarily a prerequisite. In fact, rhetorical and programmatic radicalism can, in certain instances, actually promote democratic consolidation over the long term.

Finally, this study confirms that elite convergence is often a long and tumultuous process. In Greece the earliest signs of convergence—the first phase of the left's moderation—far preceded the 1967 dictatorship. It originated in the immediate aftermath of the communists' defeat in the civil war as mutual recriminations broke out between various factions of the left over the causes of their defeat. As time passed many communists who participated in parliamentary elections in precoup Greece began to see their exiled leadership abroad as dogmatic, sectarian, and out of touch with current reality. They thus began to question the value of revolutionary forms of struggle when, in their view, the Greek electorate desired a return to peaceful, democratic parliamentary life. Thus, by the time the dictatorship was launched in 1967, a significant portion of the left had already recognized the importance of national reconciliation and had pledged its support for democracy.

Moreover, Karamanlis and certain sections of the democratic right had also begun to incrementally moderate their vehement opposition to the left during Karamanlis' precoup tenure in office. As time passed and as the civil war receded deeper into history, certain members of the parliamentary right began to question the need for the monarchy, the autonomy of the armed forces, and the appropriateness of certain repressive post–civil war measures. Later, seven years of dictatorial rule reinforced both the left's and the right's commitment to reconciliation as both sides found themselves fighting a common enemy, having contacts with each other as they resisted the colonels, sharing the same prison cells, and—in the case of the right—being persecuted by many of the same measures they had used against the left. This analysis of the Greek case thus indicates that the origins of elite convergence need not be limited to the transition and consolidation processes alone, but rather can extend further back than the original convergence theory indicates—even to the years preceding the breakdown of democracy when the divisions needing to be healed predate the actual authoritarian regime. In sum, convergence can indeed take decades or more before old animosities are healed and prodemocratic and conciliatory attitudes emerge.

In short, then, the political learning spawned by the passing of time and changing political circumstances was critically important to the process of elite convergence. This points up the importance of long-term structural historical variables—variables that often affect the process of learning that contributes to convergence. Such variables, to be discussed below, should not be ignored in analyses of democratic consolidation that focus primarily on the more contingent factors of elite motivations, decisions, actions, and interactions.

Specifically, this analysis clearly highlights the important point that elites do not act in a political vacuum devoid of contextual influences and effects. As stated elsewhere in this study, elites make the important decisions and take the decisive actions, however, environmental variables clearly constrain or facilitate their decisions. As we have seen, such variables played a key role in the Greek right's moderation. As a result of domestic and international pressure on ERE, as well as of a climate of increasing internal security as the civil war receded into the annals of history, rightist persecutions of communists and other leftists became increasingly less extensive and brutal during the precoup period. Such contextual factors also played a role in the moderation of the precoup left in Greece. For their part, EDA deputies argued that a number of "practical factors"—the geographic distance between communists living in Greece and their leadership abroad, the danger faced by "interiors" each time they attempted to meet with "exteriors," and the problems associated with maintaining the clandestine party organs of the KKE—effected moderation from a significant portion of the left.

More recently, we have also seen that events taking place in the Soviet Union and other East European countries had an important effect on all Southern European communists. As I have argued, the collapse of socialism propelled both the Italian and Spanish communist parties toward a more thorough ideological cleansing—a cleansing that was already well underway in both countries. In Greece and Portugal, too, socialism's collapse compelled their more orthodox Marxist-Leninist parties to initiate a process of ideological moderation, even though it proved ultimately short-lived and was later reversed. The rise to power of Mikhail Gorbachev and the reformist nature of his *perestroika* program resulted in a corresponding moderation of the KKE in Greece. Later, as Gorbachev's popularity—and that of *perestroika*—declined in the Soviet Union, the KKE began its swing back to the hard left. Thus, just as the rise of Gorbachev contributed to the Greek communists' moderation, his subsequent decline and fall coincided with the KKE's reradicalization in the 1990s.

As deputies of the right and left were influenced by contextual, environmental factors, so too was Papandreou's PASOK. The realities and responsibilities of governing meant that PASOK's ability to bring about radical programmatic reform was seriously curtailed once the party acceded to power. Furthermore, the fact that Greece was already a full member of the European Community by the time PASOK came to office in 1981 made withdrawal from the EC a matter of such complexity and practical difficulty that it was never seriously contemplated by the party leadership thereafter. A similar realism tempered both PASOK's as well as the Spanish PSOE's promises to remove Greece and Spain from NATO. Put simply, the contradictions between ambitions and possibilities seriously constrained elite actions—demonstrating that elite action, while often decisive, is rarely completely determinative, irrespective of wider contextual factors.

The prime focus of this study, however, has been on the critical role played in democratic transition and consolidation processes by elites, their attitudes and behavior. It has demonstrated that the anonymous Athenian quoted in chapter 1 was fundamentally correct in arguing the benefits of "moderation," "patience," and "unity," rather than "verbal braggadocio" or "a taste for spectacular and immediate results." He was correct in diagnosing Greece's basic political weakness as an abundance of the latter and a shortage of the former. As this study has argued, for democratic consolidation to be achieved, all significant political actors—civilian politicians and military officers alike—must come to value and respect a pluralistic democratic regime founded on the principles of mutual respect and the rule of law. It has demonstrated that political extremism of an antisystemic nature—whether it come from the right, the left, or the military—is fundamentally antithetical to the achievement or long-run persistence of democratic politics. For in Greece partisan demagoguery and antisystem extremism (on both the right and left of the political spectrum), coupled with the military's interventionist attitudes, produced a limited democracy and an eventual *coup d'état*. But it was also in Greece that the value of moderation was proven. In the end dramatic transformations of political and military elite attitudes in support of the legitimacy of existing institutions and conformity with norms of democratic behavior produced a stable and consolidated democratic regime.

NOTES

1. Juan J. Linz and Alfred Stepan, *Problems of Democratic Transition and Consolidation: Southern Europe, South America, and Post-Communist Europe* (Baltimore: The Johns Hopkins University Press, 1996), "Toward Consolidated Democracies," *Journal of Democracy* 7:2 (April 1996), pp. 14–13; and Andreas Schedler, "What is Democratic Consolidation?" *Journal of Democracy* 9:2 (April 1998), pp. 91–107.

2. *Problems of Democratic Transition and Consolidation*, p. 137.

3. OECD, *OECD Economic Surveys: Greece, 1990–1991* (Paris: OECD, 1991), p. 81; and *OECD Economic Surveys: Greece, 1995–1996* (Paris: OECD, 1996), pp. 59, 81.

4. Neovi M. Karakatsanis, "Relying on Stop-Gap Measures: Coping with Unemployment in Greece," *South European Society and Politics* 4:3 (Winter 1999), p. 249.

5. One should note, however, that under the current Simitis government, the budget deficit has been greatly reduced in an effort to achieve economic and monetary union with the EU.

6. Soledad García and Neovi M. Karakatsanis, "Social Policy, Democracy and Citizenship in Southern Europe," in Richard Gunther, P. Nikiforos Diamandouros, and Gianfranco Pasquino, eds., *Changing Functions of the State in the New Southern Europe* (forthcoming).

7. See Yorgos A. Kourvetaris and Betty Dobratz, *A Profile of Modern Greece: In Search of Identity* (Oxford: Clarendon Press, 1987); and Nicos Mouzelis, *Modern Greece: Facets of Underdevelopment* (New York: Holmes S. Meier Publishers, 1978), p. 143.

8. See, for example, Michael Burton, Richard Gunther, and John Higley, "Elites and Democratic Consolidation in Latin America and Southern Europe: An Overview," in John Higley and Richard Gunther, eds., *Elites and Democratic Consolidation in Latin America and Southern Europe* (Cambridge: Cambridge University Press, 1992), pp. 335–47.

9. Roy C. Macridis, *Greek Politics at a Crossroads: What Kind of Socialism?* (Stanford: Hoover Institution Press, 1984), p. 48.

10. See J.C. Loulis, "New Democracy: The New Face of Conservatism," in Howard R. Penniman, ed., *Greece at the Polls: The National Elections of 1974 and 1977* (Washington: American Enterprise Institute for Public Policy Research, 1981), p. 75.

Bibliography

Agüero, Felipe. "The Assertion of Civilian Supremacy in Post-Authoritarian Contexts: Spain in Comparative Perspective," Ph.D. Dissertation, Duke University, 1991.

———. "Democratic Consolidation and the Military in Southern Europe and South America" in Richard Gunther, P. Nikiforos Diamandouros, and Hans-Jürgen Puhle, eds. *The Politics of Democratic Consolidation: Southern Europe in Comparative Perspective* (Baltimore: Johns Hopkins University Press, 1995).

———. "The Military and the Limits to Democratization in South America," in Scott Mainwaring, Guillermo O'Donnell, and Samuel Valenzuela, eds., *Issues in Democratic Consolidation: The New South American Democracies in Comparative Perspective* (Notre Dame: University of Notre Dame, 1992).

———. *Soldiers, Civilians, and Democracy: Post-Franco Spain in Comparative Perspective* (Baltimore: Johns Hopkins University Press, 1995).

Alexander, G. M. *The Prelude to the Truman Doctrine: British Policy in Greece 1944–47* (New York: Oxford University Press, 1982).

———. and J. C. Loulis. "The Strategy of the Greek Communist Party 1934–1944: An Analysis of Plenary Decisions," *East European Quarterly*, 15:3 (Fall 1981), pp. 377–89.

Alivizatos, Nicos C. "The Difficulties of 'Rationalization' in a Polarized Political System: the Greek Chamber of Deputies," in Ulrike Liebert and Maurizio Cotta, eds., *Parliament and Democratic Consolidation in Southern Europe: Greece, Italy, Portugal, Spain and Turkey* (London: Pinter Publishers, 1990).

———. "The Emergency Regime and Civil Liberties," in John O. Iatrides, ed., *Greece in the 1940s: A Nation in Crisis* (Hanover, NH: University Press of New England, 1981).

———. "The Greek Army in the Late Forties: Towards an Institutional Autonomy," *Journal of the Hellenic Diaspora* 5:3 (Fall 1978), pp. 37–45.

———. *Hoi Politikoi Thesmoi se Krise, 1922–74: Opseis tes Ellenikes Emperias* (Political Institutions in Crisis, 1922–1974: Survey of the Greek Experience) (Athens: Themelio, 1983).

————. "The Presidency, Parliament and the Courts in the 1980s," in Richard Clogg, ed., *Greece, 1981–89: The Populist Decade* (New York: St. Martin's Press, 1993).

Almond, Gabriel and Sydney Verba. *The Civic Culture* (Princeton: Princeton University Press, 1963).

Amen, Michael Mark. "American Institutional Penetration into Greek Military and Policymaking Structures: June, 1946–October, 1949," *Journal of the Hellenic Diaspora* 5:3 (Fall 1978), pp. 89–113.

Anastasi, Paul. "Soviet Manipulation of the Press and Political Opinion in Greece 1974–88," in Nikolaos A. Stavrou, ed., *Greece under Socialism: A NATO Ally Adrift* (New Rochelle, NY: Orpheus Publishing, 1988).

Andrews, Kevin. *Greece in the Dark... 1967–1974-* (Amsterdam: Adolf M. Hakkert, 1980).

"Apo to 1967 os to 1974: Diktatoria, Antistase, Diamorfose tou KKE (esot.)" (From 1967 to 1974: Dictatorship, Resistance, Formation of the KKE [int.]), *Kommounistike Theoria kai Politike* (February–March 1976).

Arvanitopoulos, Constantine. "The Political Economy of Regime Change: A Case Study of Greece," Ph.D. Dissertation, American University, 1989.

Athenian (Rodis Roufos). *Inside the Colonels' Greece* (New York: Chatto and Windus, 1972).

Averoff-Tossizza, Evangelos. *By Fire and Axe: The Communist Party and the Civil War in Greece, 1944–1949* (New Rochelle, NY: Caratzas, 1978).

Axt, Heinz-Jürgen. "On the Way to Self-Reliance? PASOK's Government Policy in Greece," *Journal of Modern Greek Studies* 2:2 (October 1984), pp. 198–208.

Baerentzen, Lars and David H. Close. "The British Defeat of EAM, 1944–5," in David H. Close, ed., *The Greek Civil War, 1943–1950: Studies of Polarization* (New York: Routledge, 1993).

Bank of Greece. *Ta Prota Penenta Chronia tes Trapezas tes Ellados: 1928–1978* (The First Fifty Years of the Bank of Greece: 1928–1978) (Athens: Bank of Greece, 1978).

Barkman, Carl. *Ambassador in Athens, 1969–1975: The Evolution from Military Dictatorship to Democracy in Greece* (London: Merlin, 1984).

Bartolini, Stephano and Roberto D'Alimonte. "Plurality Competition and Party Realignment in Italy: The 1994 Parliamentary Elections," *European Journal of Political Research* 29:1 (January 1996), pp. 105–42.

Bermeo, Nancy. "Democracy and the Lessons of Dictatorship," *Comparative Politics* 24:3 (April 1992), pp. 273–91.

Binder, Leonard, James S. Coleman, Joseph LaPalombara, Lucian W. Pyle, Sidney Verba, and Myron Winer. *Crises and Sequences in Political Development* (Princeton: Princeton University Press, 1971).

Bosco, Anna and Carlos Gaspar. "Four Actors in Search of a Role: The South European Communist Parties," in P. Nikiforos Diamandouros and Richard Gunther, eds., *Democratic Politics in the New Southern Europe*, forthcoming.

Brooks, Joel E. "Mediterranean Neo-Democracies and the Opinion-Policy Nexus," *West European Politics* 11:3 (July 1988), pp. 126–40.

Brown, James. "Greek Civil-Military Relations: A Different Pattern," *Armed Forces and Society* 6:3 (Spring 1980), pp. 389–413.

————. "The Military in Politics: A Case Study of Greece," Ph.D. Dissertation, State University of New York at Buffalo, 1971.

Burton, Michael G. and John Higley. "Elite Settlements," *American Sociological Review*, 52:3 (June 1987), pp. 295–307.

————. "The Elite Variable in Democratic Transitions and Breakdowns," *American Sociological Review* 54:1 (February 1989), pp. 17–32.

———. "Political Crises and Elite Settlements," in Mattei Dogan and John Higley, eds., *Elites, Crises, and the Origins of Regimes* (Lanham, MD: Rowman & Littlefield, 1998).

Burton, Michael G., Richard Gunther, and John Higley. "Introduction: Elite Transformations and Democratic Regimes," in John Higley and Richard Gunther, eds., *Elites and Democratic Consolidation in Latin America and Southern Europe* (Cambridge: Cambridge University Press, 1992).

Calligas, Constantine. "The Center—Decline and Convergence," in Kevin Featherstone and Dimitrios K. Katsoudas, eds., *Political Change in Greece Before and After the Colonels* (New York: St. Martin's Press, 1987).

Campbell, John K. and Philip Sherrard. *Modern Greece* (New York: Praeger, 1968).

Charalambis, Dimitris. *Stratos kai Politike Exousia: He Dome tes Exousias sten Metemfyliake Ellada* (Army and Political Power: The Structure of Power in Post–Civil War Greece) (Athens: Exantas, 1985).

Chilcote, Ronald H. *Transitions from Dictatorship to Democracy: Comparative Studies of Spain, Portugal, and Greece* (London: Taylor and Francis, 1990).

Christodoulides, Theodore. "Greece and European Political Cooperation: The Intractable Partner," in Nikolaos A. Stavrou, ed., *Greece under Socialism: A NATO Ally Adrift* (New Rochelle, NY: Orpheus, 1988).

Clive, Nigel. "The 1985 Greek Election and its Background," *Government and Opposition* 20:4 (Autumn 1985), pp. 488–503.

Clogg, Mary Jo and Richard Clogg, eds. *Greece* (Santa Barbara: American Bibliographical Center, Clio Press, 1980).

Clogg, Richard. "The Enigma of PASOK: Greek Socialism Reviewed," *Modern Greek Studies Yearbook* 8 (1992), pp. 439–45.

———. "The Ideology of the 'Revolution of 21 April 1967'," in Richard Clogg and George Yannopoulos, eds., *Greece Under Military Rule* (New York: Basic Books, 1972).

———. "Introduction: The PASOK Phenomenon," in Richard Clogg, ed., *Greece, 1981–89: The Populist Decade* (New York: St. Martin's Press, 1983).

———. "Karamanlis' Cautious Success: The Background," *Government and Opposition* 10:3 (Summer 1975), pp. 332–53.

———. *Parties and Elections in Greece: The Search for Legitimacy* (Durham, NC: Duke University Press, 1987)

———. *A Short History of Modern Greece* (Cambridge: Cambridge University Press, 1979).

———. "Troubled Alliance: Greece and Turkey," in Richard Clogg, ed., *Greece in the 1980s* (New York: St. Martin's Press, 1983).

———, ed. *Greece, 1981–89: The Populist Decade* (New York: St. Martin's Press, 1993).

———, ed. *Greece in the 1980s* (New York: St. Martin's Press, 1983).

Clogg, Richard and George Yannopoulos, eds. *Greece Under Military Rule* (New York: Basic Books, 1972).

Close, David H. "Introduction," in David H. Close, ed., *The Greek Civil War, 1943–1950: Studies of Polarization* (New York: Routledge, 1993).

———. "The Legacy," in David H. Close, ed., *The Greek Civil War, 1943–1950: Studies of Polarization* (New York: Routledge, 1993).

———. "The Reconstruction of a Right-Wing State," in David H. Close, ed., *The Greek Civil War, 1943–1950: Studies of Polarization* (New York: Routledge, 1993).

———, ed. *The Greek Civil War, 1943–1950: Studies of Polarization* (New York: Routledge, 1993).

Close, David H. and Thanos Veremis. "The Military Struggle, 1945–9," in David H. Close, ed., *The Greek Civil War, 1943–1950: Studies of Polarization* (New York: Routledge, 1993).

Colomer, Josep M. "Transitions by Agreement: Modelling the Spanish Way," *American Political Science Review* 85:4 (December 1991), pp. 1283–1302.

Cotta, Maurizio. "Unification and Democratic Consolidation in Italy: An Historical Overview," in John Higley and Richard Gunther, eds., *Elites and Democratic Consolidation in Latin America and Southern Europe* (Cambridge: Cambridge University Press, 1992).

Coufoudakis, Van. "The Democratic Transition to Socialism in Post-War Greece," *Modern Greek Studies Yearbook* 4 (1988), pp. 15–33.

———. "Greco-Turkish Relations and the Greek Socialists: Ideology, Nationalism and Pragmatism," *Journal of Modern Greek Studies* 1:2 (October 1983), pp. 373–92.

———. "Greece and the Problem of Cyprus: 1974–1986," in Speros Vryonis, Jr., ed., *Greece on the Road to Democracy: From the Junta to PASOK 1974–1986* (New Rochelle, NY: Caratzas, 1991).

———. "Greek Foreign Policy, 1945–1985: Seeking Independence in an Interdependent World—Problems and Prospects," in Kevin Featherstone and Dimitrios K. Katsoudas, eds., *Political Change in Greece: Before and After the Colonels* (New York: St. Martin's Press, 1987).

———. "PASOK and Greek-Turkish Relations," in Richard Clogg, ed., *Greece 1981–89: The Populist Decade* (New York: St. Martin's Press, 1993).

Couloumbis, Theodore A. "Conclusion," in Howard R. Penniman, ed., *Greece at the Polls: The National Elections of 1974 and 1977* (Washington: American Enterprise Institute for Public Policy Research, 1981).

———. "Defining Greek Foreign Policy Objectives," in Howard R. Penniman, ed., *Greece at the Polls: The National Elections of 1974 and 1977* (Washington: American Enterprise Institute for Public Policy Research, 1981).

———. "Greek-American Relations since 1974," in Speros Vryonis, Jr., ed., *Greece on the Road to Democracy: From the Junta to PASOK 1974–1986* (New Rochelle, NY: Caratzas, 1991).

———. "The Greek Junta Phenomenon," *Polity* 6:3 (Spring 1974), pp. 345–74.

———. *Greek Political Reaction to American and NATO Influences* (New Haven: Yale University Press, 1966).

———. "PASOK's Foreign Policies, 1981–89: Continuity or Change?" in Richard Clogg, ed., *Greece, 1981–89: The Populist Decade* (New York: St. Martin's Press, 1993).

———. "The Structures of Greek Foreign Policy," in Richard Clogg, ed., *Greece in the 1980s* (New York: St. Martin's Press, 1983).

Couloumbis, Theodore A., John A. Petropoulos, and Harry J. Psiomades. *Foreign Interference in Greek Politics: An Historical Perspective* (New York: Pella Pub. Co., 1976).

Couloumbis, Theodore A. and Yannis M. Prodromos. "The Stability Quotient of Greece's Post-1974 Democratic Institutions," *Journal of Modern Greek Studies* 1:2 (October 1983), pp. 359–72.

Couloumbis, Theodore A. and John O. Iatrides, eds. *Greek-American Relations: A Critical Review* (New York: Pella Pub. Co., 1980).

Craig, Phyllis R. "The U.S. and the Greek Dictatorship: A Summary of Support," *Journal of the Hellenic Diaspora* 3:4 (December 1976), pp. 5–16.

Danopoulos, Constantine P. "Beating a Hasty Retreat: The Greek Military Withdraws from Power," in Constantine P. Danopoulos, ed., *The Decline of Military Regimes: The Civilian Influence* (Boulder: Westview, 1988).

———. "Democratic Undercurrents in Praetorian Regimes: The Greek Military and the 1973 Plebiscite," *Journal of Strategic Studies* 12:3 (September 1989), pp 349–68.

———. "Democratizing the Military: Lessons from Mediterranean Europe," *West European Politics* 14:4 (October 1991), pp. 25–41.

———. "Farewell to Man on Horseback: Intervention and Civilian Supremacy in Modern Greece," in Constantine P. Danopoulos, ed., *From Military to Civilian Rule* (London: Routledge, 1992).

———. "From Balconies to Tanks: Post-Junta Civil-Military Relations in Greece," *Journal of Political and Military Sociology* 13:1 (Spring 1985), pp. 83–98.

———. "From Military to Civilian Rule in Contemporary Greece," *Armed Forces and Society* 10:2 (Winter 1984), pp. 229–50.

———. "The Greek Military Regime (1967–1974) and the Cyprus Question: Origins and Goals," *Journal of Political and Military Sociology* 10:2 (Fall 1982), pp. 257–74.

———. "The Military and Bureaucracy in Greece, 1967–1974," *Public Administration and Development* 8:2 (April–June 1988), pp. 219–32.

———. "Military Professionalism and Regime Legitimacy in Greece, 1967-1974," *Political Science Quarterly* 98:3 (Fall 1983), pp. 485–506.

———. "Regional Security Organizations and National Interests: Analyzing the NATO-Greek Relationship," *Journal of Political and Military Sociology* 16:2 (Fall 1988), pp. 263–77.

———. *Warriors and Politicians in Modern Greece* (Chapel Hill: Documentary Publications, 1985).

Danopoulos, Constantine P. and Kant Patel. "Military Professionals as Political Governors: A Case Study of Contemporary Greece," *West European Politics* 8:2 (May 1980), pp. 198–202.

Danopoulos, Constantine P. and Larry N. Gerston. "Democratic Currents in Authoritarian Seas: The Military in Greece and the Philippines," *Armed Forces and Society* 16:4 (Summer 1990), pp. 529–45.

De Grand, Alexander. *The Italian Left in the Twentieth Century: A History of the Socialist and Communist Parties* (Bloomington: Indiana University Press, 1989).

Del Campo, Salustiano, Manuel Navarro and J. Félix Texanos. *La Cuestión Regional Espanola* (Madrid: Editorial Cuadernos para el Diálogo, 1977).

Delepetros, Nikos D. *Apofasisa Na Mileso* (I Decided to Speak) (Athens: Estia, 1988).

Demertzis, Efstratios. "Factionalism in the Greek Communist Party," Ph.D. Dissertation, New York University, 1979.

Dertilis, George. *Koinonikos Metaschimatismos kai Stratiotike Epemvase: 1880–1909* (Social Transformation and Military Intervention: 1880–1909) (Athens: Exantas, 1985).

Deutsch, Karl W. "Social Mobilization and Political Development," *The American Political Science Review* LV:3 (September 1961).

Diamandouros, P. Nikiforos. "Beyond Consolidation: The Quality of Democracy in Contemporary Greece," Paper presented at Symposium '95, Modern Greek Studies Association, Cambridge, Massachusetts, November 1995.

———. "Greek Political Culture in Transition: Historical Origins, Evolutions, Current Trends," in Richard Clogg, ed., *Greece in the 1980s* (New York: St. Martin's Press, 1983).

————. "PASOK and State-Society Relations in Post-Authoritarian Greece," in Speros Vryonis, Jr., ed., *Greece on the Road to Democracy: From the Junta to PASOK 1974–1986* (New Rochelle, NY: Caratzas, 1991).

————. "Politics and Constitutionalism in Greece: the 1975 Constitution in Historical Perspective," in Houchang E. Chebabi and Alfred Stepan, eds., *Totalitarianism, Authoritarianism, and Democracy: Essays in Honor of Juan J. Linz* (forthcoming).

————. "Politics and Culture in Greece, 1974-91: An Interpretation," in Richard Clogg, ed., *Greece, 1981–89: The Populist Decade* (New York: St. Martin's Press, 1993).

————. "Regime Change and the Prospects for Democracy in Greece: 1974–1983," in Guillermo O'Donnell, Philippe C. Schmitter and Laurence Whitehead, eds., *Transitions from Authoritarian Rule: Southern Europe* (Baltimore: Johns Hopkins University Press, 1986).

————. "Transition to, and Consolidation of, Democratic Politics in Greece, 1974–1983: A Tentative Assessment," in Geoffrey Pridham, ed., *The New Mediterranean Democracies: Regime Transition in Spain, Greece and Portugal* (London: Frank Cass, 1984).

————. "Transition to, and Consolidation of, Democratic Rule in Greece, 1974–83: A Tentative Assessment," *West European Politics* 7:2 (April 1984), pp. 50–71.

Diamond, Larry. *Developing Democracy: Toward Consolidation* (Baltimore: The Johns Hopkins University Press, 1999).

————. "Economic Development and Democracy Reconsidered," in Gary Marks and Larry Diamond, eds., *Reexamining Democracy: Essays in Honor of Seymour Martin Lipset* (Newbury Park, CA: Sage Publications, 1992).

Diamond, Larry, Juan J. Linz, and Seymour Martin Lipset, eds. *Democracy in Developing Countries* (Boulder: Lynne Rienner, 1989).

Diati Eginai He Epanastase tes 21 Apriliou 1967 (Why the Revolution of 21 April 1967 Occurred) (Athens: Government Printing Office, 1968).

Dimitras, Panayote E. "Changes in Public Attitudes," in Kevin Featherstone and Dimitrios K. Katsoudas, eds., *Political Change in Greece: Before and After the Colonels* (New York: St. Martin's Press, 1987).

————. "Greek Public Attitudes: Continuity and Change," *International Journal of Public Opinion Research* 2:2 (Summer 1990), pp. 92–115.

————. "The Radicals Prevailed over Papandreou," *Greek Opinion* 2:4 (August 1985).

————. "Social and Electoral Behavior in Greece," *Greek Opinion* 2:5 (August 1985).

————, ed. *He Diaspasis tou KKE* (The split of the KKE), 1 (Athens: n.p., n.d.).

Di Palma, Giuseppe. "Founding Coalitions in Southern Europe: Legitimacy and Hegemony," *Government and Opposition* 15:2 (Spring 1980), pp. 162–89.

Di Scala, Spencer. *Renewing Italian Socialism: Nenni to Craxi* (New York: Oxford University Press, 1988).

Dobratz, Betty A. "Party Preferences and 'Erratic' Issues in Greece." *Political Studies* 38:2 (June 1990), pp. 345–54.

————. "The Role of Class and Issues in Shaping Party Preferences in Greece," *Journal of Social, Political and Economic Studies* 12:1 (Spring 1987), pp. 51–76.

Dogan, Mattei and John Higley. "Elites, Crises, and Regimes in Comparative Analysis," in Mattei Dogan and John Higley, eds., *Elites, Crises and the Origins of Regimes* (Lanham, MD: Rowman & Littlefield Publishers, Inc., 1998).

————, eds. *Elites, Crises, and the Origins of Regimes* (Lanham, MD: Rowman & Littlefield, 1998).

Doulis, Thomas. *Disaster and Fiction: Modern Greek Fiction and the Impact of the Asia Minor Disaster of 1922* (Berkeley: University of California Press, 1977).

Downs, Anthony. *An Economic Theory of Democracy* (New York: Harper and Row, 1957).

Drakopoulos, Babis. "He Politike tes EADE stes Semerines Synthekes" (The Politics of EADE in Today's Conditions), *Kommounistike Theoria kai Politike* (Communist Theory and Politics), 3 (March 1975), pp. 5–20.

Drakos, George. "The Socialist Economic Policy in Greece: A Critique," in Zafiris Tzannatos, ed., *Socialism in Greece: The First Four Years* (Aldershot: Gower Publishing, 1986).

Economou, Nikos and Thanos Veremis. "Parties of the Liberal Center and the Greek Elections of 1981," *Journal of the Hellenic Diaspora* 11:4 (Winter 1984), pp. 33–46.

Elephantis, Angelos. *He Epaggelia tes Adunates Epanastases* (The Promise of an Impossible Revolution) (Athens: Olkos, 1976).

————. "PASOK and the Elections of 1977: The Rise of the Populist Movement." in Howard R. Penniman, ed., *Greece at the Polls: The National Elections of 1974 and 1977* (Washington: American Enterprise Institute for Public Policy Research, 1981).

"To Elleniko Kommounistiko Kinema apo to 1949 os to 1967" (The Greek Communist Movement from 1949 to 1967), *Kommounistike Theoria kai Politike: Periodiko tes K.E. tou K.K.E (es.)* (Communist Theory and Politics: Periodical of the Central Committee of the KKE-int), 9 (February–March 1976).

Facts on File (New York: Facts on File News Service, various years).

Featherstone, Kevin. "Elections and Parties in Greece," *Government and Opposition* 17:2 (Spring 1982), pp. 180–94.

————. "Elections and Voting Behavior," in Kevin Featherstone and Dimitrios K. Katsoudas, eds., *Political Change in Greece: Before and After the Colonels* (New York: St. Martin's Press, 1987).

————. "The Greek Socialists in Power," *West European Politics* 6:3 (July 1983), 237–50.

————. "Introduction," in Kevin Featherstone and Dimitrios K. Katsoudas, eds., *Political Change in Greece: Before and After the Colonels* (New York: St. Martin's Press, 1987).

————. "PASOK and the Left." In Kevin Featherstone and Dimitrios K. Katsoudas, eds., *Political Change in Greece: Before and After the Colonels* (New York: St. Martin's Press, 1987).

————. "Political Parties and Democratic Consolidation in Greece," in Geoffrey Pridham, ed., *Securing Democracy: Political Parties and Democratic Consolidation in Southern Europe* (London: Routledge, 1990).

Featherstone, Kevin and Dimitrios K. Katsoudas. "Change and Continuity in Greek Voting Behavior," *European Journal of Political Research* 13:1 (March 1985), pp. 27–40.

Field, G. Lowell and John Higley. "Imperfectly Unified Elites: The Cases of Italy and France," in R. Tomasson, ed., *Comparative Studies in Sociology* (Greenwich, CT: JAI Press, 1978).

Filinis, Kostas. "Ho Demokratikos Dromos pros ton Sossialismo kai he EADE" (The Democratic Road towards Socialism and EADE), *Kommounistike Theoria kai Politike* (Communist Theory and Politics), 10 (April 1976), pp. 57–59.

Finer, Samuel E. *The Man on Horseback: The Role of the Military in Politics* (New York: Praeger, 1962).

Fitch, J. Samuel. "Towards a Democratic Model of Civil-Military Relations for Latin America," paper presented to the International Political Science Association, Washington, DC, August 1988.

Fleischer, Hagen. "The 'Anomalies' in the Greek Middle East Forces, 1941–1944," *Journal of the Hellenic Diaspora* 5:3 (Fall 1978), pp. 5–36.

Fleming, Amalia. *A Piece of Truth* (London: Cape, 1972).

Florakis, Charilaos. "For Closer International Cooperation," *World Marxist Review* 22:3 (March 1979), pp. 72–75.

———. "Our Epoch and Lenin's Teaching on the New Type of Party," *World Marxist Review* 23:4 (April 1980), pp. 10–14.

———. "Turning Away From Dogmas, Forging a Closer Link With Reality," *World Marxist Review* 31:4 (April 1988), pp. 5–12.

Foreign Broadcast Information Service. *Daily Reports: Western Europe* 7 (1 March 1983–22 March 1983) (Washington: Foreign Broadcast Information Service).

Frank, Andre Gunder. *Capitalism and Underdevelopment in Latin America: Historical Studies of Chile and Brazil* (New York: Monthly Review Press, 1967).

———. *Latin America: Underdeveloped or Revolution* (New York: Monthly Review Press, 1969)

Frederica, Queen, of the Hellenes. *A Measure of Understanding* (London: Macmillan, 1971).

García, Soledad and Neovi M. Karakatsanis. "Social Policy, Democracy and Citizenship in Southern Europe," in Richard Gunther, P. Nikiforos Diamandouros, and Gianfranco Pasquino, eds., *Changing Functions of the State in the New Southern Europe* (forthcoming).

Genevoix, Maurice. *The Greece of Karamanlis* (London: Doric Publications Ltd., 1973).

Gerolymatos, Andre. "The Role of the Greek Officer Corps in the Resistance," *Journal of the Hellenic Diaspora* 11:3 (Fall 1984), pp. 69–80.

———. "The Security Battalions and the Civil War," *Journal of the Hellenic Diaspora* 12:1 (Spring 1985), pp. 17–28.

Giannaris, George. *Mikis Theodorakis: Music and Social Change* (New York: Praeger, 1972).

Ginis, Giannis. *Ho Allos Karamanlis* (The Other Karamanlis) (Athens: I. Natsos, 1986).

Graham, Lawrence S. "Redefining the Portuguese Transition to Democracy," in John Higley and Richard Gunther, eds., *Elites and Democratic Consolidation in Latin America and Southern Europe* (Cambridge: Cambridge University Press, 1992).

Gregoriades, Solon N. *He Historia tes Diktatorias* (The History of the Dictatorship) (Athens: Kapopoulos, 1975).

Gunther, Richard. "Spain: The Very Model of the Modern Elite Settlement," in John Higley and Richard Gunther, eds., *Elites and Democratic Consolidation in Latin America and Southern Europe* (Cambridge: Cambridge University Press, 1992).

———. "The Spanish Socialist Party: From Clandestine Position to Party of Government," in Stanley Payne, ed., *The Politics of Democratic Spain* (Chicago: Council on Foreign Relations, 1986).

Gunther, Richard, Giacomo Sani, and Goldie Shabad. *Spain after Franco: The Making of a Competitive Party System* (Berkeley: University of California Press, 1986).

Gunther, Richard and José R. Montero. "The Anchors of Partisanship: A Comparative Analysis of Voting Behavior in Four Southern European Democracies," (unpublished manuscript).

Gunther, Richard, P. Nikiforos Diamandouros, and Hans-Jürgen Puhle, eds. *The Politics of Democratic Consolidation: Southern Europe in Comparative Perspective* (Baltimore: Johns Hopkins University Press, 1995).

Harrison, Martin, ed. *French Politics* (Lexington, MA: Heath, 1969).

Hatzis, Thanasis. *He Nikifora Epanastase pou Chatheke* (The Victorious Revolution that Lost the Way), vols. 1–3 (Athens: Papazeses, 1977–1979).

Herz, John H., ed. *From Dictatorship to Democracy: Coping with the Legacies of Authoritarianism and Totalitarianism* (Westport, CT: Greenwood Press, 1982).

Higley, John, Judith Kullberg, and Jan Pakulski. "The Persistence of Postcommunist Elites," *Journal of Democracy* 7:2 (April 1996), pp. 133–47.

Higley, John and Michael G. Burton. "Elite Settlements and the Taming of Politics," *Government and Opposition* 33:1 (Winter 1998), pp. 98–115.

Higley, John, and G. Lowell Field. "In Defense of Elite Theory: A Reply to Cammack," *American Sociological Review* 55:3 (June 1990), pp. 421–26.

Higley, John and Richard Gunther, eds. *Elites and Democratic Consolidation in Latin America and Southern Europe* (Cambridge: Cambridge University Press, 1992).

Holden, Philip. *Greece Without Columns: The Making of the Modern Greeks* (Philadephia: Lippincott, 1972).

Hondros, John L. "Greece and the German Occupation," in David H. Close, ed., *The Greek Civil War, 1943–1950: Studies of Polarization* (New York: Routledge, 1993).

———. "The Greek Resistance, 1941–1944: A Reevaluation," in John O. Iatrides, ed., *Revolt in Athens: The Greek Communist "Second Round," 1944–1945* (Princeton: Princeton University Press, 1972).

Huntington, Samuel P. "Armed Forces and Democracy: Reforming Civil Military Relations," *Journal of Democracy* 6:4 (October 1995), pp. 9–17.

———. *Political Order in Changing Society* (New Haven: Yale University Press, 1968).

———. *The Third Wave: Democratization in the Late Twentieth Century* (Norman, OK: University of Oklahoma Press, 1991).

———. "Will More Countries Become Democratic?" *Political Science Quarterly* 99:2 (Summer 1984), pp. 193–218.

Iatrides, John O. *Ambassador MacVeagh Reports: Greece, 1933–1947* (Princeton: Princeton University Press, 1980).

———. "Beneath the Sound and Fury: US Relations with the PASOK Government," in Richard Clogg, ed., *Greece, 1981–1989 The Populist Decade* (New York: St. Martin's Press, 1993).

———. "Britain, the United States, and Greece, 1945–9," in David H. Close, ed., *The Greek Civil War, 1943–1950: Studies of Polarization* (New York: Routledge, 1993).

———. "Greece and the United States: The Strained Partnership," in Richard Clogg, ed., *Greece in the 1980s* (New York: St. Martin's Press, 1983).

———. "Papandreou's Foreign Policy," in Theodore C. Kariotis, ed., *The Greek Socialist Experiment: Papandreou's Greece 1981–1989* (New York: Pella, 1992).

———, ed. *Greece in the 1940s: A Nation in Crisis* (Hanover, NH: University Press of New England, 1981).

———, ed. *Revolt in Athens: The Greek Communist "Second Round," 1944–1945* (Princeton: Princeton University Press, 1972).

Ioakeimidis, P.K. *Ho Metaskhimatismos tes EOK: Apo ten 'Entole' sten Eniaia Europaeke Praxe* (The Transformation of the EEC: From the 'Mandate' to the Single European Act) (Athens, 1988).

Johnson, John J. *Political Change in Latin America* (Stanford: Stanford University Press, 1958).

Kalogeropoulou, Efthalia. "Election Promises and Government Performance in Greece: PASOK's Fulfillment of its 1981 Election Pledges," *European Journal of Political Research* 17:3 (1989), pp. 289–311.

Kanellopoulos, Panayiotes. *Ta Chronia tou Megalou Polemou, 1939–1944* (The Years of the Great War, 1939–1944) (Athens: n.p., 1964).

———— (Narration to Nineta Kontrarou-Rassia). *He Zoe Mou: He Aletheia gia tis Krisimes Stigmes tes Istorias tou Ethnous apo to 1915–1980* (My Life: The Truth About the Critical Moments in the History of the Nation from 1915 to 1980) (Athens: Dion. Gialleles, 1985).

Kapetanyannis, Basil. "The Making of Greek Eurocommunism," *Political Quarterly* 50:4 (October/December 1979), pp. 445–60.

————. "The Communists," in Kevin Featherstone and Dimitrios K. Katsoudas, eds., *Political Change in Greece: Before and After the Colonels* (New York: St. Martin's Press, 1987).

————. "The Left in the 1980s: Too Little, Too Late," in Richard Clogg, ed., *Greece, 1981–89: The Populist Decade* (New York: St. Martin's Press, 1983).

Kappos, Kostas. *He Epanastase pou Erchetai: Apantese sta Pseude tes Kyriarches Ideologias* (The Revolution That is Coming: An Answer to the Lies of the Dominant Ideology) (Athens: Gnoseis, 1991).

Kapsis, Yannis. "Philosophy and Goals of PASOK's Foreign Policy," in Nikolaos A. Stavrou, ed., *Greece under Socialism: A NATO Ally Adrift* (New Rochelle, NY: Orpheus Publishing, 1988).

Karakatsanis, Neovi. "Do Attitudes Matter? The Military and Democratic Consolidation in Greece," *Armed Forces and Society* 24:2 (Winter 1997), pp. 289–313.

————. "Relying on Stop-Gap Measures: Coping with Unemployment in Greece," *South European Society and Politics* 4:3 (Winter 1999), pp. 238–60.

Kariotis, Theodore C., ed. *The Greek Socialist Experiment: Papandreou's Greece 1981–1989* (New York: Pella, 1992).

Karl, Terry Lynn. "Dilemmas of Democratization in Latin America," *Comparative Politics* 23 (1990).

Karl, Terry Lynn and Philippe C. Schmitter. "Modes of Transition and Types of Democracy in Latin America, Southern and Eastern Europe" (unpublished manuscript).

Katris, John A. *Eyewitness in Greece: The Colonels Come to Power* (St. Louis: New Critics Press, 1971).

Katsaros, Panagiotes B. *He Eukairia pou Chatheke: Politikes Katagrafes kai Skepseis* (The Opportunity that was Lost: Political Writings and Thoughts) (Athens: Etairia Ellenikou Vivliou, 1990).

Katsoudas, Dimitrios K. "The Conservative Movement and New Democracy: From Past to Present," in Kevin Featherstone and Dimitrios K. Katsoudas, eds., *Political Change in Greece: Before and After the Colonels* (New York: St. Martin's Press, 1987).

————. "The Constitutional Framework," in Kevin Featherstone and Dimitrios K. Katsoudas, eds., *Political Change in Greece: Before and After the Colonels* (New York: St. Martin's Press, 1987).

————. "New Democracy: In or Out of Social Democracy?" in Speros Vryonis, Jr., ed., *Greece on the Road to Democracy: From the Junta to PASOK 1974–1986* (New Rochelle, NY: Caratzas, 1991).

Keesing's Contemporary Archives (London: Keesing's Limited, various years).

Keesing's Record of World Events (London: Keesing's Limited, various years).

Kitsikis, Dimitri. "Greece: Communism in a Non-Western Setting," in David E. Albright, ed., *Communism and Political Systems in Western Europe* (Boulder: Westview, 1978).

————. "Greek Communists and the Karamanlis Government," *Problems of Communism* 26:1 (Jan/Feb 1977), pp. 42–56.

————. "Populism, Eurocommunism and the KKE: The Communist Party of Greece," in Michael Waller and Meindert Fennema, eds., *Communist Parties in Western Europe: Decline or Adaptation?* (Oxford: Basil Blackwell, 1988).

Kleinman, Judith. "Socialist Policies and the Free Market: An Evaluation of PASOK's Economic Performance," in Nikolaos A. Stavrou, ed., *Greece under Socialism: A NATO Ally Adrift* (New Rochelle, NY: Orpheus Publishing, 1988).

Kohler, Beate. *Political Forces in Spain, Greece and Portugal* (Sevenoaks, Kent: Butterworth and Co., 1982).

Kohn, Richard H. "How Democracies Control the Military," *Journal of Democracy* 8:4 (October 1997), pp. 140–53.

Kokkos, A. and A. Mourike-Kostopoulou, eds. *Metavase sto Sosialismo* (Transition to Socialism) (Athens: Aletri Publishers, 1981).

Koliyannis, Kostas. "Leninism and the Experience of the Communist Party of Greece," *World Marxist Review* 13:4 (April 1970), pp. 48–53.

Kommounistiko Komma tes Helladas (Communist Party of Greece). "*Apofase tou 9ou Synedriou tou Kommounistikou Kommatos tes Helladas pano sten Ekthese Drases tes Kentrikes Epitropes*" (Decision of the 9th Congress of the Communist Party of Greece on the Report of the Central Committee on Its Activities), *Neos Kosmos* (New World), 3:4 (1974), pp. 17–38.

Kommounistiko Komma tes Helladas-Esoterikou (Communist Party of Greece-Interior). "To Helleniko Kommounistiko Kinema apo to 1949 os to 1967" (The Greek Communist Movement from 1949 to 1967), *Kommounistike Theoria kai Politike: Periodiko tes K.E. tou K.K.E (es.)* (Communist Theory and Politics: Periodical of the Central Committee of the KKE-I) 9 (February–March 1976).

Konstans, Dimitri C. "Greek Foreign Policy Objectives: 1974–1986," in Speros Vryonis, Jr., ed., *Greece on the Road to Democracy: From the Junta to PASOK 1974–1986* (New Rochelle, NY: Caratzas, 1991).

Kordatos, Giannis. *Historia tes Neoteres Elladas: 20os Aionas* (History of Modern Greece: 20th Century) (Athens: n.p., 1957).

Korovessis, Pericles. *The Method: A Personal Account of the Tortures in Greece* (London: Allison and Busby, 1970).

Koumoulides, John, ed. *Greece in Transition* (London: Zeno, 1977).

Kourvetaris, George A. "The Greek Army Officer Corps: Its Professionalism and Political Interventionism," in John Johnson, ed., *The Role of the Military in Underdevloped Countries* (Princeton: Princeton University Press, 1962).

————. "The Greek Officer Corps," in Constantine Tsoukalas, ed., *The Greek Tragedy* (Baltimore: Penguin, 1969).

————. "Professional Self-Images and Political Perspectives in the Greek Military," *American Sociological Review* 36:6 (December 1971), pp. 1043–57.

————. "The Role of the Military in Greek Politics," *International Review of History and Political Science* 8:3 (August 1971), pp. 95–114.

————. "The Southern Flank of Nato: Political Dimensions of the Greek-Turkish Conflict since 1974," *East European Quarterly* 21:4 (Winter 1987), pp. 431–46.

————. *Studies on Modern Greek Society and Politics* (Boulder: East European Monographs, 1999).

Kourvetaris, George and Betty A. Dobratz. "Political Clientelism in Athens, Greece: A Three Paradigm Approach to Political Clientelism," *East European Quarterly* 18:1 (March 1984), pp. 35–59.

———— *A Profile of Modern Greece: In Search of Identity* (Oxford: Clarendon, 1987).

Kousoulas, D. George. *Greece: Uncertain Democracy* (Washington: Public Affairs Press, 1973).

————. *Modern Greece: Profile of a Nation* (New York: Scribner, 1974).

————. "The Origins of the Greek Military Coup, April 1967," *Orbis* 13:1 (Spring 1969), pp. 332–50.

————. *Revolution and Defeat: The Story of the Greek Communist Party* (London: Oxford University Press, 1965).

Kyrkos, Leonidas. "EADE kai Demokratike Synergasia" (EADE and Democratic Cooperation), *Kommounistike Theoria kai Politike* (Communist Theory and Politics), 8 (January 1976), pp. 3–9.

———— . "Poios—Poion? He Ethnike Antidiktatorike Enoteta; Axonas tes Politikes tou KKE-esot" (Who—whom? The National Anti-dictatorial Unity; The Axis of Politics of the KKE-int.), *Kommounistike Theoria kai Politike* (Communist Theory and Politics), 1 (March 1975).

Lambrias, Takis. *Ste Skia Enos Megalou: Meletontas 25 Chronia ton Karamanli* (In the Shadow of a Great One: 25 Years of Studying Karamanlis) (Athens: Morfotike Estia, 1989).

Legg, Keith. *Politics in Modern Greece* (Stanford: Stanford University Press, 1969).

Legg, Keith and John M. Roberts. *Modern Greece: A Civilization on the Periphery* (Boulder: Westview Press, 1997).

Lentakes, Andreas. *Parakratikes Organoseis kai 21e Apriliou* (Parastate Organs and the 21st of April) (Athens: Ekd. Kastaniote, 1975).

Lerner, Daniel. *The Passing of Traditional Society* (New York: Free Press, 1958).

Lijphart, Arend. "Consociational Democracy," *World Politics* 21:2 (January 1969), pp. 207–25.

————. *Democracies in Plural Societies: A Comparative Exploration* (New Haven: Yale University Press, 1977).

————. "A Mediterranean Model of Democracy? The Southern European Democracies in Comparative Perspective," *West European Politics* 11:1 (January 1988), pp. 7–25.

————. *The Politics of Accommodation: Pluralism and Democracy in the Netherlands* (Berkeley: University of California Press, 1968).

————. "The Southern European Examples of Democratization: Six Lessons for Latin America," *Government and Opposition* 25:1 (Winter 1990), pp. 68–84.

Limberes, Nicholas M. "The Greek Election of June 1985: A Socialist Entrenchment," *West European Politics* 9:1 (January 1986), pp. 142–47.

Linz, Juan J. "Transitions to Democracy," *Washington Quarterly* 13:3 (Summer 1990), pp. 143–64.

Linz, Juan J. and Alfred Stepan. *Democratic Transitions and Consolidation: Eastern Europe, Southern Europe and Latin America* (Baltimore: The Johns Hopkins University Press, 1996).

Linz, Juan J. and Arturo Valenzuela. *The Failure of Presidential Democracy* (Baltimore: The Johns Hopkins University Press, 1994).

Linz, Juan J., Alfred Stepan, and Richard Gunther. "Democratic Transition and Consolidation in Southern Europe, with Reflections on Latin America and Eastern Europe," in Richard Gunther, P. Nikiforos Diamandouros, and Hans-Jürgen Puhle, eds., *The Politics of Democratic Consolidation: Southern Europe in Comparative Perspective* (Baltimore: Johns Hopkins University Press, 1995).

Linz, Juan J. and Alfred Stepan, eds. *The Breakdown of Democratic Regimes* (Baltimore: Johns Hopkins University Press, 1978).

Lipset, Seymour Martin. "Some Social Requisities of Democracy: Economic Development and Political Legitimacy," *American Politial Science Review* 53:1 (March 1959), pp. 69–105.

Lipset, Seymour Martin and Aldo Solari. *Elites in Latin America* (New York: Oxford University Press, 1967).

Loulis, John C. "New Democracy: The New Face of Conservatism," in Howard R. Penniman, ed., *Greece at the Polls: The National Elections of 1974 and 1977* (Washington: American Enterprise Institute for Public Policy Research, 1981).

———. "Papandreou's Foreign Policy," *Foreign Affairs* 63:2 (Winter 1984), pp. 375–91.

Lyrintzis, Christos. "PASOK in Power: From 'Change' to Disenchantment," in Richard Clogg, ed., *Greece, 1981–89: The Populist Decade* (New York: St. Martin's Press, 1993).

———. "PASOK in Power: The Loss of the 'Third Road to Socialism'," in Tom Gallagher and Allan M. Williams, eds., *Southern European Socialism: Parties, Elections and the Challenges of Government* (New York: St. Martin's Press, 1989).

———. "Political Parties in Post-Junta Greece: A Case of 'Bureaucratic Clientelism'?" in Geoffrey Pridham, ed., *The New Mediterranean Democracies: Regime Transition in Spain, Greece and Portugal* (London: Frank Cass, 1984).

———. "The Rise of PASOK and the Emergence of a New Political Personnel," in Zafiris Tzannatos, ed., *Socialism in Greece* (Aldershot: Gower Publishing, 1986).

Macridis, Roy C. "Elections and Political Modernization in Greece," in Howard R. Penniman, ed., *Greece at the Polls: The National Elections of 1974 and 1977* (Washington: American Enterprise Institute for Public Policy Research, 1981).

———. *Greek Politics at a Crossroads: What Kind of Socialism?* (Stanford: Hoover Institution Press, 1984).

Maguire, Diarmuid. "The Recent Birth of Modern Italy," in James Kurth and James Petras, eds., *Mediterranean Paradoxes: Politics and Social Structure in Southern Europe* (Providence, RI: Berg Publishers, Inc., 1993).

Mainwaring, Scott and Donald Share. "Transitions through Transaction: Democratization in Brazil and Spain," in Wayne Selcher, ed., *Political Liberalization in Brazil: Dynamics, Dilemmas, and Future Prospects* (Boulder: Westview Press, 1986).

Mainwaring, Scott and Eduardo Viola. "Transitions to Democracy: Brazil and Argentina in the 1980s," *Journal of International Affairs* 38:2 (Winter 1985), pp. 193–219.

Mainwaring, Scott, Guillermo O'Donnell, and J. Samuel Valenzuela, eds. *Issues in Democratic Consolidation: The New South American Democracies in Comparative Perspective* (Notre Dame: University of Notre Dame Press, 1992).

Mangakis, George A. "The Revision of the Consitution," *Spotlight*, 23 (June 15, 1985).

Maravall, José María. "What Is Left? Social Democratic Policies in Southern Europe," Working Paper 36 (Madrid: Instituto Juan March, 1992).

——— and Julián Santamaría. "Political Change in Spain and the Prospects for Democracy," in Guillermo O'Donnell, Philippe C. Schmitter, and Laurence Whitehead, eds., *Transitions from Authoritarian Rule: Southern Europe* (Baltimore: Johns Hopkins University Press, 1986).

Markezinis, Spyridon V. *Anamneseis* (Reminiscences) (Athens: Ekdoseis Sp. V. Markezine A.E., 1979).

———. *Politike Istoria tes Neoteras Hellados* (Political History of Modern Greece) (Athens: Papyros, 1968).

Matthews, Kenneth. *Memories of a Mountain War: Greece 1944–1949* (London: Longman, 1972).

Mavri Vivlos: To Chronikon tou Eklogikou Praxikopimatos tis 29/10/61 (Black Book: The Chronicle of the Electoral Coup of 29/10/61) (Athens, n.p., 1962).

Mavrogordatos, George Th. "Civil Society under Populism," in Richard Clogg, ed., *Greece, 1981–89: The Populist Decade* (New York: St. Martin's Press, 1993).

————. "Downs Revisited: Spatial Models of Party Competition and Left-Right Measurements," *International Political Science Review* 8:4 (October 1987), pp. 333–42.

————. "The Emerging Party System," in Howard R. Penniman, ed., *Greece at the Polls: The National Elections of 1974 and 1977* (Washington: American Enterprise Institute for Public Policy Research, 1981).

————. "The Greek Party System: A Case of 'Limited but Polarised Pluralism'?" *West European Politics* 7:4 (October 1984), pp. 156–69.

————. *Rise of the Green Sun: The Greek Election of 1981* (London: Centre of Contemporary Greek Studies, King's College, 1983).

————. *Stillborn Republic: Social Coalitions and Party Strategies in Greece, 1922–1936* (Berkeley: University of California Press, 1983).

Maxwell, Kenneth. "Regime Overthrow and the Prospects for Democratic Transition in Portugal," in Guillermo O'Donnell, Philippe C. Schmitter, and Laurence Whitehead, eds., *Transitions from Authoritarian Rule: Southern Europe* (Baltimore: Johns Hopkins University Press, 1986).

McCaskill, Charles W. "PASOK's Third World/Nonaligned Relations," in Nikolaos A. Stavrou, ed., *Greece under Socialism: A NATO Ally Adrift* (New Rochelle, NY: Orpheus Publishing, 1988).

McClelland, David. *The Achieving Society* (Princeton: Von Nostrand, 1962).

McNeill, William Hardy. *The Greek Dilemma: War and Aftermath* (Philadelphia: Lippincott, 1947).

————. *The Metamorphosis of Greece Since World War II* (Chicago: University of Chicago Press, 1978).

Mercouri, Melina. *I Was Born Greek* (Garden City, NJ: Doubleday, 1971).

Meynaud, Jean. *Rapport sur l'Abolition de la Democratie en Grèce* (Montreal: n.p., 1970).

Michalopoulos, Demetres. "PASOK and the Eastern Bloc: A Growing Relationship," in Nikolaos A. Stavrou, ed., *Greece under Socialism: A NATO Ally Adrift* (New Rochelle, NY: Orpheus Publishing, 1988).

Morlino, Leonardo. *Costruire la Democrazia: Gruppie partiti in Italia* (Bologna: Società editrice il Mulino, 1991).

————. "Crisis of Parties and Change of Party System in Italy," *Party Politics* 2:1 (1996), pp. 5–30.

————. "Political Parties and Democratic Consolidation in Southern Europe," in Richard Gunther, P. Nikiforos Diamandouros, and Hans-Jürgen Puhle, eds. *The Politics of Democratic Consolidation: Southern Europe in Comparative Perspective* (Baltimore: Johns Hopkins University Press, 1995).

Morlino, Leonardo and José R. Montero. "Legitimacy and Democracy in Southern Europe," in Richard Gunther, P. Nikiforos Diamandouros, and Hans-Jürgen Puhle, eds. *The Politics of Democratic Consolidation: Southern Europe in Comparative Perspective* (Baltimore: Johns Hopkins University Press, 1995).

Moskos, Charles C. "Institutional and Occupational Trends in Armed Forces," in Charles C. Moskos and Frank R. Wood, eds., *The Military: More than a Job?* (New York: Pergamon-Brassey's International Defence Publishers, 1988).

Moskos, Charles C. and Frank R. Wood, eds. *The Military: More than a Job?* (New York: Pergamon-Brassey's International Defence Publishers, 1988).

Mouzelis, Nicos. "Continuities and Discontinuities in Greek Politics—From Elefterios Venizelos to Andreas Papandreou," in Kevin Featherstone and Dimitrios K. Katsoudas, eds., *Political Change in Greece: Before and After the Colonels* (New York: St. Martin's Press, 1987).

————. "The Greek Elections and the Rise of PASOK," *New Left Review* 108 (March–April 1978), pp. 59–75.

————. *Modern Greece: Facets of Underdevelopment* (New York: Holmes and Meier, 1978).

————. "On the Analysis of Social Stratification in Greece," *Journal of the Hellenic Diaspora* 11:4 (Winter 1984), pp. 69–78.

Murtagh, Peter. *The Rape of Greece: The King, the Colonels, and the Resistance* (London: Simon and Schuster, 1994).

Mylonas, George. *Escape From Amorgos* (New York: Charles Scribner's Sons, 1974).

Nefeloudis, Vassiles A. *He Ethnike Antistase ste Mese Anatole* (The National Resistance in the Middle East), vols. 1–2 (Athens: Themelio, 1981).

Nelson, Brian R. *Western Political Thought: From Socrates to the Age of Ideology* (Englewood Cliffs, NJ: Prentice Hall, 1982).

Nicolacopoulos, Ilias. *Kommata kai Vouleutikes Ekloges sten Ellada, 1946–1964* (Parties and Parliamentary Elections in Greece, 1946–1964) (Athens: Ethniko Kentro Koinonikon Ereunon, 1985).

Nieto, Lourdes López. *Alianza Popular: Estructura y evolución electoral de un partido conservado (1976–1982)* (Madrid: Centro de Investigaciones Sociológicas, 1988).

Nimetz, Matthew. "Introduction," in Nikolaos A. Stavrou, ed., *Greece under Socialism: A NATO Ally Adrift* (New Rochelle, NY: Orpehus Publishing).

Nordlinger, Eric. "Political Development, Time Sequences and Rates of Change," in Jason L. Finkle and Robert W. Gable, eds., *Political Development, Times Sequences and Rates of Change* (New York: John Wiley, 1971).

O'Donnell, Guillermo. "Illusions About Consolidation," *Journal of Democracy* 7:2 (April 1996), pp. 34–51.

————. "Introduction to the Latin American Cases," in Guillermo O'Donnell, Philippe C. Schmitter, and Laurence Whitehead, eds. *Transitions from Authoritarian Rule: Latin America* (Baltimore: Johns Hopkins University Press, 1986).

O'Donnell, Guillermo and Philippe C. Schmitter. *Transitions from Authoritarian Rule: Tentative Conclusions about Uncertain Democracies* (Baltimore: Johns Hopkins University Press, 1986).

O'Donnell, Guillermo, Philippe C. Schmitter, and Laurence Whitehead, eds. *Transitions from Authoritarian Rule: Comparative Perspectives* (Baltimore: Johns Hopkins University Press, 1986).

————, eds. *Transitions from Authoritarian Rule: Latin America* (Baltimore: Johns Hopkins University Press, 1986).

————, eds. *Transitions from Authoritarian Rule: Southern Europe* (Baltimore: Johns Hopkins University Press, 1986).

OECD. *OECD Economic Surveys: Greece* (Paris: OECD, various years).

Paidoussi, Eleni. "Why Caramanlis Won the Election in Greece," *Journal of the Hellenic Diaspora* 2:1 (January 1975), pp. 5–8.

Papacosma, S. Victor. "The Historical Context," in Richard Clogg, ed., *Greece in the 1980s* (New York: St. Martin's Press, 1983).

————. "The Military in Greek Politics: A Historical Survey," in John Koumoulides, ed., *Greece in Transition: Essays in the History of Modern Greece 1821–1974* (London: Zeno Booksellers and Publishers, 1977).

————. *Politics and Culture in Greece* (Ann Arbor: Center for Political Studies, Institute for Social Research, University of Michigan, 1988).

Papadopoulos, Yannis. "Parties, the State and Society in Greece: Continuity Within Change," *West European Politics* 12:2 (April 1989), pp. 55–71.

Papandreou, Andreas. *Democracy at Gunpoint: The Greek Front* (Garden City, NY: Doubleday, 1970).

———. "Farewell to the Diaspora Resistance," *Journal of the Hellenic Diaspora* 1:4 (Winter 1974), pp. 9–15.

———. Gia mia Sosialistike Koinonia: Koinonekopoiese, Autodiacheirise, Apokentrose, Topike Autokioikise, Syndikalismos (For a Socialist Society: Socialization, Self-management, Decentralization, Local Self Government, Syndicalism) (Athens: PASOK Press Office, 1977).

———. "Greece and the Atlantic Alliance," *Harvard International Review* 9 (November/December 1986).

———. "If Capitalism Can't, Can Socialism?" *New Perspective Quarterly* 4:3 (Fall 1987).

———. *Imperialismos kai Ekonomike Anaptexe* (Imperialism and Economic Development) (Athens: Nea Sinora, 1975).

Papandreou, Margaret. "Dynamic Socialism in Greece," *World Affairs Journal* 3 (Summer 1984), pp. 19–27.

———. *Nightmare in Athens* (Englewood Cliffs, NJ: Prentice-Hall, 1970).

Papayannakis, Michalis. "The Crisis in the Greek Left," in Howard R. Penniman ed., *Greece at the Polls: The National Elections of 1974 and 1977* (Washington: American Enterprise Institute for Public Policy Research, 1981).

Pappas, Peter. "The Eighteenth October of Andreas Papandreou: Some Thoughts on a Democratic Cult of Personality," in Theodore C. Kariotis, ed., *The Greek Socialist Experiment: Papandreou's Greece 1981–1989* (New York: Pella, 1992).

Pappas, Takis S. *Making Party Democracy in Greece* (New York: St. Martin's Press, Inc., 1999).

Paraskeuopoulos, Potes. *Ho Karamanlis sta Chronia 1974–1985* (Karamanlis in the Years 1974–1985) (Athens: O Typos, n.d.).

Parsalidis, Dimitris. "The Communist Party of Greece in the Struggle for Democratic Change," *World Marxist Review* 5:1 (January, 1962), pp. 26–33.

PASOK. *Proclamation of Basic Principles and Goals of the Panhellenic Socialist Movement* (Athens: 3 September 1974).

———. "Programmatic Declaration of the Government" (Athens: 22 November 1981).

Pasquino, Gianfranco. "The Demise of the First Fascist Regime and Italy's Transition to Democracy: 1943–1948," in Guillermo O'Donnell, Philippe C. Schmitter, and Laurence Whitehead, eds., *Transitions from Authoritarian Rule: Southern Europe* (Baltimore: Johns Hopkins University Press, 1986).

———. "Political Leadership in Southern Europe: Research Problems," *West European Politics* 13:4 (October 1990), pp. 118–30.

Payne, Stanley G. "Dictatorship and Democratization in Southern Europe: A Historian's Perspective," *Modern Greek Studies Yearbook* 4 (1988).

Penniman, Howard R. *Greece at the Polls: The National Elections of 1974 and 1977* (Washington: American Enterprise Institute for Public Policy Research, 1981).

Pérez-Díaz, Víctor M. *The Return of Civil Society: The Emergence of Democratic Spain* (Cambridge, MA: Harvard University Press, 1993).

Petras, James. "The Contradictions of Greek Socialism," *New Left Review* 16:3 (May/June 1987), pp. 3–25.

———. "Greece: Democracy and the Tanks," *Journal of the Hellenic Diaspora* 4:1 (March 1977), pp. 3–30.

———. "Greek Socialism: Walking the Tightrope," *Journal of the Hellenic Diaspora* 9:1 (Spring 1982), pp. 7–15.

Pharakos, Grigoris. "Banner of Struggle and Victory," *World Marxist Review* 12:11 (November 1978), pp. 26–36.

Pion-Berlin, David. "Between Confrontation and Accommodation: Military and Government Policy in Democratic Argentina," *Journal of Latin American Studies* 23:3 (October 1991), pp. 543–71.

To Pistevo Mas (Our Creed) (Athens: Greek Government Printing Office, 1968).

Pollis, Adamantia "The Political Implications of the Modern Greek Concept of Self," *British Journal of Sociology* 16 (March 1985), pp. 29–47.

———. "Socialist Transformation in Greece," *Telos: A Quarterly Journal of Critical Thought* 61 (Fall 1984), pp. 101–11.

———. "The State, the Law, and Human Rights in Modern Greece," *Human Rights Quarterly* 9:4 (November 1987), pp. 587–614.

Pranger, Robert J. "U.S.-Greek Relations under PASOK," in Nikolaos A. Stavrou, ed., *Greece under Socialism: A NATO Ally Adrift* (New Rochelle, NY: Orpehus Publishing, 1988).

Pridham, Geoffrey. "The International Context of Democratic Consolidation: Italy, Spain, Greece and Portugal in Comparative Perspective," in Richard Gunther, P. Nikiforos Diamandouros, and Hans-Jürgen Puhle, eds. *The Politics of Democratic Consolidation: Southern Europe in Comparative Perspective* (Baltimore: Johns Hopkins University Press, 1995).

———. "Southern European Socialism and the State: Consolidation of Party Rule of Consolidation of Democracy?" in Tom Gallagher and Allan M. Williams, eds., *Southern European Socialism: Parties, Elections and the Challenges of Government* (New York: St. Martin's Press, 1989).

———, ed. *The New Mediterranean Democracies: Regime Transition in Spain, Greece and Portugal* (London: Frank Cass, 1984).

———, ed. "Political Actors, Linkages and Interactions: Democratic Consolidation in Southern Europe," *West European Politics* 13:4 (October 1990), pp. 103–17.

———, ed. *Securing Democracy: Political Parties and Democratic Consolidation in Southern Europe* (New York: Routledge, 1990).

———, ed. "Special Issue on the New Mediterrean Democracies: Regime Transition in Spain, Greece, and Portugal," *West European Politics* 7:2 (April 1984), pp. 1–19.

Przeworski, Adam. *Democracy and the Market: Political and Economic Reforms in Eastern Europe and Latin America* (Cambridge: Cambridge University Press, 1991).

Psomiades, Harry J. "Greece: From the Colonels' Rule to Democracy," in John H. Herz, ed., *From Dictatorship to Democracy: Coping with the Legacies of Authoritarianism and Totalitarianism* (Westport, CT: Greenwood Press, 1982).

Psychares, Stavros P. *Ta Paraskenia tes Allaghes* (Behind the Scenes of the Transition) (Athens: Ekdoseis Papazese, 1975).

Rallis, Georgios I. *Politikes Ekmystereuseis, 1950–1989* (Political Revelations, 1950–1989) (Athens: Proskenio, 1990).

Rostow, Walt W. *The Stages of Economic Growth* (New York: Cambridge University Press, 1960).

Roufos, Rodis. "Culture and the Military," in Richard Clogg and George Yannopoulos, eds., *Greece under Military Rule* (New York: Basic Books, 1972).

Rousseas, Stephen W. *Death of a Democracy: Greece and the American Conscience* (New York: Grove Press, 1968).

———. "Memoire on the 'Second Solution'," *Journal of the Hellenic Diaspora* 2:1 (January 1975), pp. 22–35.

———. "Zorba Abandoned, Theodorakis Plays On," *Worldview* 16 (October 1973), pp. 13–19.

Rustow, Dankwart. "Transitions to Democracy: Toward a Dynamic Model," *Comparative Politics* 2:3 (April 1970), pp. 337–63.

Safran, William. *The French Polity*, Second Edition (New York: Longman, 1985).

Samatas, Minas. "Greek McCarthyism: A Comparative Assessment of Greek Post-Civil War Repressive Anticommunism and the U.S. Truman-McCarthy Era," *Journal of the Hellenic Diaspora* 13:3–4 (Fall–Winter 1986), p. 41

Schaffer, Jeffrey. "Andreas Papandreou: [Political] Portrait of a Modern Socialist," in Nikolaos A. Stavrou, ed., *Greece under Socialism: A NATO Ally Adrift* (New Rochelle, NY: Orpheus Publishing, 1988).

Schedler, Andreas. "What is Democratic Consolidation?" *Journal of Democracy* 9:2 (April 1998), pp. 91–107.

Schmitter, Philippe C. "The Consolidation of Political Democracy in Southern Europe" (unpublished manuscript).

Seferiades, Seraphim. "Polarization and Nonproportionality: The Greek Party System in the Post-War Era," *Comparative Politics* 19:1 (October 1986), pp. 69–93.

Share, Donald. "Transitions to Democracy and Transition through Transaction," *Comparative Political Studies* 19:4 (January 1987), pp. 525–48.

———— and Scott Mainwaring. "Transitions from Above: Democratization in Brazil and Spain," in Wayne Selcher, ed., *Political Liberalization in Brazil: Dynamics, Dilemmas, and Future Prospects* (Boulder, CO: Westview Press, 1986).

Simitis, Kostas. *He Domike Antipoliteuse* (Structural Opposition) (Athens: Kastiniotis, 1979).

Smith, Ole L. "'The First Round'—Civil War during the Occupation," in David H. Close, ed., *The Greek Civil War, 1943–1950: Studies of Polarization* (New York: Routledge, 1993).

————. "The Greek Communist Party, 1945–9," in David H. Close, ed., *The Greek Civil War, 1943–1950: Studies of Polarization* (New York: Routledge, 1993).

————. "Marxism in Greece: The Case of the KKE," *Journal of Modern Greek Studies* 3:1 (May 1985), pp. 45–64.

Smokovitis, Dimitrios. "Greece," in Charles C. Moskos and Frank R. Wood, eds., *The Military: More than a Job?* (New York: Pergamon-Brassey's International Defence Publishers, 1988).

Smothers, Frank, William Hardy McNeill, and Elizabeth Darbishire McNeill. *Report on the Greeks Findings of a Twentieth Century Fund Team which Surveyed Conditions in Greece in 1947* (New York: Twentieth Century Fund, 1948).

Spourdalakis, Michalis. *The Rise of the Greek Socialist Party* (London: Routledge, 1988).

Spraos, John. "Government and the Economy: The First Term of PASOK 1982–1984," in Speros Vryonis, Jr., ed., *Greece on the Road to Democracy: From the Junta to PASOK 1974–1986* (New Rochelle, NY: Caratzas, 1991).

Stavrou, Nikolaos A. *Allied Politics and Military Interventions: The Political Role of the Greek Military* (Athens: Papazisis, 1976).

————. "Ideological Foundations of the Panhellenic Socialist Movement," in Nikolaos A. Stavrou, ed., *Greece under Socialism: A NATO Ally Adrift* (New Rochelle, NY: Orpheus Publishing, 1988).

————, ed. "Appendix on Defense Policies," in Nikolaos A. Stavrou, ed., *Greece under Socialism: A NATO Ally Adrift* (New Rochelle, NY: Orpehus Publishing, 1988).

————, ed. *Greece Under Socialism: A NATO Ally Adrift* (New Rochelle, NY: Orpheus Publishing, 1988).

Stepan, Alfred. "Paths toward Redemocratization: Theoretical and Comparative Considerations," in Guillermo O'Donnell, Philippe C. Schmitter, and Laurence Whitehead, eds. *Transitions from Authoritarian Rule: Comparative Perspectives* (Baltimore: Johns Hopkins University Press, 1986).

————. *Rethinking Military Politics* (Princeton: Princeton University Press, 1988).

Stern, Laurence. *The Wrong Horse   The Politics of Intervention and the Failure of American Diplomacy* (New York: Times Books, 1979).

"The Strategy of Coalition: Greek Communists and Their Partners Say . . ." *World Marxist Review* 32:10 (October 1989), pp. 70–73.

Tezanos, Félix. *Sociología del Socialismo Espanol* (Madrid: Tecnos, 1983).

Theodoracopulos, Taki. *The Greek Upheaval: Kings, Demagogues and Bayonets* (London: Stacey International, 1976).

Theodorakis, Mikis. *Journal of Resistance* (New York: Coward, McCann and Geoghegan, 1973).

Threlfall, Monica. "Social Policy towards Women in Spain, Greece and Portugal," in Tom Gallagher and Allan M. Williams, eds., *Southern European Socialism: Parties, Elections and the Challenges of Government* (New York: St. Martin's Press, 1989).

Todorov, Nikolai. *The Ambassador as Historian: An Eyewitness Account of Bulgarian-Greek Relations in the 1980s* (New Rochelle, NY: Aristide D. Caratzas, Publisher, 1999).

Treholt, Arne. "Europe and the Greek Dictatorship," in Richard Clogg and George Yannopoulos, eds., *Greece Under Military Rule* (New York: Basic Books, 1972).

Tsatsos, Konstantinos. *Ho Agnostos Karamanlis: Mia Prosopografia* (The Unknown Karamanlis: A Personal Account) (Athens: Ekdotike Athenon A.E., 1989).

Tsingos, Basilios Evangelos. "The Breakdown of Authoritarian Regimes: The Political Evolution of the Greek Military Dictatorship, 1967–1974," Honors Thesis, Harvard College, April 1990.

Tsoukalas, Constantine. *The Greek Tragedy* (Baltimore: Penguin, 1969).

———. "The Ideological Impact of the Civil War," in John O. Iatrides, ed., *Greece in the 1940s: A Nation in Crisis* (Hanover, NH: University Press of New England, 1981).

———. *Kratos, Koinonia, Ergasia ste Metapolemike Hellada* (State, Society, Labor in Postwar Greece) (Athens: Themelio, 1986).

Tsoukalis, Loukas. "The Austerity Programme: Causes, Reactions and Prospects," in Speros Vryonis, Jr., ed., *Greece on the Road to Democracy: From the Junta to PASOK 1974–1986* (New Rochelle, NY: Caratzas, 1991).

Tsoumis, George J. "The Defense Policies of PASOK," in Nikolaos A. Stavrou, ed., *Greece under Socialism: A NATO Ally Adrift* (New Rochelle, NY: Orpheus Publishing, 1988).

Tzannatos, Zafiris. "Socialism in Greece: Past and Present." In Zafiris Tzannatos, ed., *Socialism in Greece: The First Four Years* (Aldershot: Gower Publishing Co., 1986).

———, ed. *Socialism in Greece: The First Four Years* (Aldershot: Gower Publishing, 1986).

Tzermias, Paulos N. *He Politike Skepse tou Konstantinou Karamanli: Mia Anichneuse* (The Political Thought of Konstantine Karamanlis: An Investigation) (Athens: Hellenike Euroekthotike, 1990).

Valenzuela, J. Samuel. "Democratic Consolidation in Post-Transitional Settings: Notion, Process, and Facilitating Conditions," in Scott Mainwaring, Guillermo O'Donnell, and J. Samuel Valenzuela, eds., *Issues in Democratic Consolidation: The New South American Democracies in Comparative Perspective* (Notre Dame, IN: University of Notre Dame Press, 1992).

Vatikiotis, P.J. *Greece: A Political Essay* (Beverly Hills: Sage, 1974).

———. "Greece: The Triumph of Socialism?" *Survey* 26:2 (1982).

Venetsanopoulos, Vasilis. "Triumph of Leninist National Policy," *World Marxist Review* 15:10 (October 1972), pp. 112–14.

Venetsanopoulos, Vasilis, Vladimir Guliev, Sylwester Zawadzki, and Jaime Schmirgeld. "Notes on the History of the Idea of Proletarian Dictatorship," *World Marxist Review* 17:7 (July 1974), pp. 64–75.

Ventires, Georgios. *He Hellas tou 1910–1920* (The Greece of 1910–1920) (Athens: Ikaros, 1970).

Veremis, Thanos. "Defence and Security Policies under PASOK," in Richard Clogg, ed., *Greece 1981–89: The Populist Decade* (New York: St. Martin's Press, 1993).

———. *Hoi Epemvaseis tou Stratou sten Ellenike Politike, 1916–1936* (The Interventions of the Army in Greek Politics, 1916–1936) (Athens: Exantas, 1977).

———. "Greece," in Douglas T. Stuart, ed., *Politics and Security in the Southern Region of the Atlantic Alliance* (London: Macmillan, 1988).

———. "Greece and NATO," in Speros Vryonis, Jr., ed., *Greece on the Road to Democracy: From the Junta to PASOK 1974–1986* (New Rochelle, NY: Caratzas, 1991).

———. "The Greek Army in Politics, 1922–1935," Ph.D. Dissertation, Oxford University, 1974.

———. "The Military," in Kevin Featherstone and Dimitrios K. Katsoudas, eds., *Political Change in Greece: Before and After the Colonels* (New York: St. Martin's Press, 1987).

———. *The Military in Greek Politics: From Independence to Democracy* (Montreal: Black Rose Books, 1997).

———. "Security Considerations and Civil-Military Relations in Post-War Greece," in Richard Clogg, ed., *Greece in the 1980s* (New York: St. Martin's Press, 1983).

———. "Some Observations on the Greek Military in the Inter-War Period, 1918–25," *Armed Forces and Society* 4:3 (Spring 1978), pp. 527–42.

———. "The Union of the Democratic Center," in Howard R. Penniman, ed., *Greece at the Polls: The National Elections of 1974 and 1977* (Washington: American Enterprise Institute for Public Policy Research, 1981).

Verney, Susannah. "Between Coalition and One-Party Government: The Greek Elections of November 1989 and April 1990," *West European Politics* 13:4 (October 1990), pp. 131–38.

———. "From the 'Special Relationship' to Europeanism: PASOK and the European Community, 1981–89," in Richard Clogg, ed., *Greece, 1981–89: The Populist Decade* (New York: St. Martin's Press, 1993).

———. "Greece and the European Community," in Kevin Featherstone and Dimitrios K. Katsoudas, eds., *Political Change in Greece: Before and After the Colonels* (New York: St. Martin's Press, 1987).

———. "The New Red Book of the KKE," *Journal of Communist Studies* 4:4 (December 1988), pp. 170–73.

———. "Political Parties and the European Community in Regime Consolidation in Greece," Paper presented to the Political Studies Association, 1987.

———. "The Spring of the Greek Left: Two Party Congresses," *The Journal of Communist Studies* 3:4 (December 1987), pp. 166–70.

———. "To Be or Not to Be within the European Community: The Party Debate and Democratic Consolidation in Greece," in Geoffrey Pridham, ed., *Securing Democracy: Political Parties and Democratic Consolidation in Southern Europe* (London: Routledge, 1990).

Vlachos, Helen. "The Colonels and the Press," in Richard Clogg and George Yannopoulos, eds., *Greece Under Military Rule* (New York: Basic Books, 1972).

———. *Free Greek Voices: A Political Anthology* (London: Doric Publications Ltd., 1971).

———. *House Arrest* (Boston: Gambit, 1970).

Vournas, Tasos. *Goudi—To Kinima tou 1909* (Goudi—The 1909 Coup) (Athens: Tolides, 1957).

Vryonis, Speros, ed. *Greece on the Road to Democracy: From the Junta to PASOK 1974–1986* (New Rochelle, NY: Caratzas, 1991).

Wallerstein, Immanuel. *The Modern World-System: Capitalist Agriculture and the Origins of the European World-Economy in the 16th Century* (New York: Academic Press, 1974).

Welch, Claude E. "Civilian Control of the Military: Myth and Reality," in Claude E. Welch, ed., *Civilian Control of the Military* (Albany: State University of New York Press, 1976).

———. *No Farewell to Arms?* (Boulder, CO: Westview Press, 1987).

Woodhouse, C. M. *Apple of Discord: A Survey of Recent Greek Politics in Their International Settings* (London: Hutchinson, 1948).

———. "Greece and Europe," in Richard Clogg, ed., *Greece in the 1980s* (New York: St. Martin's Press, 1983).

———. *Karamanlis: The Restorer of Greek Democracy* (Oxford: Clarendon Press, 1982).

———. *Modern Greece: A Short History* (London: Faber and Faber, 1991).

———. "The 'Revolution' in its Historical Context," in Richard Clogg and George Yannopoulos, eds., *Greece Under Military Rule* (New York: Basic Books, 1972).

———. *The Rise and Fall of the Greek Colonels* (New York: Franklin Watts, 1985).

———. *The Story of Modern Greece* (London: Faber and Faber, 1977).

———. *The Struggle for Greece, 1941–1949* (London: Hart-Davis-MacGibbon, 1976).

Xydis, A.G. "The Military Regime's Foreign Policy," in Richard Clogg and George Yannopoulos, eds., *Greece Under Military Rule* (New York: Basic Books, 1972).

Xydis, Stephen G. "Coups and Countercoups in Greece, 1967–1973 (With Postscript)," *Political Science Quarterly* 89:3 (Fall 1974), pp. 507–38.

Yannopoulos, George. "The State of the Opposition Forces Since the Military Coup," in Richard Clogg and George Yannopoulos, eds., *Greece Under Military Rule* (New York: Basic Books, 1972).

Young, Kenneth. *The Greek Passion: A Study in People and Politics* (London: Dent, 1969).

Zaharopoulos, George. "Politics and the Army in Post-War Greece," in Richard Clogg and George Yannopoulos, eds., *Greece Under Military Rule* (New York: Basic Books, 1972).

Zografos, Zisis. "Some Lessons of the Civil War in Greece," *World Marxist Review* 7:11 (November 1964), pp. 43–50.

Index

About the Author

NEOVI M. KARAKATSANIS is Assistant Professor of Political Science at Indiana University, South Bend and Fellow of the Southern European Research Group, Princeton University. Her articles have appeared in *Armed Forces and Society* and *South European Society and Politics*.